MIKE M[...] [...]TION

Pass[port] ★

Java 2™

EXAM
310-025

CINDY GLASS, JANE GRISCTI,
MARGARITA ISAYEVA,
AJITH KALLAMBELLA, AND
KATHY SIERRA

OSBORNE

New York • Chicago • San Francisco
Lisbon • London • Madrid • Mexico City
Milan • New Delhi • San Juan
Seoul • Singapore • Sydney • Toronto

McGraw-Hill/Osborne
2600 Tenth Street
Berkeley, California 94710
U.S.A.

To arrange bulk purchase discounts for sales promotions, premiums, or fund-raisers, please contact **McGraw-Hill**/Osborne at the above address.

Mike Meyers' Java 2™ Certification Passport (Exam 310-025)

34567890 DOC DOC 0198765432

Book p/n 0-07-219597-5 and CD p/n 0-07-219596-7
parts of
ISBN 0-07-219366-2

Publisher	**Technical Editor**	**Series Design and**
Brandon A. Nordin	Karl Moss	**Production**
	Peter den Haan	epic
Vice President &		
Associate Publisher	**Copy Editor**	**Illustrators**
Scott Rogers	Sally Engelfried	Lyssa Seiben-Wald
		Beth Young
Acquisitions Editor	**Proofreader**	
Francis Kelly	Marian Selig	**Cover Design**
		Ted Holladay
Project Manager	**Indexer**	
Jenn Tust	Claire Splan	
Acquisitions Coordinator		
Alex Corona		

This book was composed with QuarkXPress™.

About the Authors

Cindy Glass, St. Clair, MI, is a Senior Information Specialist for Electronic Data Systems (EDS). She has been working on the GM account in the Detroit, Michigan, area for 16 years. Cindy has a BS in Chemistry from the University of Michigan, and a BS in Math from Michigan State University. Cindy is the mother of three daughters and a moderator at JavaRanch.com.

Jane Griscti is a Sun Certified Java Programmer and a Certified Lotus Professional. She works part-time for a Toronto HelpCentre where she develops software tools for internal use. In her spare time she co-moderates the Programmer Certification Study Forum at www.javaranch.com.

Margarita Isayeva is a Sun Certified Java Programmer and IBM Certified XML Developer and holds a bachelor's degree in Math. She has worked for more than ten years for "Dipol" Inc, Russia, primarily in the field of information system design. Her interests include linguistics, information theory, psychology, and particularly human interactions with computers. Margarita is a co-moderator of the "Programmer Certification Study" forum on JavaRanch.com and she spends her free time watching progress in the IT industry from this safe place and occasionally helping others to survive its consequences.

Ajith Kallambella is a Sun Certified Java Programmer and IBM Certified XML Developer. He holds a bachelor's degree in Computer Science and a post-graduate degree in Software Engineering from Harvard Extension school. He has been writing software for the past eight years. At present, Ajith works as a Systems Consultant for Analysts International in the Enterprise Solutions Group. Based in Research Triangle Park, North Carolina, he specializes in developing fault-tolerant systems, object-oriented frameworks, and heuristics-based solutions. Ajith is a professional flute player and while not sipping Java, he enjoys listening to music, stargazing, and camping. His second home is JavaRanch.com where he can be spotted moderating the XML forum or stomping in a dozen other discussion forums.

Kathy Sierra is a senior Java instructor at Sun Microsystems, Inc. She spent the last four years helping others learn everything from Jini to J2EE through courses, articles, online discussions, and evangelism. Kathy believes that learning Java should be fun, and founded one of the world's largest Java websites, javaranch.com, to build a friendly, learning-centered Java community. She also claims to know, for a fact, that Java programmers are more attractive and have more fun than C++ coders.

Dedication

Cindy Glass   I would like to dedicate this book to the multi-national, ethnic and religious participants at JavaRanch.com who were so supportive of the U.S. after the terrorist attacks on the World Trade Center.

Jane Griscti   I would like to dedicate my chapters to my fellow JavaRanchers: greenhorns, ranch hands, bartenders and sheriffs, all of whom make JavaRanch the friendliest place in cyberspace.

Margarita Isayeva   To my parents.

Ajith Kallambella   I dedicate my chapters to all Java enthusiasts around the world.

Kathy Sierra   To Albert James Bates IV for evolving from C to Java and making life so much fun.

Contents

v

Acknowledgments

Cindy Glass   I would like to thank Dr. Peter den Haan for his expertise in insuring that the technical content of this book was excellent. Also, thanks to JavaRanch.com for bringing us together and providing a forum for folks interested in Java-related technologies to interact in a uniquely personal environment.

Jane Griscti   My personal thanks to Peter den Haan for the time and care he took in his technical review of the manuscript; the editorial team at McGraw-Hill/Osborne Media Group: Claire Splan, Sally Engelfried, Alex Corona, and especially Francis (Franny) Kelly, without whose encouragement I would never have dared to write my chapters; and to my co-worker, Glen Jansen, for his willingness to read through my muddled first drafts. Any errors are solely my own.

Margarita Isayeva   I'd like to thank both the JavaRanch community and the editorial team at Osborne without whom my work would not be possible. My personal thanks to: Jane Griscti for her friendship, patience and great help; Peter den Haan for priceless nitpicking; Jim Yingst for a constant inspiring demonstration of inconceivable knowledge of Java tenets; and Sahir Shah, whose brilliant sense of humor saved me from a heavy depression due to an inability to keep up with Jim, Peter and Jane. Thanks to my husband Christopher for sacrificing his computer and helping my work.

Ajith Kallambella   I would like to thank my wife, Harsha, for all her support and inspiration and Dr. Peter for his nit-picking and excellent technical reviews. Thanks to folks at Osborne for giving me an opportunity to be a part of this great team.

Kathy Sierra   Thanks to the whole Passport team, especially Franny (kept us going), Mike (kept us laughing), and Peter (kept us technically correct). Thanks also to my co-authors and the whole wonderful javaranch world, including the cows. And a huge thanks to my co-workers, certification specialists, and fellow java gurus at Sun Educational Services, especially Simon.

Check-In

May I See Your Passport?

What do you mean you don't have a passport? Why, it's sitting right in your hands, even as you read! This book is your passport to a very special place. You're about to begin a journey, my friend, a journey towards that magical place called CERTIFICATION! You don't need a ticket, you don't need a suitcase. Just snuggle up and read this passport—it's all you need to get there. Are you ready? Let's go!

Your Travel Agent—Mike Meyers

Hello! My name's Mike Meyers. I've written a number of popular certification books and I'm the President of Total Seminars, LLC. On any given day, you'll find me replacing a hard drive, setting up a website, or writing code. I love every aspect of this book you hold in your hands. It's part of a powerful new book series called the *Mike Meyers' Certification Passports*. Every book in this series combines easy readability with a condensed format. In other words, the kind of book I always wanted when I went for my certifications. Putting this much information in an accessible format is an enormous challenge but I think we have achieved our goal and I am confident you'll agree.

   I designed this series to do one thing and only one thing—to get you only the information you need to achieve your certification. You won't find any fluff in here—the authors packed every page with nothing but the real nitty gritty of the certification exam. Every page is packed with 100 percent pure concentrate of certification knowledge! But we didn't forget to make the book readable. I hope you enjoy the casual, friendly style. I want you to feel as though the authors are speaking to you, discussing the certification—not just spewing facts at you.

You may e-mail the authors of this book at **cowgirl@javaranch.com.**
My personal e-mail address is **mikem@totalsem.com**. Please feel free to
contact me directly if you have any questions, complaints, or compliments.

Your Destination—Java 2

This book is your passport to the Java 2 exam. You'll learn about basic language rules and OOP concepts, including declarations and access control;
overloading, overriding, runtime types, and object orientation; garbage
collection; and the java.lang package. You'll then learn how to put Java into
practice, using operators, assignments, flow control, exceptions, and
threads. Finally, you'll learn how to use the Java API, including the java.awt
package, the java.io package, and the java.util package.

Why the Travel Theme?

One of my favorite topics is the parallel of gaining a certification to taking
a trip. All of the elements are the same: preparation, an itinerary, a route—
even mishaps along the way. Let me show you how it all works.

This book is divided into 12 chapters. Each chapter begins with an
"Itinerary" which provides objectives covered in each chapter and an
"ETA" to give you an idea of the time involved learning the skills in that
chapter. Each chapter is broken down by real exam objectives, either
those officially stated by the certifying body or, if the vendor doesn't
provide these, our expert take on the best way to approach the topics.
Also, each chapter contains a number of helpful items to bring out
points of interest:

Exam Tip

Points out critical topics you're likely to see on the actual exam.

Travel Assistance

Shows you additional sources such as books and websites to give you
more information.

Local Lingo

Describes special terms in detail in a way you can easily understand.

Travel Advisory

Warns you of common pitfalls, misconceptions, and downright physical peril!

The end of the chapter gives you two handy tools. The "Checkpoint" reviews each objective covered in the chapter with a handy synopsis—a great way to quickly review. Plus, you'll find end-of-chapter questions to test your newly acquired skills.

But the fun doesn't stop there! After you've read the book, pull out the CD and take advantage of the free practice questions! Use the full practice exam to hone your skills and keep the book handy to check answers.

If you want even more practice, log on to **http://www.Osborne.com/ Passport,** and for a nominal fee you'll get additional high-quality practice questions.

When you're passing the practice questions, you're ready to take the exam—go get certified!

The End of the Trail

The IT industry changes and grows constantly—and so should you. Finishing one certification is just a step in an ongoing process of gaining more and more certifications to match your constantly changing and growing skills. Read the Career Flight Path at the end of the book to see where this certification fits into your personal certification goals. Remember, in the IT business, if you're not moving forward, you are way behind!

Good luck on your certification! Stay in touch!

Mike Meyers
Series Editor
Mike Meyers' Certification Passport

Basic Language Rules and OOP Concepts

Language Fundamentals

CHAPTER 1

NEWBIE	SOME EXPERIENCE	EXPERT
40 hours	20 hours	5 hours

Java is a high-level, general purpose, object-oriented programming language that is similar to other *object-oriented programming* (OOP) languages. Programs written in Java are not compiled directly into machine-executable code; they are compiled into *bytecode*, a machine independent instruction set. Each Java enabled system includes a *Java Runtime Environment* (JRE) specifically designed to work with the system's operating software. Each JRE includes a "software-execution engine," the *Java Virtual Machine* (JVM). The JVM acts as an interpreter, translating bytecode into machine-specific instructions which are then executed on the host platform. Multiplatform applications written in other languages have many distribution versions because a different, machine-executable version must exist for each targeted operating platform. Java programs are compiled to one bytecode version which can then be executed on any Java enabled system. This is Java's ultimate strength and the source of its *write once, run anywhere* (WORA) reputation.

Whew! That was a mouthful! Feeling a little like you did the first time you looked at the Java documentation? Wondering how on earth you're going to remember all that? Relax! You don't have to. Feel better? Good. Now take a deep breath…you have to *understand* it! The exam doesn't test your memory. It's full of code exhibits—10-, 20-, and 30-line code examples—and you're expected to know what they do. That means you have to know how to write code the compiler will understand *and* know how the compiler will interpret it.

And that is what this chapter is all about. It ain't fascinating reading, but it will introduce you to the layout of typical Java programs and the language we use to construct them: the language you'll use everyday as a Java programmer. So, are you ready? Let's go!

Objective 1.01

Identify Correctly Constructed Source Files and Declarations

Writing a Java source file is simple; all you need is a text editor. Writing source files that will compile without error is a little trickier. The Java compiler is a specialized application that reads source files and translates them into bytecode. Because the compiler is, in essence, a translation machine, it expects your files to be written in the Java language and it expects the contained statements to be written according to the rules of the Java language. Just as an English speaking person would have difficulty understanding an English sentence written in accordance with the rules of French grammar, the compiler will have difficulty translating statements written following the rules of Basic, C, or another programming language. In this objective, you'll learn how source files and their contained statements are written and how the compiler deals with nonconforming text.

Travel Assistance

You can learn more about the Java Language Specification by going to **http://java.sun.com/docs/books/jls/second_edition/html/j.title.doc.html**.

Organizing Java Source Files

Java applications are organized into *packages*. A package is composed of compilation units or *source files*. Source files are plain, vanilla text files that describe defined types: classes and interfaces. A *defined type* is a template that your programs can use over and over again to create objects. *Objects* are individual software entities, *instances* of a class. It helps to think of a class as an ice cube tray. Every time you want ice cubes, you fill the tray with water, stick it in the freezer, and a few hours later you pop out a dozen nicely formed cubes of ice. A class is very similar, but you are not limited to creating a dozen or ten dozen ice cubes at a time; you can create as many as you like, as often as you like, and better yet, you don't have to wait a few hours for them to freeze into shape!

Packages let you organize source files (the text files containing your class definitions) into related groups. Package names are hierarchical and correspond to the directory structure of the hard drive where your source files are stored. They are generally grouped according to their use. For example, classes created by Sun for the *Java Development Kit* (JDK) bear the package name `java` and are further organized into subgroups: `awt` (Abstract Window Toolkit), `lang` (language), `math` (mathematics), `io` (input/output), and so on. The original source files would have been stored in a matching directory structure :

```
directory      ........java
subdirectory   ...awt
subdirectory   ...lang
subdirectory   ... math
subdirectory   ... io
```

Package names are written using dot notation. The preceding packages would be written as : `java.awt`, `java.lang`, `java.math`, and `java.io`.

The JDK install files include an archive (`src.jar`) of all the source files used to create the JDK. To view a source file for a particular class, unpack the file from the `src.jar` archive. For example, to unpack the source file for `java.awt.Button` on a Win32 platform, open a DOS prompt and switch to the JDK directory. Then enter the following command:

```
jar xf src.jar src/java/awt/Button.java
```

The new directories: `src`, `java`, and `awt` will be created. You may view the `Button.java` file using any text editor. You'll find that any given source file follows a standard structure.

The Structure of a Java Source File

A source file has the file extension `.java`. (compiled source files are given the file extension `.class`). A source file has three basic sections, all of which are optional:

- A *package* declaration
- *Import* declarations
- Defined type (class or interface) declarations

The following is an example of a simple Java source file:

```
/** SimpleJava.java */
package ch36601;
import java.io.*;
public class SimpleJava {
    // class body
}
```

You can view the compiled bytecode of any `.class` file using the `javap.exe` utility that ships with the JDK. For example, executing `javap -c ch36601.SimpleJava`, where `-c` is the option to disassemble code, displays the following on a Win32 system:

```
Compiled from SimpleJava.java
public class ch36601.SimpleJava extends java.lang.Object {
    public ch36601.SimpleJava();
```

```
}
Method ch36601.SimpleJava()
   0 aload_0
   1 invokespecial #1 <Method java.lang.Object()>
   4 return
```

Travel Advisory

An empty file with the `.java` extension will compile without error, although it will be useless.

Descriptive text included in a source file is referred to as a *comment*. Java treats as comments any single-line text following the `//` characters and any block of text between the `/*` and `*/` characters. Comments enclosed between the `/**` and `*/` characters are used by the `javadoc.exe` utility to create *Application Programming Interface* (API) documentation. The documentation installed with the JDK is an example of API documentation generated by the JavaDoc utility. Comments are not included in compiled code.

Exam Tip

Java documentation (JavaDoc) is not specifically covered on the exam. You do, however, need to be able to distinguish a comment from an executable statement.

The `package` Declaration

You can use a `package` declaration (remember, it's optional) to group-related source files. The declaration has the following syntax:

```
package packageName;
```

Exam Tip

All complete Java statements end with a semicolon (`;`). A line which only consists of a semicolon is an *empty* statement.

The *fully qualified name* of any defined type includes its package name. For example, the JDK contains the `String` type, which is defined in the `java.lang` package. The fully qualified name of the `String` type is `java.lang.String`. Its *simple name* is `String`.

Travel Advisory

Package names, by convention, are based on reverse URLs and are written in lowercase. For example, packages written by IBM begin with `com.ibm` (the `www` is dropped), while those written by Intel might start with `com.intel`. Source files may also be stored in databases. In such cases the package naming rules may be slightly different.

A source file does not have to include a package declaration; however, if one is used:

- It must be the first noncomment line in the source file.

and

- It must be the *only* package declaration in the source file.

Package naming merely provides you with a convenient way to organize and locate source files. A package has no special relationship to its subpackages in terms of how the source files they contain are implemented. If a package name is not declared, the type becomes part of the *default unnamed package*. A default package is equivalent to the directory in which the source file is stored. For example, all source files in the `myutils` directory that do not include an explicit package name belong to the default package for `myutils`. The majority of Java-enabled systems allow one default package per directory, and only one default package—the one related to the current directory—is visible at any given time. How do you access a type defined in a different package? You import it!

The `import` Declaration

The `import` declaration allows you to make use of defined types (classes and interfaces) created by you or other programmers and defined in separate packages. The declaration may take two forms:

- Single-type import
- Import-on-demand

A *single-type import* declares the fully qualified name of a type that is used by the source file. The declaration tells the compiler where to look for the referenced type. The following statement notifies the Java compiler that if the current source file or package does not contain a definition for the `DataInputStream` type, it should search the `java.io` package:

```
import java.io.DataInputStream;
```

An *import-on-demand* declaration uses the wild card character, an asterisk (*):

```
import java.awt.*;
```

The preceding statement advises the Java compiler to search the `java.awt` package if it cannot find a referenced type within the current source file.

> **Travel Advisory**
>
> Using a wild card does not result in larger compiled files; only the types actually referenced in the source file's code are included in the compiled code. In the preceding example, the compiled `.class` file will not include every type defined in the `java.awt` package; it will include only those actually used.

Import declarations are optional. If they are not included, your code may still reference other types; however, unless they are in the same package or in the `java.lang` package, they must be referenced by their fully qualified names. An import allows you to reference them by their simple names. It's a form of shorthand; having to enter `java.awt.font.TextLayout` every time you want to change the display of a string can become tedious. If you import the type, all you need to enter in your code is `TextLayout`, and the compiler will know where to find it.

If you do use import declarations, they must adhere to the following four rules:

1. `import` statements must appear directly after the package statement, or, if no `package` statement is used, they must be the first noncomment lines in the source file.
2. Single-type imports cannot have the same simple name even if they have different fully qualified names. For example, the following is illegal:

```
import java.awt.Button;
import com.acme.Button;
```

3. You cannot use a single-type import with the same simple name as a type defined in the source file. For example, the following is illegal:

```
import java.awt.Button;
public class Button { }      // new type declaration
```

4. A single-type import can have the same name as a package. For example, the following is legal:

```
import java.io.Vector;    // single-type name is "Vector"
import Vector.myType;     // package name is "Vector"
```

Exam Tip

Duplicate import statements are ignored by the compiler.

When the compiler encounters a type name, it searches for the matching definition as follows:

- Within the current source file
- Within the same package
- Within the package named in a single-type import
- Within the packages named by import-on-demand statements

Exam Tip

The `java.lang` package is automatically made available to the compiler. Your code may access any of its types without explicitly including a `java.lang.*` import statement.

Travel Assistance

You can learn more about import statements by going to **http://developer.java.sun.com/developer/TechTips/2000/tt0110.html#tip2.**

To this point we've focused on what a source file is—how we group them into packages and how we import code from external packages. Now we can get to the heart of the matter: the *why* behind source file creation. Why do we do it? Because we want to build our own software entities, define our own types, rule our own domain!

Defined Types

Applications are written to mimic real (finance, travel, health) or imaginary (Atlantis, Fredonia, Pern) *domains*. Each domain contains objects: accounts, planes, health cards, Neptune, rebels, dragons, and so on. Each object has its own state of being and is capable of various behaviors. Java allows us to define the data (information about an object's state) and capabilities (behaviors) for a new object by creating a *type definition*. The definition can be saved, used, and reused to create new objects or instances of the same type. You can use your new types in your own applications or make them available to other programmers. The JDK consists of numerous such types that Sun has made available for public use. They are not part of the language; they *extend* the language, and when you define new types, you are also extending the language. You are not, however, given a totally free hand in this area. There are some basic rules you need to follow if you want the compiler to understand your type definitions.

A defined type consists of a *type declaration* followed by a *body*. The body of a type declaration is enclosed in curly braces ({ })and can contain declarations for any of the following:

- Initialization blocks (special one-time behaviors)
- Fields (state, data)
- Methods (capabilities, behaviors)
- Constructors (a special behavior that allows an object to create itself)
- Member types (other defined types)

The following illustrates the syntax of a defined type declaration and the optional sections that may be included in the body of the declaration.

```
[modifiers] type DefinedTypeName [extends-clause] [implements-
clause] {
    [initialization blocks]
    [fields]
    [constructors]
    [methods]
    [member types]
} // end of type body
```

> **Local Lingo**
>
> Variables that hold data concerning an object's state are called *fields* in Java.

The declaration of a defined type is composed of the following parts:

- *Modifiers* qualify a type's accessibility and the manner in which it can be used.
- The *extends clause* signifies that an object created with the type definition *is* a subtype of the extended type.
- The *implements* clause signals that an object created with the type definition will have the same behaviors as the implemented type(s) and *is* a subtype of the implemented type(s).

It may seem odd that you can include a type declaration within the body of another type declaration. While types come in two basic flavors (class or interface) they also come in two different forms: top level and nested. A *nested* type is enclosed within the body of another type. The directly enclosing type is referred to as the *top-level* type. A *member* type is, by definition, a nested type. Furthermore, a nested type can take on one of four additional forms: static member type, nonstatic member type, local, and anonymous.

> **Exam Tip**
>
> Constructors and initializers are defined within a class but are not *members* of the class; they are not inherited by subclasses. For more on inheritance see Chapter 3.

Both a type's flavor (class or interface) and form (top level, static member, nonstatic member, local, or anonymous) have a role in determining exactly *where* and *how* the type can be declared. The following is an example of the placement of the various forms of types within a source file:

```
TopLevelType {
    StaticMemberType {
        // body of StaticMember
```

```
    } // end of StaticMember

    NonStaticMemberType {
        someBlockOfCode {
            LocalType {
            } // end of LocalType
        } // end of someBlockOfCode
    } // end of NonStaticMemberType
} // end of TopLevelType
```

Note that a *local* type may be declared within any block of code, not just a method. A *block of code* consists of a set of statements enclosed in curly braces.

An *anonymous* type may be declared within the body of any of the other types.

Travel Advisory

Only nonstatic, local, and anonymous types are *inner classes.* A static member type is not an inner class and is sometimes formally referred to as a *top-level nested class* (how's that for an oxymoron!).

Modifiers

Modifiers set provisions for the manner in which an object of the defined type may be accessed or used. There are seven modifiers in Java that can be used in defined type declarations: `public`, `protected`, `private`, `static`, `abstract`, `final`, and `strictfp`. The `public`, `protected`, and `private` modifiers are known as *access modifiers*. They allow or restrict interactions between objects of different types. A type may be declared with no access modifier or one of `public`, `private`, or `protected`. The remaining modifiers qualify the manner in which an object may be used.

The general meanings of the modifiers are given in Table 1.1. For detailed information on the effects of modifiers on defined types see Chapters 2 and 3.

No declaration can contain both the `abstract` and `final` modifiers. The `abstract` modifier defines a type as being incomplete, while the `final` modifier defines a type to be complete and not subject to change. The two modifiers are incompatible. Use them together and the compiler will politely tell you, via an error, that you are confused.

TABLE 1.1   General Meanings of Defined Type Modifiers

Modifier	Meaning
public	Access to the type is unrestricted.
protected	Access to the type is restricted to defined types that are part of the same package and direct subtypes regardless of their package *if* the subtype is involved in the creation of an object of the protected type.
(no access modifier)	No modifier declares the type has default access and may be accessed by any type in the same package (directory).
private	Access is restricted to objects of the same type.
static	A static type belongs to the enclosing type and is not implicitly tied to an instance of the enclosing type.
abstract	Signifies that the type definition is incomplete and it cannot be used to create (instantiate) objects.
final	Signifies that the type cannot be modified or extended (subtyped).
strictfp	Signifies that all behaviors of the type that involve floating-point operations will produce the same results, regardless of the platform used to execute the type.

Furthermore, no class may contain abstract methods unless the class itself is declared to be abstract. Interfaces are implicitly public and abstract, so including these modifiers in an interface declaration is redundant.

Travel Assistance

You can learn more about abstract classes by going to **http://developer.java.sun.com/developer/JDCTechTips/2001/tt0612.html#tip1.**

Extends Clause

An extends clause may be used in both class and interface declarations. It has two parts: the word `extends` and a type name.

If the extends clause is part of a class declaration, it may only include one class name. For example:

```
[modifiers] class NewClassName extends OneClass [implements]
```

> **Travel Advisory**
>
> By convention, class and interface names are written
> `CapitalizedWithInternalWordsCaptialized.`

If the extends clause is part of an interface declaration, it may contain a comma-delimited list of *interface* names. For example:

```
[modifiers] interface NewInterfaceName extends Interface, Interface,…
```

The new type is said to be a *subtype* (child) of the extended type. The extended type is said to be the *supertype* (parent) of the new type. This is the main means by which Java implements *inheritance*.

> **Exam Tip**
>
> Java does not allow multiple inheritance per se; that is, a class may only have one direct parent or supertype. A class may indirectly inherit the behavior of another type by implementing an interface. For more information on inheritance, see Chapter 3.

Implements Clause

An implements clause may only be used in a class declaration. It consists of two parts: the word `implements` and an interface type name. For example:

```
[modifiers] class ClassName [extends]
                    implements Interface, [Interface, Interface..]
```

Exam Tip

A class may implement more than one interface. An interface may not implement anything.

An interface type is similar to a class type in that it defines the properties and behaviors of an object; however, the behaviors in an interface are not implemented, that is, their methods do not include code statements that define how the behaviors will be executed. Any class which `implements` an interface *must* declare exactly the same methods as the interface even if it does not wish to implement the behavior. For example, the interface `Runnable` includes one method, `public void run()`. Any class which implements the `Runnable` interface must declare a `public void run()` method. Failure to do so will result in a compile error.

```
public class InterfaceExample implements Runnable {
    public void run(){
        // implementation code
    }
}
```

If the `run()` method declaration is removed from the above example the following compile error is raised:

```
InterfaceExample.java:1: InterfaceExample should be declared
abstract; it does not define run() in InterfaceExample
```

Top-Level Type Declarations

A top-level type is *not* enclosed within another type's declaration. It may have no access modifier (default access) or be declared `public`. If it is declared `public`, the source file which includes it must have a name that exactly matches the type's name. As a result of this rule, a source file may only contain *one* top-level `public` type, be it a class or an interface. Their declarations have the following syntax:

```
class ClassName [extends] [implements] {
    // body of class
```

```
}
public class ClassName [extends] [implements] {
    // body of class
}
```

> **Exam Tip**
>
> A source file may define multiple default-access top-level classes.
> If it does not contain a `public` class or interface, the file can
> have any name.

A top-level class may be either `abstract` or `final` but not both. It may also be declared `strictfp`. It may *not* be declared `private`, `protected`, or `static`.

```
public interface InterfaceName [extends] {
    // body of interface
}
```

A top-level interface may be declared as `abstract` or `strictfp`. An interface declaration may not include the modifiers `static` or `final`. All members of a top-level interface are implicitly `public`.

`Static` Member Declarations

A `static` member type is one whose declaration is enclosed within the body of another type and contains the modifier `static`. It is created when a class is first loaded and can be accessed directly; for example, `TopLevel.StaticType.method()`. It does not need an instance of the enclosing class, unlike nonstatic member classes.

```
class TopLevel {
    static class StaticMemberClass [extends] [implements] {}
    static interface StaticInterface [extends] {}
}
```

Table 1.2 details which modifiers may used in a `static` member declaration.

TABLE 1.2   Modifiers for a Static Member Type

| | A **Static** Member | | | |
| | Class Declared in Another | | Interface Declared in Another | |
Modifiers	Class	Interface	Class	Interface
public	yes	yes (implicit)	yes	yes (implicit)
protected	yes	no	yes	no
(default)	yes	no	yes	no
private	yes	no	yes	no
abstract	yes	yes	yes	yes (implicit)
final	yes	yes	no	no
strictfp	yes	yes	yes	yes

Travel Advisory

Source files containing nested classes compile to multiple .class files, with one file named for the top-level type and one file for each nested type. Nested .class filenames are written as TopLevel Type$NestedType.class.

Inner Type Declarations

An *inner type* is any type whose declaration is contained within the body of another type and which does *not* contain the static modifier.

```
typeName TopLevel {
    class InnerClass [extends] [implements] {}
    interface InnerInterface [extends] {}
}
```

Table 1.3 details which modifiers may be used in an inner type declaration.

	An Inner			
	Class Declared in Another		**Interface Declared in Another**	
Modifiers	**Class**	**Interface**	**Class**	**Interface**
public	yes	yes (implicit)	yes	yes (implicit)
protected	yes	no	yes	no
private	yes	no	yes	no
abstract	yes	yes	yes	yes (implicit)
final	yes	yes	no	no
strictfp	yes	yes	yes	yes

TABLE 1.3 Modifiers for Inner Type Declarations

Travel Advisory

A top-level class which contains an `abstract` inner class may be instantiated; however, the `abstract` inner class itself may not be.

Local Class Declarations

A *local class* is declared within the body of any other block of code. They may only be declared within a class. There is no such type as a "local interface."

```
class Inner {
    void method(){
        class Local [extends][implements] {
            // body of local class
        }
    }
}
```

A local class may *not* be declared `public`, `protected`, `private`, or `static`. It may be either `abstract` or `final` (but not both) or `strictfp`.

Anonymous Type Declarations

An *anonymous* type does not have a modifier clause, a name, an extends clause, or an implements clause. It is created using the `new` operator and the name of an existing class, which it implicitly extends, or an existing interface, which it implicitly implements.

```
new ClassName() { // implementation }
new InterfaceName() { // implementation }
```

An anonymous class is implicitly `final`. It can never be `abstract` or `static`.

The body of an anonymous class cannot declare a constructor. A constructor identifier must be the same as the class name; an anonymous class has no name and uses the constructor of the type it implicitly extends. For more on how and where anonymous classes are most commonly used, see Chapter 10.

Once you've settled on a name and declaration for your defined type you can begin to describe what instances of the type will do. You can describe the state (fields) and behaviors (methods) along with any special, one-time behavior (initializer blocks). These are the features that make your objects come to life.

Initialization Blocks

An *initialization block* is a set of statements enclosed in curly braces inside a class body; they may not be used in an interface type. They may be declared with the `static` modifier or not. An initialization block that is declared `static` belongs to the class. It will be executed only once, when the class is first loaded.

An initialization block that is not declared with the `static` modifier is an instance initializer. An instance initializer is executed once for each object created using the class. As they apply to objects, they may reference the current object using the `this` keyword and parent objects using the `super` keyword.

Exam Tip
An initialization block may not include the `return` keyword.

Field Declarations

A field is a variable that contains or references data belonging to a class or an instance of the class. Field declarations take the form:

```
[modifiers] type fieldName [= initializer] ;
```

where a modifier can be any one or more of `public`, `protected`, `private`, `static`, `final`, `transient`, or `volatile`.

The access modifiers `public`, `protected`, and `private` have the same meanings as those given in Table 1.1 for defined types. If no access modifier is declared, the field has default (package) access.

The `final` modifier may not be combined with the modifier `volatile`. A `volatile` field is constantly changing, while a `final` field never changes.

> **Exam Tip**
>
> Watch out for classes, interfaces, or methods declared with the `transient` or `volatile` modifiers. They only apply to variables.

Type Fields

A field declared to be `static` belongs to the type. Only one incarnation of a type field exists at any given time. The data referenced by or stored in a type field is shared in common by all instances of the type.

A `static final` field is a *constant*. It belongs to the type and its value may not be altered once it is initialized. Only `static final` fields (constants) may be declared in an interface type and they must be initialized when declared. Constant identifiers are commonly written with ALL_WORDS_CAPITALIZED.

Instance Fields

An instance field is any field declared *without* the `static` modifier. One incarnation of the field exists for *each object* created using the class.

Transient Fields

The `transient` modifier signifies that the field is not meant to represent a persistent object state. The field's value will be not be saved if the object is transferred to permanent storage, for example, a file, if the object is serializable. See Chapter 5 for more information on the `java.lang.Serializable` interface and Chapter 11 for information on using serializable objects.

Volatile Fields

In multithreaded applications, the JVM maintains a master copy of all fields being accessed. Newly created threads receive working copies of any referenced fields. A thread will work with its own copy of a field, transferring the result of its operations to the master copy only when the operation is complete.

Declaring a field `volatile` notifies the JVM that the value of the field may change unpredictably. In this case, the JVM will not give each thread a working copy of the field; instead all thread operations will synchronize on the field's master copy. For more information on threads and synchronization, see Chapter 8.

Table 1.4 details the combination of modifiers that may be used in field declarations.

Method Declarations

A type's methods define its capabilities or behaviors; that is, what it can do. A method declaration takes the following form:

```
[modifiers] resultType MethodSignature [throws clause] {
    [method body]
    return [value];
}
```

> **Exam Tip**
>
> `Abstract` methods or methods declared in an interface (which are implicitly `abstract`) do not have a body. Their declarations must end with a semicolon.

Method Signatures

Every method has a *method signature*: a name and formal parameters, also called *arguments*. The signature does *not* include a method's return type or the throws clause.

TABLE 1.4   Field Modifier Combinations

	public	protected	private	static	final	transient	volatile
public		no	no	yes	yes	yes	yes
protected	no		no	yes	yes	yes	yes
private	no	no		yes	yes	yes	yes
static	yes	yes	yes		yes	yes	yes
final	yes	yes	yes	yes		yes	no
transient	yes	yes	yes	yes	yes		yes
volatile	yes	yes	yes	yes	no	yes	

A method's formal parameters are written as `Type argumentName`. Multiple parameters must be separated by commas.

```
[modifiers] ReturnType methodName( [final] [Type argName],
                                   [final] [Type argName, ..] )
                                   [throws clause]
```

The order in which the parameter types are listed forms part of the signature. A type may not declare two methods with exactly the same name and parameter order. However, a method declaration using the same name as another and using the same parameter types but declared in a different order is legal. The declaration would be seen as a method overload. See Chapter 3 for more information on overloading methods.

A method must include a return type or the keyword `void` to indicate no value is returned.

Travel Advisory

A method name includes its parameter list, even if there is none. Java immediately recognizes an item as a method by the parentheses () that follow the identifier. A method can have the same name as a variable: `duplicate` and `duplicate()` are seen by the compiler to refer to a variable and a method, respectively.

Method Modifiers

There are nine method modifiers: `public`, `protected`, `private`, `abstract`, `static`, `final`, `synchronized`, `native`, and `strictfp`. The access modifiers `public`, `protected`, and `private` have the same meanings as those given in Table 1.1 for defined types.

Any method declared `static` is a class method. Any method declared without the `static` modifier is an instance method. A `final` method may not be modified by a subtype. The floating point operations of a `strictfp` method are guaranteed to produce the same results regardless of the platform used to execute the method.

The modifier `final` may be used with parameters; for example, `int method(final int arg)`. Declaring a parameter `final` lets the compiler and

JVM know that the value of the parameter will not be changed within the method. This allows the compiler to perform some optimization. It also allows the variable to be used by any local class declared within the method.

Abstract Methods

An abstract method may only be declared within an abstract class; any method declared in an interface is implicitly abstract. An abstract method cannot be declared private, static, native, or final because none of these modifiers would allow the method to be changed in a subtype, and an abstract method must be implemented by any nonabstract subtype.

Travel Advisory

It is not illegal to use the modifiers public and abstract when declaring methods in an interface; however, doing so is redundant and not recommended.

Native Methods

A native method may not be declared abstract or have a method body; its declaration must end with a semicolon (;). Native methods alert Java to the existence of a platform-dependent function written in a language other than Java. A call to a native method instructs the JVM to invoke the function via the operating system. The compiler will not check for the existence of a native method. The JVM will only check for the existence of the native method when the method is invoked during execution.

Synchronized Methods

Synchronized methods must obtain a lock before they begin execution. Only synchronized methods or code blocks may use the monitor methods wait(), notify(), and notifyAll() defined in java.lang.Object. For more on locks, monitors, synchronized methods, and code blocks, see Chapter 8.

Exam Tip

Watch out for classes, interfaces, or variables declared with the synchronized keyword. This keyword is only valid for methods or code blocks.

The Throws Clause

If an operation performed in the body of a method is likely to cause a checked exception, the method must either handle the exception in a try-catch block or declare the exception in a throws clause, indicating to the caller that it will either have to handle the exception itself or pass it on by declaring it in its own throws clause.

```
public class MethodDeclaration {
    void methodA() {
        int a = methodB();
    }
    int methodB() {
        throw new Exception();  // force an exception
    }
}
```

The preceding example will result in the compile error "unreported exception `java.lang.Exception;` must be caught or declared to be thrown." The code may be corrected by doing any of the following:

- Adding a throws clause to the declarations for both methodA and methodB:

```
void methodA() throws Exception
int methodB() throws Exception
```

- Adding a try-catch block to methodB:

```
int methodB() {
    try{
        throw new Exception();
      } catch( Exception e ) {}
```

- Adding a throws-clause to methodB and adding a try-catch block to methodA:

```
void methodA() {
    try{
        int a = methodB();
    } catch( Exception e ) {}
```

```
int methodB() throws Exception {
    throw new Exception();
}
```

For more information on exceptions and try-catch blocks, see Chapter 7.

There's one special method that every class can have. It belongs to the class, not instances of the class, and is used by the JVM.

The `main()` Method

The `main()` method holds a special position in Java. It is the first section of code to be executed when a class is used as an entry point into an application. If a properly declared `main()` is not found by the JVM, the following runtime error will occur:

```
Exception in thread "main" java.lang.NoSuchMethodError: main
```

A properly declared `main()` method takes the following form:

```
public static void main( String[] args ) { // method body }
```

- The modifiers `public` and `static` are required, although their order may be reversed. The declaration of `main()` may also legally include the modifier `final`.
- The return type `void` is required and must appear directly before the method name `main()`.
- The parameter type `String[]` is required. The parameter variable name `args` is used by convention only. It may be replaced by any legal identifier, for example, `arg`, `foo`, `fred`, and so on. The parameter may also be declared `final`.

Exam Tip

Java Language Specification (JLS) §12.1.4 states `main()` must be `public`, `static`, and `void` and take a single argument that is an array of strings. On the exam, declarations that do not include all four elements in their correct order are incorrect, despite the fact that the JDK 1.2 compiler will not complain if the method is declared with `protected` or `private` rather than `public`.

It is legal to declare a `main()` method in any class. For this reason, an application may have as many entry points as it does classes. The `main()` executed by the JVM is based on the class used to start the application.

Travel Advisory
The `main()` method can also be inherited and overridden (see Chapter 3 for method inheritance rules).

The JVM may use `main()` to start an application, but how does it create objects? The class tells it how! Each has one or more special behaviors called *constructors*. That's what's neat about classes: they take Socrates' motto "know thyself" literally.

Constructors

A constructor is similar to a method but it has a special function: it knows how to build the object defined by the class. A constructor may only be declared in class bodies; they will cause a compile error if they are declared in an interface body. A constructor declaration takes the following form:

```
[modifiers] ClassName( [parameters] ) [throws-clause]
```

Local Lingo
Constructors are commonly referred to as *ctors*.

A class may have more than one constructor, provided the types of the parameters are different or given in a different order. If a class definition does not include a constructor declaration, the compiler will provide a default constructor similar to the following:

```
public SimpleJava() {
    super();
}
```

where `SimpleJava` would be replaced by the name of the class. The compiler will also use the same access modifier used in the original class declaration.

Local Lingo

The default constructor is commonly called the *default no-arg ctor* because it does not contain a parameter (argument) list.

Travel Assistance

You can learn more about default constructors by going to **http://developer.java.sun.com/developer/TechTips/1998/ tt0811.html#tip2.**

If the class explicitly declares even one constructor, the compiler will not create a default constructor.

A constructor may only be declared with one of the three access modifiers: `public`, `protected`, or `private`, or with no modifier, indicating default package access.

The name of a constructor must be the same as the simple type name of the class in which it is declared.

The body of a constructor cannot invoke itself by using the `this` keyword. It may, however, use the `this` keyword to access its own instance fields or to invoke another constructor that has a different parameter list. If `this()` is used to invoke another constructor, it must be the first line in the constructor body.

Exam Tip

A constructor declared with a return type, for example, `int MyClassName()`, is treated as a method, not a constructor. The body of a constructor may contain a return statement such as `return`, but it may not return a value.

Travel Assistance

You can learn more about constructors and initialization ordering by going to **http://developer.java.sun.com/developer/TechTips/ 2000/tt1205.html#tip2.**

Whew! That takes care of source files and defined types. From here on the going is easier as we look at the individual pieces of the language itself.

Objective 1.02

State the Correspondence Between `main()` and Command-Line Arguments

The `main()` method is not only used to start an application, you can also give it commands! An *identifier* is the name given to an item in a program. Variables, methods, classes, and interfaces are all declared with identifiers. Keywords are reserved words which may not be used as identifiers. In this objective, you'll learn how Java handles command-line arguments and recognizes identifiers.

`main()` and Command-Line Arguments

Any command-line arguments supplied at an application's startup are stored beginning at the zeroth index of the `String[]` parameter. For example, the following code,

```java
public class TestMain{
    public static void main(String[] args){
        for( int i=0; i < args.length; i++ ) {
            System.out.println( "args[" + i + "] = " + args[i] );
        }
    }
}
```

when run from the command line using `java TestMain a b c d` will produce the following output:

```
args[0] = a
args[1] = b
args[2] = c
args[3] = d
```

Exam Tip
All arrays in Java are zero based.

Java Language Keywords

The Java language includes a limited number of keywords, as listed in Table 1.5. Keywords are reserved in Java and *may not be used as identifiers.*

TABLE 1.5	Keywords
Keyword Type	**Keywords**
Primitive types	boolean, byte, char, double, float, int, long, short
Modifiers	public, private, protected, abstract, final, native, static, strictfp, synchronized, transient, volatile
Flow control	if, else, do, while, switch, case, default, for, break, continue
OO operators	class, extends, implements, import, instanceof, interface, new, package, super, this
Exception handling	catch, finally, try, throw, throws
Method specific	return, void
*Unused	const, goto

* The keywords const *and* goto *are not currently implemented in the Java language.*

The words true and false are boolean literals, not keywords. They may not be used as identifiers.

The word "null" is a null literal, not a keyword. It may not be used as an identifier.

> ## Exam Tip
>
> All Java keywords are lowercase. Watch out for capitalized versions in keyword lists.

Identifiers

An identifier is an unlimited sequence of legal (as defined by the *Java Language Specification* [JLS]) Unicode characters. They may begin with:

- Any Unicode letter, including letters from other languages such as Chinese, Greek, Italian, and so on
- The underscore character (_)
- The dollar sign character ($)

Travel Assistance

You can learn more about Unicode by going to **http://www. unicode.org/.**

Any Unicode character may be used in the remaining identifier sequence, including the underscore, dollar sign, and digits. Identifier sequences may *not*:

- Contain a space
- Contain any character that is not part of a standard alphabet; for example, the following are illegal identifier characters: # [ ] (* ^ ~
- Begin with a number, including the ASCII characters used for the digits 0 through 9 and their Unicode equivalents \u0030-\u0039
- Have the same spelling as a keyword, either of the `boolean` literals `true` and `false`, or the null literal

---

Exam Tip

Java is case sensitive. `MyClass` and `myClass` are different identifiers.

Objective 1.03

State Effect of Using a Variable or Array Element When No Explicit Assignment Is Made

Accessing a variable, array or array element can produce different results depending on where the variable or array is declared. In this objective, you'll learn how Java handles variables declared as fields, in methods, and in code blocks and how array variables and elements are created and accessed.

Variables Declared as Fields

When a class is loaded, all its fields are initialized to the default values (see Table 1.6) of their declared types. `static` initializer statements are then executed in the order in which they appear in the source file. When an instance of the class is created, all the instance fields are initialized to the default values of their declared types, and then the instance initializers (instance initialization blocks or assignment statements) are executed in their textual order.

TABLE 1.6   Range and Default Values for Primitive Data Types

Type	Size	Range	Default Value
byte	8-bit	−128 to 127	0
short	16-bit	−32,768 to 32,767	0
int	32-bit	−2,147,483,648 to 2,147,483,467	0
long	64-bit	$-(2^{63})$ to $2^{63}-1$	0L
float	32-bit	−3.4E38 to 3.4E38 (6 or 7 digits of precision)	0.0F
double	64-bit	−1.7E308 to 1.7E308 (14 or 15 digits of precision)	0.0D
char	16-bit	0 to 65,535	\0000 (Unicode character)
boolean	undefined	true or false	false

> **Exam Tip**
>
> The default value of any object is the null literal.

The order of initialization affects the manner in which fields may reference one another:

- A class field may not reference the value of another class field whose declaration statement is later in the source file.

- Instance fields may not reference the value of another instance field whose declaration statement is later in the source file.
- An instance field initializer may be assigned the value of a class field even if the class field is declared after the instance field, since it will have been previously initialized.

```
public class FieldInitialization {
        int i = b;
    static int a = b;    // compile-error: illegal forward reference
        int j = k;    // compile-error: illegal forward reference
    static int b = 5;
        int k = 10;
}
```

In the preceding example, assigning the static field b to the instance field i does not raise a compile-time error because static field initialization occurs before instance field initialization. However, assigning the value of static field b to the static field a raises the compile-time error illegal forward reference because static field b is declared after static field a in the source file. The same rule applies in the statement that assigns the instance field k to the instance field j; an illegal forward reference compile error is raised.

Travel Assistance

You can learn more about class methods and variables by going to **http://developer.java.sun.com/developer/TechTips/2000/ tt0912.html#tip1.**

Constant and Blank Finals

The only exceptions to the preceding rules are final fields whose initialization values are known at compile time. These constants are immediately initialized to their given values and are *never* assigned the default value of their declared type.

A blank final field is a final field whose declaration does not include an initializer. A compile error will be raised if a blank static final field is not assigned a value within a static initialization block.

```
public class StaticBlankFinals {
    static final int CONSTANT; // blank final
```

```
    static {                    // initialization block
        CONSTANT = 10;
    }
}
```

If the initialization block is removed from the preceding example, the compile error "variable CONSTANT may not have been initialized" will be raised.

A blank final instance field must be assigned a value within an initialization block or in every one of the class constructors:

```
public class InstanceBlankFinal {
    final int qty;
    InstanceBlankFinal() {     // default constructor
        super();
    }
    InstanceBlankFinal( int qty ) {    // constructor
        this.qty = qty;
    }
}
```

The preceding example will produce the compile error "variable qty might not have been initialized" because the default constructor fails to assign a value to the blank final qty.

Variables Declared Within Methods

What happens when you access a variable declared in a method? Variables declared in methods are *local variables*. They must have an explicitly assigned value *before* they are accessed. They will not automatically be set to their default values as fields are.

Can a local class access the variables in its enclosing method? Only if the method variables and parameters are declared final. This prevents both the method and the local class from modifying their values and allows the compiler to optimize the code.

What happens if a field initializer invokes a method? The unexpected may happen. While a forward reference compile error will be raised if a field references another field before it is declared, the same is not true if a field initializer invokes a method that uses another field that has not yet been declared. The following example code will compile without error and display a value of zero:

```
public class TestFieldInit {
    int fieldOne = getFieldTwo();
    int fieldTwo = 20;
    int getFieldTwo() {
        return fieldTwo;
    }
    public static void main(String[] args) {
        System.out.println( "Value of fieldOne: " +
                          new TestFieldInit().fieldOne );
    }
}
Output: Value of fieldOne: 0
```

The declaration and initialization of `fieldTwo` appears after the call to `getFieldTwo()` by the initializer for `fieldOne`. No compile error is raised; the default value of `fieldTwo`, zero, is returned, not the assigned value of 20.

Variables Declared Within Code Blocks

Variables declared within code blocks must also be explicitly assigned a value before they can be accessed. The variable will only be visible within its enclosing block. For example, a variable declared and initialized in a `for-loop` is only accessible within the `for-loop` construct.

Accessing Arrays and Array Elements

Java has one non-primitive built-in type: array. Array variables are declared using the array dimension operator `[]`: `typeName [] arrayName;`

Array variables are *reference variables*. When they are declared as fields, they are initialized to `null`. When declared in methods, they are not initialized, and any attempt to access them before they are explicitly assigned a value results in a compile error.

Array declarations do *not* create array elements; these are created either through the use of the `new` operator or an initialization block:

```
int[] arrayA = new int[5];
String[] arrayB = { "Welcome", "to", "Java" };
```

In the preceding example, the array reference variable `arrayA` holds the first memory address to a chain of five integer values. The array reference variable arrayB holds the first memory address to a chain of three String objects. Array elements are always initialized to the default value of their declared type; regardless of where they are declared: as fields or local variables.

Exam Tip

Once an array is initialized, it may not be resized.

You access array elements via an *index*. All arrays are zero-based. In the preceding example, the statement arrayB[0] would access the string "Welcome", arrayB[1] would access "to", and so on. A variable may be used in the initialization statement or as an index into an array only if it evaluates to one of the integral types byte, short, char, or int. An index cannot be of type long, float, or double.

The language is very lenient with array declaration statements. Extra white space is ignored and the index operator may be placed before or after the type name. All of the following are legal array declarations:

```
int [] arrayA;
int[]arrayA;
int arrayA[];
int arrayA     [];
```

Exam Tip

Watch out for array declaration statements that include an index value; for example, int [5] arrayA; or int arrayA[5]. These are illegal in Java.

The language is less lenient with initialization statements. An array reference variable may be assigned a null value, but you cannot use empty brackets to indicate an empty array.

```
int[] arrayA = null;        // legal
int[] arrayB = new int[0];  // legal
int[] arrayC = new int[];   // illegal
```

An array initialization statement may combine the new operator and an initialization block but an initialization block may not be used once an array has been initialized using the new operator.

```
int [] arrayA = new int[] { 1, 2, 3, 4, 5 };    // legal
int [] arrayB = new int[5];
arrayB = { 1, 2, 3, 4, 5 };                     // illegal
```

An array's length is stored as a property and may be accessed using `arrayName.length`.

Exam Tip

Watch out for code using a length method to return the length of an array, for example, `array.length()`. There is no `length()` array method.

Multidimensional Arrays

Technically, all arrays in Java are one-dimensional. You may create multidimensional arrays; however, they are really arrays of arrays. The following are all legal multidimensional array declarations:

```
int[][] arrayA;
int [] arrayA [];
int arrayA [][];
```

The first array index operator represents the rows; the second, the columns. Array initialization statements may use the new operator or nested curly braces:

```
int[][] arrayA = new int[5][10];
int[][] arrayA = { {1,2,3} , {4,5,6} , {7,8,9} };
```

The rows must be initialized; columns may be initialized separately but not vice versa:

```
int[][] arrayA = new int [5][];    // legal
int[][] arrayA = new int [][10];   // illegal
```

Columns may be of different lengths:

```
int[][] arrayA = new int [3][];
arrayA[0] = new int[3];
```

```
arrayA[1] = new int[6];
arrayA[2] = new int[9];
```

Travel Advisory

Arrays may be manipulated using the `java.util.`
`Arrays` class.

Objective 1.04

State the Range of Primitive Data Types and Declare Literal Values for `String` and Primitive Types

The Java language defines eight primitive data types, each of which can be represented with a literal or constant value.

Primitive Data Types

There are four signed integral types: `byte`, `short`, `int`, and `long`; two floating-point types: `float` and `double`; one unsigned integral (character) type: `char`; and one `boolean` type. These are collectively known as the *primitive data types*. The size of memory used to store values assigned to primitive types is fixed by the language, as shown in Table 1.6.

Floating point values in Java conform to the IEEE Standard for Binary Floating-Point Arithmetic, ANSI/IEEE Standard 754-1985.

Travel Assistance

You can learn more about accessing reference types by going to
http://www-106.ibm.com/developerworks/library/praxis/
pr8.html?dwzone=java.

Literals

Literals are constant values which are known at compile-time. They do not change during the execution of a program. Every primitive type may be represented by a literal.

Integral Literals

An integral literal may be expressed in octal, decimal, or hexadecimal notation where:

- Decimal numbers are composed of the digits 0 through 9.
- Octal numbers start with the digit zero (0) followed by any of the decimal digits 0 through 7.
- Hexadecimal numbers start with the digit zero (0) and a lowercase letter *x* (0x) followed by the characters for 0 through 15 where the numbers 10 through 15 are represented by the letters *a* through *f* or *A* through *F*, respectively.

The following are all legal integral literals:

```
12     // decimal notation for the number twelve
014    // octal notation for the number twelve
0xC    // hexadecimal notation for the number twelve
```

All integral literals are assumed to be of type `int`. To create a `long` literal, append either a lowercase or uppercase letter *L*.

```
12L    // decimal representation of twelve as a "long"
014L   // octal representation of twelve as a "long"
0xCl   // hexadecimal representation of twelve as a "long"
```

> **Travel Advisory**
>
> The standard convention is to append an uppercase letter *L* as this is less likely to be confused with the digit one (1).

Floating-Point Literals

Floating-point literals are written using decimal or exponential notation. They must include at least one decimal digit and a decimal point or an exponent. The following are all valid floating-point literals:

```
0.1    10.125    5.    .2    2e5    1E1
```

They cannot, however, begin with the exponential identifiers *e* or *E*. The following would be interpreted as *identifiers*, not literal values:

```
e2    E5
```

All floating-point literals are assumed to be of type `double`. To create a float literal, append a lowercase or uppercase *F* to the number.

```
0.1f    10.125F
```

Travel Advisory

While you cannot directly represent floating-point literals using octal or hexadecimal notation, Java does provide the `intBitsToFloat` method in the `java.lang.Float` class and the `longBitsToDouble()` method in the `java.lang.Double` class. Both may take values expressed in octal or hexadecimal notation. See Chapter 5 for more information on the `Float` and `Double` classes.

`char` Literals

The `char` type is used to represent 16-bit Unicode characters. A character type literal may be written as a single character or in Unicode notation. The following are examples of legal `char` literals:

```
'a'    '\u0041'    '\177'    'Z'
```

Exam Tip

Watch out for supposed character literals enclosed in double rather than single quotes. Double quotes denote strings, not characters.

Some characters may be written using an *escape sequence* consisting of the *escape character*, a backslash (\ ), and the corresponding ASCII character, as shown in Table 1.7.

TABLE 1.7   `char` Literal Escape Sequences

Escape Sequence	Unicode Equivalent	Description
\b	\u0008	backspace BS
\t	\u0009	horizontal tab HT
\n	\u000a	linefeed LF
\f	\u000c	form feed FF
\r	\u000d	carriage return CR
\ddd	\u0000 to \u00FF	Octal escape sequence
\"	\u0022	Double quote
\'	\u0027	Single quote
\\	\u005c	Backslash

Travel Advisory

Octal escape sequences are legal; however, Unicode sequences are recommended.

The backslash and double and single quote escapes allow you to embed the characters within single-line comments and strings.

Exam Tip

Always use the escaped ASCII sequences `\n` and `\r` to represent linefeeds and carriage returns in single-line comments or `String` literals. One of the first steps in the compile process is the translation of Unicode characters. The Unicode characters for a linefeed (\u000a) or carriage return (\u000d) are interpreted literally as "end of line" and can cause compile errors.

> **Travel Assistance**
>
> You can learn more about ASCII by going to
> **http://foldoc.doc.ic.ac.uk/foldoc/foldoc.cgi?ASCII.**

As the `char` type is an unsigned integral type you can also write `char` literals using decimal, octal and hexadecimal notation.

```
109    0115    0x21
```

The preceding are all legal `char` literals.

`boolean` Literals

A `boolean` literal can take one of two values: `true` or `false`. You cannot assign the digits 1 or 0 to `boolean` literals. They do not have corresponding integral values.

`null` Literals

A `null` literal has only one value: `null`. Only nonprimitive variables may be assigned a `null` literal.

`String` Literals

`String` literals are enclosed in double quotes and may be formed by zero or more characters and escape sequences, for example:

```
""    "I am a String literal."    "\n"
```

`String` literals are implicitly created as instances of the `java.lang.String` class. `String` variables hold a *reference* to a `String` literal object. `String` objects are *immutable,* which means that once they are created, *their contents cannot be changed.* This feature allows the compiler to optimize the storage of string objects. `String` literals are stored in a special area of memory: the string constant pool. Whenever a `String` literal is encountered, the JVM will first check the string constant pool to see if it already contains a `String` object with exactly the same data (character sequence). If a match is found, a reference to the existing string is returned, and no new object is created.

A `String` created using the `new` operator is *not* a `String` literal.

```
String str = new String("Hello");
```

The `new` operator *always* generates a unique object and returns a reference to
that object. The JVM will not search the string constant pool for a match. The following code, which uses the == operator, illustrates this point:

```
public class StringLiterals {
    public static void main(String[] args){
        String strA = "Hello";
        String strB = new String("Hello");
        String strC = "Hello";
        System.out.println("strA == strB -> " + (strA == strB) );
        System.out.println("strA == strC -> " + (strA == strC) );
    }
}
Output:
strA == strB -> false
strA == strC -> true
```

The == operator (see Chapter 6) returns `false` if two reference variables, in
this example `strA` and `strB`, point to *different* objects. The variable `strA` holds
a reference to the `String` literal `Hello`, which was created in the string constant
pool. The variable `strB` holds a reference to a *new* `String` object that was created
in the general memory area. The variables point to different objects that happen
to contain the same *data,* the character sequence for the word "Hello."

The == operator returns `true` if two reference variables point to the *same*
object. The variable `strC` holds a reference to the same `String` object `Hello`,
which is stored in the string constant pool. When the compiler encountered
`String strC =   "Hello"`, it recognized this as a `String` literal and checked

the string constant pool for a match. Because one was found, a reference to the existing object was returned, and no new String object was created. The following illustrates this behavior:

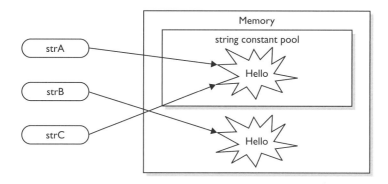

A `String` literal may also be formed by a *constant* `String` *expression*. A constant `String` expression is formed by concatenating `String` literals, as in this illustration.

```
String strA = "Hello," + "World!"
```

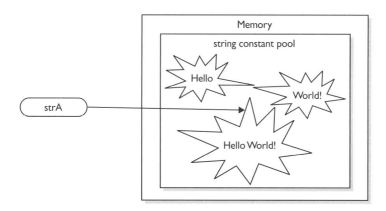

The resulting string, `Hello, World!` is a `String` literal, as are each of the words used to build it.

A string whose value results from the concatenation of two `String` variables or a `String` literal and a `String` variable is *not* a `String` literal.

```
String strA =  "Hello";
String strB = strA + "World";
```

strB in the preceding example does not reference a String literal. The result of the concatenation is a *new* String object. At runtime, the contents of the object referenced by strA are appended to the contents of the String literal object created from "World", and a new String object is returned. The contents of the object referenced by strA are not known until runtime.

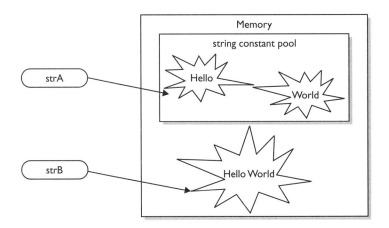

Note that the strB variable does not reference either of the objects in the string constant pool; instead, it references an entirely new object in general memory.

There is one other way to create a String literal: by using the intern() method of the java.lang.String class.

```
String str = new String("Hello").intern();
```

The intern() method instructs Java to treat the newly created string "Hello" *as if* it were a String literal. The following example code illustrates this point:

```
public class StringIntern {
    public static void main(String[] args){
        String strA = "Hello";
        String strB = new String("Hello").intern();
        System.out.println("strA == strB -> " + (strA == strB) );
    }
}
Output:
strA == strB -> true
```

The `intern()` method instructs the JVM to search the string constant pool for a matching object, and if one is found, return a reference to that object. If no matching object is found in the string constant pool, a new `String` object will be created and placed in the string constant pool, not in the general application memory area.

Travel Assistance

You can learn more about interning strings by going to **http:// developer.java.sun.com/developer/TechTips/1999/tt0114. html#tip3.**

Class Literals

There is one other literal that can be expressed in Java, the `class` literal. A `class` literal is a `java.lang.Class` object. Appending `.class` to the name of a reference or primitive type returns the `Class` object representing that type in the current runtime:

```
java.lang.String.class        // returns the Class object for String
int.class                     // returns the Class object for int
```

You may not create a `class` literal using a variable:

```
int i = 10;
i.class;                      // results in a compile-error
```

Travel Assistance

You can learn more about using class literals by going to **http:// developer.java.sun.com/developer/TechTips/1997/tt1118. html#tip3.**

That's it! You've made it through the first leg of the journey. The basics definitely aren't the fun part of any language. They are, however, what makes it tick. On the real exam, you can expect to see anywhere from 10 to 15 questions related to objectives about language fundamentals. Your understanding of them can make or break your final score. Know them well, along with the rest of the material covered in this text, and you have an excellent chance of passing with flying colors.

✔ **Objective 1.01** Identify Correctly Constructed Source Files and Declarations

- **Source Files**   Java applications are organized into packages that duplicate the directory structure of the system housing the application source files (compilation units). A source file contains three optional sections: a package declaration, import declarations, and defined type declarations.
- **Package Declarations**   A source file may only have one package statement which must be the first noncomment line in the file.
- **Import Declarations**   The import statement is used to access classes or interfaces that are not defined in the source file. A mix of multiple single-import and type-on-demand import statements is allowed. They must immediately follow the package statement, or, if no package statement exists, they must be the first noncomment lines in a source file.
- **Defined Type Declarations**   Type declarations contain three optional parts: modifiers, an extends clause, and an implements clause. A class may extend one other class and implement multiple interfaces. An interface may extend multiple interfaces but may not implement anything. Declarations may have no access modifier, indicating default package access, or they may include *one* of the three access modifiers: `public`, `protected`, or `private`. The fully qualified name of a class or interface includes its package name.
- **Top-Level Declarations**   A source file may not include more than one top-level public class or interface declaration, and the filename must exactly match the public class or interface name. A top-level class is not nested and can have either default (no access modifier) or `public` access. Top-level interfaces are implicitly public, and an interface cannot be directly nested in another interface as all interface members are implicitly `public`.
- **Nested Type Declarations**   Only nested classes or interfaces nested within a class may be declared `protected` or `private`.

- **The `static` Modifier**   The `static` modifier denotes that the class, initializer, field, or method belongs to the class or interface, not to individual instances. A top-level class or interface may not be declared `static`. A nested class declared with the `static` modifier is a `static` member class, not an inner class. All fields in an interface are implicitly `public static` and `final` constants and they must be initialized when declared. `Static final` constant fields in a class must be initialized when declared or within a `static` initializer block.

- **The `abstract` Modifier**   The `abstract` modifier denotes that the class or method is incomplete. An `abstract` method may only be declared in an `abstract` class. All `abstract` methods must have a semicolon for a body. Methods declared in an interface are implicitly `abstract`.

- **The `final` Modifier**   The `final` modifier denotes that the class, field, method, parameter or variable cannot be altered. An interface may only contain final fields. No declaration may include both the `final` and `abstract` modifiers.

- **Local Class Declarations**   A local class may not be declared `public`, `protected`, `private`, or `static`.

- **Anonymous Class Declarations**   An anonymous class is created using the `new` operator and implicitly extends a class or implements an interface. Its declaration has no name, no modifiers, and no extends clause or implements clause and is immediately followed by a set of curly braces enclosing its implementation.

- **Field and Variable Declarations**   The modifiers `volatile` and `transient` are only allowed in field or variable declarations. The `volatile` modifier may not be combined with the `final` modifier.

- **Method Declarations**   The modifier `synchronized` can only be used in method declarations or when defining a code block. The modifier `native` is only allowed in method declarations. A `native()` method has a semicolon for a body. A method declaration must include a throws clause if it invokes another method that can throw an exception or if it throws an exception of its own. If the method includes a try-catch block to handle the exception, the throws clause is not required. A method declaration must include a return type or be declared to return `void`.

- **Declaring `main()`**   The `main()` method must be declared `public static void main(String[] parameterName)`. The declaration may optionally include the modifier `final`. The parameter may optionally be declared `final`.

✔ **Objective 1.02** State the Correspondence Between `main()` and Command-Line Arguments. Identify Keywords and Identifiers

- **Index into `main()` array argument**   Command-line arguments are stored in the `String[]` array argument. The first command-line argument is stored in the zeroth index of the string argument array.
- **Correctly constructed identifiers**   Identifiers have no length restrictions. They are case sensitive and must begin with an alpha character, an underscore, or a dollar sign. The remaining characters may be standard alphabet characters of any language, digits, an underscore, or a dollar sign.
- **Java keywords**   Keywords are always lowercase. They may not be used as identifiers nor may the literals `true`, `false`, or `null` be used as identifiers.

✔ **Objective 1.03** State the Effect of Using a Variable or Array Element When No Explicit Assignment Has Been Made to It

- **Accessing fields**   Fields are initialized to the default value of their declared type. `Static` items are initialized when a class is loaded. Instance fields are initialized when an instance is created. The order of initialization follows the order in which the fields appear in the source file with all static fields initialized first. The only exception is a final field declared with a literal value. These are initialized immediately and are never assigned a default value.
- **Accessing local variables**   Variables in methods or code blocks (local variables) must be explicitly assigned a value before they can be used. They are *not* automatically initialized to the default value of their declared types.
- **Arrays**   Arrays are similar to objects. An array reference variable declared as a field is initialized to null. Array reference variables declared within a method are not initialized. An array is initialized when it is created with the `new` operator or an initialization block, not when it is declared. Array elements are initialized to the default value of their declared type whether they are declared as fields or local variables. All arrays are zero indexed. The length of an array is stored in its `length` property.

✔ **Objective 1.04** State the Range of All Primitive Data Types and Declare Literal Values for `string` and All Primitive Types

- **Primitive data types**   There are eight primitive data types: `byte`, `short`, `int`, `long`, `float`, `double`, `char`, and `boolean`. All integral literals are assumed to be of type int unless explicitly declared as long. All floating-point literals are assumed to be doubles unless explicitly declared as floats.

- **Numeric literals**   Integral literals, including char, may be written in decimal, octal, or hexadecimal notation. Floating-point literals must include one digit and either a decimal point or the exponent character *e* or *E* preceded by a digit. Character literals are enclosed in single quotes.
- **Escape characters**   The ASCII characters for a newline (\u000a) or carriage return (\u000d) may not be included in single-line comments or String literals. Use \n or \r instead.
- **String literals**   String literals are implicitly created as String objects. They are stored in the string constant pool and are only created as new pool objects if a matching String object does not already exist in the pool. Strings created with the new operator or from expressions involving variables are not String literals. They always result in the creation of new String objects.

REVIEW QUESTIONS

1. Will the following source file compile without error? Yes or No.

```
import java.io.*;
package questions;
import java.lang.*;
class ClassA {}
```

2. Will the following source file compile without error if the source filename is saved as Q36601_2.java? Yes or No.

```
package questions;
class Q36601_A {}
public class Q36601_2 {}
```

3. Which of the following type declarations are legal?

- **A.** static interface MyInterface implements Runnable {}
- **B.** class MyClass extends java.util.Date implements Runnable {}
- **C.** interface MyInterface extends MyClass {}
- **D.** public class MyClassA extends Thread, Runnable {}

4. Which of the following modifiers may be used in an inner class declaration? Select two.

   A. `public`
   B. `void`
   C. `abstract`
   D. `transient`

5. Which of the following modifiers may be used in a method declaration? Select three.

   A. `void`
   B. `protected`
   C. `volatile`
   D. `synchronized`

6. What will be the output of the following code if it is started from the command line using `java Q36601_6 one two three four`?

```
public class Q36601_6 {
    public static void main(String[] args){
        System.out.println( args[2] );
    }
}
```

   A. two
   B. three
   C. Q36601_6
   D. four

7. Which of the following are illegal identifiers? Select two.

   A. 9Letter
   B. _Name
   C. First10
   D. $dollars
   E. num#

8. Which of the following are not Java keywords? Select three.

   A. `Byte`
   B. `int`

    C. `main`
    D. `for`
    E. `goto`
    F. `then`

9. Which of the following are primitive data types? Select two.

    A. `boolean`
    B. `Integer`
    C. `float`
    D. `Char`

10. Which of the following are legal character literals? Select three.

    A. \u0031
    B. 'a'
    C. 9
    D. "z"
    E. 0x0065
    F. y

REVIEW ANSWERS

1. **No** Package declarations, if used, must be the first noncomment line in a source file.

2. **Yes** A source file must bear the same name as the `public` class it contains.

3. **B** Answer A is incorrect; an interface may not implement an interface. C is incorrect; an interface may not extend a class. D is incorrect; a class may only extend one class and cannot extend an interface.

4. **A** **C** The keyword `void` is only legal in method declarations. The modifier `transient` only applies to fields or variables.

5. **A** **B** **D** Answer C is incorrect; the modifier `volatile` may only be used with fields or variables.

6. **B** Indexes are zero-based, args[2] would index the third argument of "three". The filename is not part of the argument list.

7. **A** **E** "9Letter" is incorrect because identifiers may not begin with a digit. "num#" is incorrect because the pound sign is neither a digit nor a standard alphabet character.

8. **A** **C** **F** `byte`, not `Byte`, is a keyword. The words `main` and `then` are not keywords in Java.

9. **A** **C** `int` and `char` are primitive types, not `Integer` and `Char`.

10. **B** **C** **E** \u0031 is a Unicode escape; it must be enclosed in single quotes to qualify as a character literal; "z" is a string literal, not a character literal. The letter *y* on its own (not in single quotes) would be interpreted as a variable.

Declarations and Access Control

	NEWBIE	SOME EXPERIENCE	EXPERT
ETA	20 hours	10 hours	3 hours

55

The objectives in this section revolve around declarations. For the exam, you need to be able to declare classes (including the special variety known as *inner classes*), methods, instance variables, arrays, and local (also known as stack, automatic, or method) variables. To understand how to do these declarations, you'll need to know everything about the modifiers that can be used with each of the different things you're declaring. For example, you can mark a normal, top-level class as public by using the `public` modifier keyword, but you can't mark it as `private`. Methods, however, can be marked as private by using the `private` modifier.

This chapter covers all the modifiers you'll need to know for the exam, along with the rules for how and when to use them in declarations. It also covers other language rules for making legal (compilable and runnable) declarations for nearly everything in Java.

Objective 2.01

Write Code That Declares, Constructs, and Initializes Arrays

For this exam objective, you need to know three things: how to make an array reference variable (declare), how to make an array object (construct), and how to populate the array with elements (initialize). There are several different ways to do each of those things, and you'll need to know about all of them for the exam.

Array Overview

An array is an object on the heap, just like any other object, so to declare an array really means to declare a reference variable of some array type. One of the more confusing aspects of arrays in Java is that while an array itself is actually an object, the array object can hold primitive values or reference variables. In other words, there is no such thing as an array primitive, but you can have an array which holds primitives. If you think of a single (non-array) variable as a cup (holding either a primitive value or an object reference), an array is like a tray of multiple cups, each cup holding either a primitive value or a reference.

In Java, each cup in the array is called an element, with the index starting at zero. The first element in an array is at index zero, the second at index one, and so on. You must remember that all elements in an array are *always* given a default value. Always. It doesn't matter if the array is an instance variable or a local variable. When an array is constructed, something is put into each element. If the array holds primitives, each element in the array is given its default value (we'll look at the default values later in this chapter), and if the array holds object references, each element is initialized to null (an object reference referring to no actual object).

Declaring an Array

You can declare an array to either hold primitives or object references. Regardless of what the array will hold, you must declare the type (int, String, Dog, etc.) at the time you declare the array reference variable.

Declaring an Array

```
int [] testScores;
int testScores [];
Animal [] pets;
Animal pets[];
```

Although the preferred style is the first one in each of these two examples (where the brackets come after the type but before the variable name), for the exam you need to know that both are legal.

Legal Array Types

Array types live in a unique world provided by the Java language; for *any* type in Java (int, String, Button, Dog, char, and so on), whether primitive or object, you can declare an array object reference of that type simply by adding brackets either before or after the variable name. For example, to declare an array that holds ints, you write:

```
int [] testScores;
```

If the array will hold references to String objects, then you still just add brackets to the class name String as follows:

```
String [] students;
```

Travel Advisory

Don't forget that for each of the above examples, the brackets could also go after the variable name.

But what about classes that *you* write? The Java language automatically provides a mechanism for dynamically creating array types for any class type. For example, if you create a class Dog, then you declare an array that will hold references to Dogs using the same syntax used for String:

```
Dog [] dogList;
```

Travel Advisory

You must never include the size of the array in your declaration. For example, the following is illegal in Java:

```
int [5] testScores;
```

Constructing an Array

Constructing an array means creating the array object on the heap. In other words, doing a new on the array type. To create a new object on the heap, Java needs to know how big the object should be based on its instance variables. You can think of the elements in an array as the instance variables of the array object, so in order to create/construct the new array object, you must specify the size of the array. The size of the array is the number of elements the array will hold, or to use the earlier analogy, the number of cups in the tray.

Constructing an Array of Primitives

To construct an array that holds primitives, use the keyword new followed by the primitive type, with a bracket specifying how many elements of that primitive type the array will hold.

Constructing a Previously Declared Array

```
testScores = new int[12];
```

This code puts one new object on the heap, an array object holding 12 elements, each element containing an int with a default value of 0. Think of this code as saying to the compiler, "Create an array object on the heap that will hold 12 primitives of type int, and assign it to the previously declared array variable named testScores."

```
pets = new Animal [5];
```

This code puts one new object on the heap, an array object holding five elements, each element containing a reference variable (of type Animal) with a default value of null. Think of this code as saying to the compiler, "Create an array object on the heap that will hold five Animal object references, and assign it to the previously declared array variable named pets."

Declaring and Constructing on One Line

```
int [] testScores = new int[12];
```

This code puts one new object on the heap, an array object holding 12 elements, each element containing an `int` with a default value of 0.

```
Animal [] pets = new Animal [5];
```

This code puts one new object on the heap, an array object holding five elements, each element containing a reference variable (of type Animal) with a default value of null.

Initializing an Array

Initializing an array means putting things in it. *Things* in the array represent the elements of the array and are either primitive values (2, 'g', 27.90, and so on) or objects referenced by the reference variables in the array elements (cups). For example, an array constructed in the following way creates only one object on the heap, the array object itself:

```
Animal [] pets = new Animal[5];
```

There are still no actual animals!

Assigning Values to an Array of Object References

Array elements are always given default values when the array is constructed, and for arrays of object references, the default value is null. The next step is to create some Animal objects and assign them to index positions in the array, as follows:

```
pets[0] = new Animal();
pets [1] = new Animal();
pets[2] = new Animal();
```

This code puts three new Animal objects on the heap and assigns those new objects to three of the five index positions (elements) of the `pets` array, leaving two elements in the array (index 3 and 4) with null references, waiting to refer to animal objects not yet created (or created but not yet assigned to those indexes).

Assigning Values to an Array of Primitives

Remember, array elements are always given a default value. In other words, elements in an array are always initialized, at the moment the array is constructed. As we just stated, with an array of object references, the default value of each element in the array is null. However, with an array of primitives, all elements are given the default value for the particular type of the array. For example, `int` arrays are constructed with all elements given a default value of zero:

```
int [] testScores = new int[5];
```

creates one object on the heap, the array object referenced by the variable testScores, and puts the value zero in each of the five elements.

Default values for primitives and object references are shown in Table 2.1.

TABLE 2.1   Default Values for Array Elements

Element Type	Default Value
`byte, short, int, long`	0
`float, double`	0.0
`boolean`	false
`char`	'\u0000'
Object reference	null

Declaring, Constructing, and Initializing on One Line

You can use two different syntax shortcuts to both initialize (put values into the elements of the array) and construct an array at the same. The first shortcut lets you declare, construct, and initialize an array as one statement, while the second lets you construct and initialize a previously declared array.

```
int [] testScores = {5,22,89};
```

Given this code, Java counts up the number of items between the braces (in this example, three) and creates a new array with three elements, each element initialized to the values in the bracket. The code above is functionally identical to the following longer code:

```
int [] testScores = new int[3];
testScores [0] = 5;
testScores [1] = 22;
testScores [2] = 89;
```

With object references rather than primitives, it works exactly the same way:

```
Animal [] pets = {new Animal(), new Animal(), new Animal(), new
Animal()};
```

The code above creates an array of type Animal (an array that holds references to objects of type Animal), with four elements, each element holding a reference to four newly created Animal objects.

The second shortcut lets you construct and initialize a previously declared array, as follows:

```
testScores = new int[] {5,22,89};
pets = new Animal [] {new Animal(), new Animal(), new Animal(), new
Animal()};
```

What Can You Put in a Particular Array?

For the exam, you need to know that arrays can have only one declared type (int [], Animal[], String[], and so on), but that doesn't necessarily mean that only things of that declared type can be placed in the array.

Legal Elements for Arrays of Primitives

Primitive arrays can accept any value which can be promoted implicitly to the declared type of the array. Chapter 6 covers the rules for this in detail, but for example, an `int` array can hold any value that can fit in a 32-bit sized `int` cup. Thus, the following code is legal:

```
int [] foo = 5new int[5];
byte b = 4;
char c = 'c';
short s = 7;
foo[0] = b;
foo[1] = c;
foo[2] = s;
```

and of course, an `int` literal:

```
foo[3] = 890;
```

or an `int` variable:

```
int i = 1200;
foo[4] = i;
```

Legal Elements for Arrays of Object References

If the array type is a class, you can put objects of any subclass of that type into the array. For example, if Dog is a subclass of Animal, you can put both Animals and Dogs into an Animal array. The rules are exactly the same as those for non-array variable assignments:

```
class Animal {}
class Dog extends Animal {}
class Cat extends Animal {}
Animal [] pets = new Animal[3];
pets[0] = new Animal();
pets[1] = new Dog();
pets[2] = new Cat();
```

If the array type is an interface, the array can hold instances of any class that implements the interface. Again, the rules are exactly the same as those for non-array variable assignments.

```
public interface FriendlyPet {
 public void beFriendly();
}
class Beagle implements FriendlyPet {
 public void beFriendly() {
 System.out.println("wagging tail");
  }
}
FriendlyPet[] nicePets = new FriendlyPet[4];
nicePets[0] = new Beagle();
Beagle bert = new Beagle();
nicePets[1] = bert;
```

Multidimensional Arrays

Arrays can also be created with multiple dimensions, but these are nothing more than arrays of arrays. In other words, an element in an array can be a reference to another array object on the heap. You need to be familiar with the syntax, which uses additional brackets to indicate the number of dimensions. For example, an array of `ints` representing test scores would be useful only for one particular course or set of students. But what if the teacher had three different courses? You could represent this with three separate array variables:

```
int [] courseOneScores;
int [] courseTwoScores;
int [] courseThreeScores;
```

Or you could create a single array reference variable, courseScores, which referred to an array holding three references to `int` arrays. That second dimension, the `int` arrays, would hold the actual scores. The following code demonstrates this example:

```
int [][] courseScores = new int[3][];
```

This code declares an array variable that is not an `int` array at all, but rather an array of references to *three* int arrays. The additional int arrays don't yet exist until you construct them as follows:

```
courseScores[0] = new int[12];
```

Imagine the teacher's first course has 12 students. The array would need to hold 12 `ints` representing the test scores for that course.

```
courseScores[1] = new int[14];
courseScores[2] = new int[9];
```

You can see from this code that the additional dimensions can be of different sizes. For this reason, you are permitted to leave all brackets except the first one empty when you construct the initial array.

To access the added dimensions, you can use multiple brackets with the array index notation:

```
courseScores[1][5] = 19;
```

This code assigns the value 19 to the array element at index 5 in the first array referenced by the variable courseScores.

Watch out for the following example of declaring a multidimensional array:

```
int [] myList [];
```

It's legal! Strange as it looks, it's nothing more than a declaration of a two-dimensional `int` array named myList. Where you place the brackets *really* doesn't matter.

Declaring, Constructing, and Initializing a Multidimensional Array on One Line

Yes, you can do it. The following code examples demonstrate legal, and not legal, syntax for doing this:

```
int [][] testScores = {5,22,89}; // not legal
```

But you can do this:

```
int [] [] testScores = {{7,2,5}, {5,9,3,7,9}};
```

This code creates a two dimensional array of `ints`, with the testScores array having a size of two (in other words, two elements are in the array). Each of those two elements is an object reference to an `int` array. The array `testScores[0]` holds three elements (three `ints`) while `testScores[1]` holds five elements, again all `ints`.

Declare Classes, Inner Classes, Methods, Instance Variables, Static Variables, and Automatic (Method Local) Variables

Objective 2.02

If you're going to make a class, method, variable, and so on, you have to declare it. This section covers the rules for declaring all types of classes, variables, methods, and constructors, including which modifiers can be used for each.

Declaration Basics

Before tackling the modifiers, you need to know the minimum requirements for declaring the components of a Java program.

Class

To declare a class, you must use the keyword `class` followed by the name of the class:

```
class Dog { }
```

Inner Class

With the exception of a special case known as an *anonymous inner class*, inner classes are declared as a normal class (shown in the previous section) except the declaration happens somewhere within the enclosing curly braces of another class:

```
class Dog {
 class Collar { }
}
```

Methods

The term *method*, used on its own, refers to instance methods. In this chapter, static methods will be explicitly referred to using the term *static*, so you may assume that in this chapter any use of the term "method" without the word "static" refers to a non-static instance method of class.

To declare a method, you must have the return type followed by the method name and parentheses.

```
int getSize() { }
```

You can also include arguments for the method, which are separated by commas with the type followed by the name:

```
int addNums (int first, int second) {
 return first + second;
}
```

Instance Variables

Instance variables are declared within the class (that is, inside the curly braces of the class declaration) but outside any method or other code block.

To declare an instance variable, you must use the variable type followed by the variable name.

```
int size;
Dog pet;
```

Static Variables

Static variables are declared in the same way instance variables are, but with the addition of the keyword `static` in front of the type. The static modifier will be covered later in this chapter.

```
static int numOfObjects;
```

Automatic (Method Local) Variables

Automatic (also known as *local* or *stack*) variables are declared within the curly braces of a method or as part of the argument list of a method.

Declaring automatic variables is similar to declaring instance variables, except for the use of modifiers, which are covered later in this chapter.

```
int size;
```

One key difference between local and instance variable declarations is that instance variables are given a default value but local variables are not. This means you must give a local variable a value before trying to use it, or you won't be able to compile.

Modifers

The examples in the previous section show you the minimum requirements for declaring classes, variables, methods, and so on. But there are modifiers you can use with your declarations to *modify* the thing you're declaring. You might think of modifiers as adjectives that further describe, or qualify, the method, variable, or whatever it is you're declaring. For example, marking a variable with the final keyword means that the variable's value can't be changed. Modifiers come in two flavors:

- Access modifiers
- Other modifiers

This section covers both modifier types to the extent to which they're covered on the exam.

Travel Advisory

In this section, the term *class* refers to normal (non-nested) top-level classes. Thus, the special types of classes known as inner or nested classes will be referred to explicitly. Also in this section, the term *method* refers to instance methods (methods that are not static) and static methods will be explicitly referred to as *static methods*.

Access Modifers

For the exam, you'll need to understand what the access modifiers mean, and you'll also need to know which access modifiers can be used on the different types of things you're declaring.

There are four levels of access visibility, but only three of them are designated with keyword access modifiers. The fourth, the *default* modifier, is what you get when you don't type any access modifier at all (next to something that *can* have an access modifier specified, that is). In other words, even if you don't type in an access modifier, using one of the three keyword modifiers (`public`, `protected`, and `private`), you are still *implicitly* specifying a level of access (called *default* access, which is discussed in the following sections).

You can think of access modifiers as describing who sees what. When designing a class, ask yourself questions such as, "Who should be allowed to invoke this method?" or, "Who should be allowed to create objects of this class?" Access modifiers are the way in which you implement the answers to such questions.

In order of restriction, the access levels are as follows:

- `private`
- default (not a keyword; you'll never type this in code)
- `protected`
- `public`

Private

`Private` means *private to the class*. Only other parts of the class can access something marked with the `private` modifier. For example, an instance variable marked as `private` can only be accessed by methods of the class, but no other class (with the special exception of inner classes) will be able to access it.

```
class Dog {
 private int size = 27;
}
class TestDog {
 public static void main (String [] args) {
 Dog d = new Dog();
 System.out.println(d.size); // won't compile
// because class TestDog can't access the private variable of class
Dog.
// Only code within Dog instances can access the size variable.
 }
}
```

Things You Can Mark as Private

- Inner (including nested) classes
- Methods
- Instance variables

- Static variables
- Constructors
- Static methods

Things You Cannot Mark as Private

- Classes
- Interfaces
- Automatic (method local) variables

Default (Package-Level Access)

Remember that the default access level is not a keyword; it's the access level you get when you don't explicitly type in one of the other three modifiers (`private`, `protected`, or `public`). It helps if you think of default as meaning "package." Anything using default access is accessible only from code within the same package as the default-restricted thing.

For example, a class with default/package access cannot be used from code in a different package, which means you can't use that default class as a type.

Imagine a class Dog, in the package `com.wickedlysmart.pets`:

```
package com.wickedlysmart.pets;
public class Dog {
 void adjustCollar() { }
 public void getSize() { }
}
```

And, in another class, Trainer:

```
package com.wickedlysmart.workers;
public class Trainer {
public static void main (String [] args) {
// can access about the Dog class because Dog is public
 Dog d = new Dog();
// can access the getSize method because it is public
 d.getSize();
// but can not access (won't compile) the adjustCollar method
because
// adjustCollar has no explicit access modifier, which implicitly
// marks the method with default access which means package-level
```

```
// restriction. Since Dog and Trainer are in different packages,
// Trainer code is out of luck.
```

Default/package access is really like restricting your secrets to just close family and friends—the people in your immediate circle or package. Private, on the other hand, is like restricting your secrets to just you and your twins (other instances of the same class).

Things You Can Mark as Default

By not typing in an explicit access modifier, the following things will use default/package access restriction:

- Classes
- Inner and nested classes
- Methods
- Instance variables
- Static variables
- Constructors
- Static methods
- Interfaces

Things You Cannot Mark as Default

- Automatic (method local) variables

Protected

The protected modifier can be thought of as *default plus kids*. Protected works just like default, except it adds one more level of permission for children/subclasses of the class. When you think protected, think subclasses and inheritance because that's the only way it makes sense. For example, a variable marked protected is inherited by subclasses, including those in a package different from the one in which the parent (superclass) lives. Resist the tendency to think of protected as more restrictive than default. The very word *protected* sounds intuitively more restrictive, but it is actually *less* restrictive than default since it adds on an additional level of access (for subclasses).

```
package com.wickedlysmart.pets;
public class Dog {
 protected int tailWagFactor;
 void adjustCollar() { }
```

```
 public void getSize() { }
}
package com.wickedlysmart.animals;
public class Beagle extends Dog {
 void wagTail() {
 if (tailWagFactor < 10) { // this compiles
 // because Beagle extends Dog
// even though the Beagle class is in a different package.
 }
}
```

Things You Can Mark as Protected

- Inner and nested classes
- Methods
- Instance variables
- Static variables
- Static methods

Things You Cannot Mark as Protected

- Classes
- Interfaces
- Automatic (method local) variables

Public

Public means anybody, anytime, anywhere. A public method can be accessed by any code that has a valid reference to an object of the type with the public method. A public class can be declared as a type in code from any other class in any other package. It gets a little more interesting when you mix and match modifiers within a class. For example, a public class doesn't automatically give any code the right to instantiate objects of that type, unless the constructor of that class is also accessible.

Things You Can Mark as Public

- Classes
- Interfaces

- Inner and nested classes
- Methods
- Instance variables
- Static variables
- Constructors
- Static methods

Things You Cannot Mark as Public

- Automatic (method local) variables

Other Modifiers

Access modifiers define who gets access to which parts of code, but the other modifiers describe other characteristics and restrictions on code. For example, marking a method as `abstract` means that particular method must be overridden by a non-abstract subclass, while marking a method as `final` has the opposite effect: the method cannot be overridden by any subclass.

The other modifiers covered on the exam include:

- `Final`
- `Abstract`
- `Synchronized`
- `Native`
- `Transient`

There are other modifiers in Java, but they are beyond the scope of the programmer's exam and won't be covered in this section. They include:

- `Volatile`
- `Strictfp`

Final

`Final` is a descriptive modifier that means "end of the line/no further changes." Exactly what "no further changes" means depends on whether you're modifying a method, variable, or class. For example, a `final` method cannot be overridden by a subclass. A `final` variable's value cannot be changed once initialized. A final class can't have any subclasses. Anything can be marked `final` except a constructor or an interface. (It doesn't make sense to have a final constructor, since constructors are not inherited and thus can't be overridden.)

What It Means to Have a Final Variable

A variable marked `final` means you cannot change the contents of the variable (its value) once the value has been set, and there are rules about when a value must be set. `Final` instance variables can be initialized in one of two ways, either as a "blank final" or explicitly when declared. Instance variables are always given a default value if not explicitly initialized (*explicitly initialized* means assigned a value at the time the variable is declared). However, with `final` variables, you must provide an explicit value rather than relying on the default value, even if the default value is what you want anyway (say, zero for an `int`).

To compile a class with a `final` instance variable, you will usually give it an explicit value at declaration time:

```
class Foo {
private final int size = 23;
}
```

But what if you need more information before you can provide that value? For example, what if the constructor arguments determine the variable's value? For just that reason, Java gives you one last chance to provide a value for a final instance variable during the run of the constructor:

```
class Foo {
 private final int size;
 Foo(int size) {
 this.size = size; // last chance to give size a value
 }
}
```

If the compiler sees that you haven't initialized the value on declaration, or in the constructor, you won't be able to compile.

What about static `final` variables? Obviously, the constructor wouldn't work (since there won't be any object, so the constructor won't run), but you can still make a "blank final" by leaving the static variable uninitialized at declaration time and assigning it a value in a static code block:

```
class TestFinal {
 public static final int foo;
 static {
 foo = 12;
 }
}
```

What does it actually mean to say, "The value can't be changed"? For a primitive value, you simply can't assign any new value, by any means. For example, the following code is illegal for the int value size:

```
class Foo {
 private final int size;
 Foo(int size) {
 this.size = size; // last chance to give size a value
 }
// so far, the code above is OK, but it goes wrong below…
 public void badMethod() {
size = 28; // can't assign a new value to final size
 size++; // this still changes foo, so you can't do it
 size = size + 3; // you guessed it. Not allowed!
 }
}
```

What if the final variable is a reference to an object? Does this mean you can't invoke any setter methods or change any variable values? Of course not. Remember, Java uses pass-by-value semantics, and final means "can't change the value of the variable." So you must ask yourself, "What's the value of a reference variable? Is it the object or the reference?" The answer is "the reference." The object is stored on the heap, and the reference variable's value is simply the reference. You don't know what the reference actually looks like, since that's VM-dependent, but you can imagine something like a 32- or 64-bit number that the VM can use (perhaps a pointer to a pointer to a…) to get to the actual object, and it is the reference that you can't change if the reference variable is final. For example, you can't do the following:

```
final Dog myDog = new Dog("Bert");
public void badMethod() {
 myDog = new Dog(); // can't make myDog refer to some other Dog!
 myDog = null; // changes the value of myDog reference, so its illegal
}
```

But you *can* change the object referred to by the final reference variable:

```
final Dog myDog = new Dog("Bert");
```

```
public void goodMethod() {
 myDog.changeSize(45);
 myDog.changeSpots(2);
}
```

Bottom line: there are no final objects in Java, only final variables.

Things You Can Mark as Final

- Classes
- Inner and nested classes
- Methods
- Instance variables
- Static variables
- Automatic (method local) variables
- Method parameters
- Static methods

Things You Cannot Mark as Final

- Constructors
- Interfaces

Static

Imagine you've got a utility class with a method that always runs the same way; its sole function is to return the next number in a sequence. It wouldn't matter which instance of that class performed the method—it would always behave exactly the same way with no dependency on instance variable state. In this case, it might be a waste of heap space to instantiate an object just to run that method. Why not let the class itself simply run the code?

Now imagine that you want to keep a count of all the instances created from a particular class. Where do you keep that variable? It doesn't make sense to keep it as an instance variable of the class whose instances you're counting, since the count will be reinitialized each time a new instance is created.

The answer to both of these issues is the keyword (and concept of) `static`. Variables and methods marked as `static` belong to the class, rather than any particular instance. In fact, you can use a `static` method or variable without having any instances of that class at all. You need only have the class available. `Static` variables and methods are shared by all instances of the particular class, and there is just one copy.

A simplified class with a counter might look something like this:

```
public class Dog {
 static int dogCount = 0;
 public Dog() {
 dogCount++;
 }
}
```

In this example, the static `dogCount` variable would be set to 0 when the Dog class is loaded, *before* any instances of Dog are created! (You do not need to initialize the variable to 0, since 0 is the default value for an `int` and will be assigned to `dogCount` when the Dog class is loaded. We've done it in this example just for clarity.)

Whenever a Dog instance is created, the Dog constructor runs and increments the `dogCount` static variable.

So how do `static` methods work? A `static` method runs independent of any particular instance, even if no instances of that class have been created. That means that a `static` method can't use any instance variable values (unless a reference to an instance happened to be passed in to the method, of course). To continue the Dog example:

```
public class Dog {
 static int dogCount = 0;
 public static int getDogCount() {
 return dogCount;
}
 public Dog() {
 dogCount++;
 }
}
```

The previous code is legal because the `static` method `getDogCount()` can access the `static` variable `dogCount`.

How to Access Static Variables and Methods

Since you aren't required to have an instance in order to invoke a `static` method or access a `static` variable, what's the syntax? Normally, you invoke a method by using the reference variable that refers to the object/instance you're trying to access:

```
Cat c = new Cat();
c.chaseMouse();
int size = c.getSize();
```

In the previous example, a `Cat` instance is instantiated and referenced by the variable c, and the variable c is used to access two `Cat` methods: `chaseMouse()` and `getSize()`.

But this is not appropriate with `static` methods (or `static` variables) because you might not have any instances at all. The way you access `static` methods is by using the class name:

```
int numOfDogs = Dog.getDogCount()
```

It works the same way for variables:

```
int numOfDogs = Dog.dogCount;
```

Given the previous code, you can probably see that a `static` method, such as `getDogCount()`, would not be able to make use of any Dog instance variables. Think about it: if all you use to invoke a `static` method is the name of the class, how would a `static` method ever know which Dog instance variables it was supposed to be using? *There is no Dog object in the picture when you invoke a* `static` *method, so you can't use any Dog object (instance) variables!* That means the following code is not legal:

```
public class Dog {
 static int dogCount = 0;
 int numOfSpotsForThisDog;
 public static int getDogCount() {
 return dogCount;
 }

 public static int getDogSpots() {
 return numOfSpotsForThisDog; // won't compile!
 // Which Dog's spot number would be used here?
 }
 public Dog(int spotNum) {
 dogCount++;
 numOfSpotsForThisDog = spotNum;
 }
}
```

On the exam, if you see any `static` method trying to access a non-static (instance) variable, the code is illegal and won't compile. For the same reasons, a `static` method can't access normal instance methods, since instance methods implicitly can (and do) use instance variable values dependent on which instance was used to invoke the method. For example, a `static` method would not be able to call a `getSize()` method on a Dog instance, since the return value of the `getSize()` method would be a particular Dog instance's size instance variable value.

One point to be aware of for the exam, or for code you might occasionally come across, is that the Java language allows you to use an object reference to invoke a `static` method:

```
Dog d = new Dog();
int dogsMade = d.getDogCount();
```

Even though here we are using a specific Dog instance to invoke a `static` method, the rules haven't changed. This is merely a syntax trick to allow you to invoke a Dog's `static` method through a particular Dog instance, but the `static` method is still unaware of the particular Dog instance used to invoke the method. The compiler knows that the reference variable d is of type Dog, and the Dog class `static` method is run with no awareness of or concern for the Dog instance at the other end of that d reference. In other words, the compiler only cares that variable d is of type/class Dog.

So again, because Java will not know about any particular instance of Dog when the `static` method is running, the `static` method cannot access any non-static variables or methods.

One last point to remember about `static` methods is that `static` methods cannot be overridden. This does not mean that they can't be redefined in a subclass. Just be aware that `static` methods are not polymorphic (discussed in Chapter 3) but are bound at compile-time based on the reference variable type rather than the actual object type.

Things You Can Mark as Static

- Inner classes
- Methods (this makes the method a `static` method)
- Variables (this makes the variable a `static` variable)

Things You Cannot Mark as Static

- Constructors (constructors always mean an instance is being created; it makes no sense to have a `static` constructor)

- Classes
- Interfaces
- Inner classes (unless you want them to become top-level nested classes)
- Inner class methods and instance variables
- Automatic (method local) variables

Abstract

The `abstract` keyword is associated with inheritance and implementation. Abstract really means "the abstract characteristics that must be concretely defined or realized." What does *that* mean? Imagine a class Animal. What does an animal look like? What is the shape of its head, ears, legs? What kind of fur does it have? How tall is it? What does it eat? You can't know the answers, if you are thinking about the abstract notion of an animal. The idea of animal is too vague, too…*abstract*. To answer the specific questions, you'll need to know what *kind* of animal we're talking about.

In Java, marking a class as `abstract` means a concrete subclass must be made in order to make use of the abstract class. In the Animal class example, you'd need to make a more specific subclass, such as Dog, in order to answer the specific, detailed questions about the fur, ears, teeth, and so on.

```
public abstract class Animal {
 // instance variables which all animals will have
 protected int size;
 protected String name;
 protected Sound noiseSnd;
 public Animal() {
 // initialization that applies to animals of any type / subclass
 }
 // two abstract methods that all animals will have, but that
 // subclasses must implement
 public abstract void eat();
 public abstract void makeNoise();
 // one concrete (non-abstract) method that all Animal types will
 // inherit
 public String getName() {
 return name;
 }
}
```

In order to be of any use, any `abstract` class must be subclassed by a concrete type, with all `abstract` methods overridden by the subclass.

```
public class Dog extends Animal {
 // everything is inherited except the
 // abstract methods must be overridden
 public void makeNoise() {
 // Dog-specific barking code
 }

 public void eat() {
 // Dog-specific eating code
 }
}
```

Why Make Abstract Classes?

Suppose you have a group of classes in your program such as Dog, Cat, Horse, and so on with common code. Your good OO (object-oriented) design might encourage you to take the common code, things which apply to all animals, and place it in a superclass. This not only helps prevent code duplication (and allows you to make changes to common code in just one place), but it also allows you to take advantage of polymorphism. For example, you might have an array of type Animal, but the elements in the array are all concrete animal subtypes. With your design, you could loop through the array and call `eat()` on each of the elements in the array, knowing that each element will in fact be able to respond to the `eat()` method invocation, regardless of the element's actual type. The point of marking the class `abstract` is to take full advantage of the OO characteristics of inheritance and polymorphism without allowing anyone to actually construct an instance of the `abstract` type.

Rules About Abstract Classes and Methods

- `Abstract` classes cannot be instantiated! You can never say, for example, `new Animal()`.
- Abstract classes can contain both `abstract` and non-`abstract` methods.
- If a class has any `abstract` methods (directly or through inheritance), the class must be declared `abstract`.
- `Abstract` classes still have constructors because of the superchaining of constructors. (A constructor will always invoke the constructor of its immediate superclass, and `abstract` classes are always superclasses to some other class.)

- You can subclass one `abstract` class with another abstract class, but the first concrete (non-`abstract`) class in the inheritance tree must override/ implement all the `abstract` methods from any and all of the `abstract` superclasses.
- `Abstract` methods must not be marked `private` or `final`, since neither `private` nor `final` methods can be overridden, and `abstract` methods must be overridden.

Things You Can Mark as Abstract

- Classes
- Methods
- Interfaces (this is discouraged; interfaces are always implicitly `abstract`)

Things You Cannot Mark as Abstract

- Constructors
- Instance variables
- Static variables
- Static methods
- Automatic (method local) variables

Synchronized

The `synchronized` modifier applies only to method code and is covered in Chapter 8. Only non-`abstract` methods (including `static` methods) and blocks of code can be marked as `synchronized`.

Native

The `native` modifer applies only to methods and designates that the method code is not compiled Java bytecode but is in a library compiled for a particular machine type. For the purposes of the exam, you need only know that the `native` modifier can be applied to methods but not to anything else.

Transient

The `transient` modifier applies only to variables. A variable marked with the `transient` modifier is not saved as part of an object's state when the object is serialized. Serialization, which is not covered on the exam, is a way of saving an object to persistent storage (such as writing it to a file). For the exam you need only know that instance variables marked `transient` are not saved during object serialization and that variables are the *only* things that can be marked `transient`.

Table 2.2 provides an at-a-glance summary of modifiers as covered in this section.

TABLE 2.2 Modifiers

	public	protected	default	private	final	static	abstract
Class	X		X		X		X
Inner Class	X	X	X	X	X	X	X
Method	X	X	X	X	X	X	X
Variable	X	X	X	X	X	X	
Constructor	X	X	X	X			
Automatic					X		

Determine If a Default Constructor Will Be Created

Objective 2.03

Every class has a constructor. This is a crucial point—burn it into your brain now. But this does *not* necessarily mean that you, the programmer, must type it in.

Rules for Constructors

The following summarizes rules for constructors that you'll need to know for the exam:

- If you don't type a constructor, a *default* constructor will be automatically inserted by the compiler.
- The default constructor is always a no-arg constructor.
- If you want a no-arg constructor and you've typed in other constructors, you'll have to type in the no-arg constructor yourself.
- Every constructor must have as its first line either a call to an overloaded constructor or a call to the super constructor. If you do make a constructor (rather than relying on the default constructor) and if you do not have a call to an overloaded constructor or super(), the compiler will implicitly put in the call to super() as the first line of your constructor. It will do this for each overloaded constructor in your class (as well as the default, of course).
- A call to a super() constructor can be no-arg or include arguments passed to the super constructor:

```
class Dog extends Animal {
Dog() {
super("Fido"); // pass a String to Dog's super constructor
}
}
```

How Do You Know if a Default Constructor Will Be Created?

Because *you* didn't write any constructors at all in your class.

How do you know what that constructor will look like? It will have the same access modifier as your class (public or default) and it will be no-arg with a no-arg call to super.

Given the following class:

```
public class Dog {
}
```

the compiler will put in a constructor that looks like this:

```
public Dog() {
 super();
 }
```

Objective 2.04

State the Legal Return Types

The rules are simple for knowing what you can have as a return type; but it all depends on whether you're overriding or overloading the method. Since those topics are covered more deeply in Chapter 3, this section covers it only briefly.

Overloading

Method overloading means using the same name for two different methods. In Java, you must vary the argument list in order to overload a method. The following code shows an overloaded change() method for the Dog class:

```
public class Dog {
public void change(int size, String name) {
 }

public void change(int size, String name, int numOfDots) {
 }
}
```

The change() method is an overloaded method because both methods are named change(), but the argument lists are different. Overloaded methods must vary the argument list in a way that makes them distinguishable from one another, so that means the order and/or type of the arguments must vary in a meaningful way.

Overloaded methods allow you to vary the return type, although *changing the return type alone is not enough to make an overloaded method*! You'll need to know for the exam that overloaded methods can have different return types and it's perfectly legal to do the following:

```
class Foo {
 public int go(int x, int y) {

}

 public String go(double x, String y) {

 }
```

Overriding

When a method is inherited from a superclass and the subclass wants to change the method implementation (or in the case of abstract methods, because the subclass *must* provide an implementation), the subclass code must define a method which matches the overridden method. The main difference, for the purposes of this exam objective, is that overloaded methods can change the return type, but overriding methods cannot.

The following is an example of overriding:

```
public class Animal {
 protected void eat(String foodToEat) {
 // generic eating code
 }
}

public class Dog extends Animal {
 public void eat(String foodToEat) {
 //Dog-specific eating code
 }
}
```

Travel Assistance

For more information, check out the following sources: The JavaTM 2 Platform, Standard Edition, v 1.3.1 API Specification at **http://java.sun.com/j2se/1.3/docs/api/index.html;** *The Java Class Libraries, Second Editon, Volume 1* by Patrick Chan, Rosanna Lee and Douglas Kramer, Addison-Wesley, 1998; *The Java Programming Language, Second Edition* by Ken Arnold and James Gosling, Addison-Wesley, 7th printing, February 2000 (also available on the web at **http://java.sun.com /docs/books/jls/**)

CHECKPOINT

✔ **Objective 2.01** **Write code that declares, constructs, and initializes arrays of any base type using any of the permitted forms both for declaration and for initialization.** Arrays are objects that can hold primitive or object reference values. To use an array, you'll need to declare the array reference variable, construct the new array object, and populate the array elements with values. All array elements are given default values.

✔ **Objective 2.02** **Declare classes, inner classes, methods, instance variables, static variables, and automatic (method local) variables making appropriate use of all permitted modifiers (such as `public`, `final`, `static`, `abstract`, and so forth). State the significance of each of these modifiers both singly and in combination, and state the effect of package relationships on declared items qualified by these modifiers.** Modifiers are like adjectives that further describe, or qualify, the method, variable, class, or interface you're declaring. Modifiers include access modifiers (`public`, `private`, and so on) which restrict the visibility of code, and several non-access modifiers (`static`, `final`, and so on) that describe other characteristics of the code.

✔ **Objective 2.03** **For a given class, determine if a default constructor will be created, and if so, state the prototype of that constructor.** If you don't type a constructor into your class, the compiler will provide a default constructor. It will always be a no-arg constructor with a call to super with no arguments.

✔ **Objective 2.04** **State the legal return types for any method given the dec-larations of all related methods in this or parent classes.** Overloaded methods are allowed to vary the return type. Overriding methods must have the same return type as the overridden method in the superclass.

REVIEW QUESTIONS

1. Which of the following is legal for using one line to declare, construct, and initialize an array?

   A. `int [] myList = {"a", "b", "c"};`
   B. `int [] myList = (5,8,2);`
   C. `int [][] myList = {4,9,7,0};`
   D. `int [] myList = {4,3,7};`
   E. `int myList [] = [3,5,6];`
   F. `int [] myList = [4;6;5];`

2. Which of the following defines the correct default values for array elements of the type indicated? (Select four.)

   A. int   →   0
   B. String   →   "null"
   C. Dog   →   null
   D. char   →   '\u0000'
   E. float   →   0.0f
   F. boolean   →   true

3. Which of the following are legal array declarations? (Select three.)

   A. `int [] [] myScores [];`
   B. `char [] myChars;`
   C. `int [6] myScores;`
   D. `Dog myDogs [];`
   E. `Dog myDogs [7];`

4. What would be the output of the following code?

```
public class Test {
 public static void main(String[] args){
 String [] names = new String [5];
```

```
System.out.println( names [2] );
 }
}
```

    A. names
    B. compiler error
    C. runtime exception
    D. null

5. What would be the output of the following code?

```
public class Test {
 public static void main(String[] args){
  Dog [][] theDogs = new Dog[3][];
     System.out.println(theDogs[2][0].toString());


 }
}
```

    A. Compiler error
    B. Runtime error
    C. null

6. Which of the following are legal, given the class hierarchy described? (Select three.)

Dog extends Animal
Cat extends Animal
Tiger extends Cat

    A. Animal [] animals = {new Cat(), new Dog(), new Animal()};
    B. Animal [] animals = new Animal [3]; animals[0] = new Cat();
    C. Dog [] animals = new Dog[3]; animals[0] = new Cat();
    D. Animal [] animals = new Animal [8]; animals [0] = new Tiger();

7. Which of these shows the correct order of access modifiers, beginning with the least restrictive and ending with the most restrictive?

    A. Public → Default → Protected → Private
    B. Default → Public → Private → Protected

   C. Default → Public   → Protected → Private
   D. Public → Protected → Default   → Private

8. Would the following code compile?

```
public class Dog {
 private int dogCount = 0;
 public static int getDogCount() {
 return dogCount;
 }
}
```

   A. Yes
   B. No

9. Which of the following are true statements? (Select two.)

   A. An abstract class is allowed to have non-abstract methods.
   B. If a class has abstract methods, it must be declared abstract.
   C. A non-abstract class is allowed to have abstract methods.
   D. A non-abstract class is allowed to have abstract methods as long as those methods are also static.

10. Which of these statements are true about the private access modifer? (Select two.)

   A. Private means "private to the class."
   B. Private means "private to the instance."
   C. Static methods must not be marked private.
   D. Abstract methods must not be marked private.

REVIEW ANSWERS

   1. **D** Answer A is wrong because the initial values it puts in the array are Strings, not ints . B is wrong because of the parenthesis. C is wrong because it's trying to initialize a two-dimensional array with values for only one dimension. E is wrong because of the square brackets. F is wrong because of both the square brackets and the semicolon separators.

2. **A** **C** **D** **E** Answer F is wrong because the `boolean` default value is false. Answer B is wrong because Strings are object references and default to the null reference, not the string literal "null."

3. **A** **B** **D** Answer C and E are both wrong because you can't define the size of an array at the time you declare the array reference variable. You only specify an array size at the time you construct the array (when the JVM needs to know how much space to allocate).

4. **D** When an array is constructed, each of its elements is given a default value. Since this is an array of String objects, each element in the array initializes to null (no String objects are created, so the array elements are references holding a value of null).

5. **B** This code results in a `NullPointerException`. The array reference variable named theDogs references an array of Dog arrays. But the second dimension is not yet created when `System.out.println` runs, so there is no array object at theDogs [2][0]. But even if the second dimension had been created, you would still get a `NullPointerException` since there aren't yet any Dog objects, so invoking a `toString()` method on the Dog at index 0 of the Dog array at index 2 of theDogs would fail at runtime.

6. **A** **B** **D** C is wrong because the array is declared to hold Dog objects, and a Cat does not pass the "is-a" test (since Cat does not have Dog as a superclass). An array declared as type Dog can hold only objects of type Dog or one of Dog's subclasses (unless Dog were an interface, in which case any object implementing Dog could go into the array).

7. **D** A is a common misconception because many people assume that Protected is more restrictive than the default access level.

8. **B** A is wrong because static methods don't have an explicit reference to any particular instance, so the static method doesn't know which instance's values to use. Static methods can use static variables, but to use instance variables, a static method needs a reference to an object.

9. **A** **D** C is wrong because even a single abstract method makes a class `abstract`, and the compiler will force you to acknowledge by marking the class `abstract`. D is wrong because static methods cannot be `abstract`. Remember that abstract *methods must be overridden* (or they have no use whatsoever) whereas static methods *can't be overridden*.

10. **A** **D** B is a common misconception about the concept of Private, but multiple instances of a class are free to access one another's private methods and data. In fact, even objects instantiated from an inner class are free to access the private members of the outer class.

CHAPTER 3

Overloading, Overriding, Runtime Type, and Object Orientation

	NEWBIE	SOME EXPERIENCE	EXPERT
ETA	18 hours	8 hours	2 hours

The objectives in this section revolve (mostly) around object-oriented (OO) concepts including encapsulation, inheritance, and polymorphism. For the exam, you'll need to recognize whether a code fragment is correctly or incorrectly implementing some of the key OO features in Java. You'll also need to recognize the difference between an overloaded and overridden method; although overloaded methods and constructors aren't usually considered a key feature of OO, they're covered in this section (and in the exam objective) because of their close relationship to the OO concepts.

Since the focus of this book is on passing the programmer's exam, only the critical exam-specific aspects of OO will be covered here. If you're not already well-versed in OO concepts, then as a developer you could (and should) study a dozen books on the subject of OO to get a broader and deeper understanding of both the benefits and the techniques for analysis, design, and implementation. But for passing the exam, the relevant concepts and rules you'll need to know are covered in this section.

State the Benefits of Encapsulation in Object-Oriented Design

Imagine you wrote some code, a class, and another 12 programmers from your company wrote programs that used the class you wrote. Now imagine you decided that you didn't like the way that class was functioning because some of the instance variables in your objects were being set (by the other programmers) to values you hadn't anticipated and it was causing errors in their programs. Well, it *is* a Java program, so you should be able to simply ship out a newer version of your class, which they could drop in without changing any of their own code.

That scenario highlights two of the promises/benefits of OO: flexibility and maintainability. But you don't get those benefits automatically. You have to design and write your classes and code in a way that supports that flexibility. For example, if you had made your classes with public instance variables, then those other programmers might have been setting the variable values directly, as the following code demonstrates:

```
public class BadOO {
 public int size;
 public int weight;
  ...
}
```

```
public class ExploitsBadOO {
   public static void main (String args[]) {
       BadOO b = new BadOO();
       b.size = -5;   ← legal, but not good!
    }
}
```

And now you're in trouble. How are you going to change the class in a way that lets you handle the issues that come up when somebody changes the size variable to a value that might cause problems? Your only choice is to write method code for adjusting the size (a `setSize()` method, for example), and then protect the size variable with, say, a private or protected access modifier. But as soon as you make the change, *you break everyone else's code*!

This example brings up one of the key benefits of encapsulation: the ability to make changes in your implementations without breaking the code of others who use your code. *You want to hide implementation details behind a public API* (accessible methods). That way, you're free to change your implementation details by reworking your method code without changing the calling code.

But it means you'll have to start out that way from the beginning. If you design for maintainability, flexibility, and extensibility, you should keep your instance variables protected (using the protected, private, or default access levels) and allow access to those variables only from methods. The methods used to read or change instance variable values are referred to as *getters* and *setters*, or the fancier (more impressive at dinner parties) terms *accessors* and *mutators*. Regardless of what you call them, they're methods that let you get at the instance variable values or other data.

They look simple:

```
public class Dog {
 // protect the instance variable so that
 // only subclasses can use it (by inheriting it)
 protected int size;
 // now provide public getters and setters
 public int getSize() {
 return size;
 }

 public void setSize (int newSize) {
 size = newSize;
 }
}
```

So how useful is the previous code? It doesn't even do any tests or validation on the data in the setter method, for example. What benefit can there be from having getters and setters that look as useless as the ones above? The point is this: even if you don't actually do any work in your getters and setters, you give yourself *the ability to change your mind without breaking anyone's code later.* Even if you don't think you need any validation or checking on the variables, good OO design says you need to plan for the future, and to be safe, allow others to access your object's data *only* through methods. That way, you can rework the implementation details of those methods without breaking the calling code (in other words, without forcing the code that uses your objects to be rewritten).

"Is–A" Relationships

In OO, the concept of "is-a" relies on inheritance. It's a way of saying "this one thing is a type of this other thing." For example, a beagle is a type of dog. A Subaru is a type of vehicle. Broccoli is a type of vegetable (not my favorite, but it still counts).

The way you express this in Java is through the keyword `extends`:

```java
public class Car {
 // important car code goes here
}


public class Subaru extends Car {
 // important Subaru-specific Car stuff goes here
}
```

Of course, the Car class is a vehicle, so the inheritance tree might start from a Vehicle class:

```java
public class Vehicle { …}
public class Car extends Vehicle { …}
public class Subaru extends Car { … }
```

In OO terms, you can say the following:

- Vehicle is the superclass of Car
- Car is the subclass of Vehicle
- Car is the superclass of Subaru
- Subaru is the subclass of Vehicle
- Vehicle is the parent (or *parent class*) of Car

- Car is the child (or child class) of Vehicle
- Car is the parent of Subaru
- Subaru is the child of Car

The terms "superclass" and "parent" are used interchangeably. Some folks also use the term *base* class to represent the superclass/parent and *derived* class to represent the subclass/child.

And returning to our is-a relationship, the following statements are true:

"Car extends Vehicle" means "Car is-a Vehicle."

"Subaru extends Car" means "Subaru is-a Car."

What Does Inheritance Buy You?

Think about it: if you abstract out the code that's common to all vehicles and put it in a Vehicle class, then all subtypes (*subtypes* is another way of saying *subclasses*) can use that code. Otherwise, you would most likely have duplicate code in several classes, and if you wanted to modify that code you'd have to track it down everywhere and make all the changes (a maintenance nightmare). With common code in a superclass, all you have to do is make a change in the superclass, and suddenly all the subtypes using that code behave better, without ever reworking or recompiling any of the subclasses.

"Has-A" Relationships

Is-a relationships are based on inheritance, whereas has-a relationships are based on *usage*. In other words, object one "has-a" second object if object one has a way to invoke methods on the second object, usually with an instance variable referencing that second object. For example, you could say the following:

A Dog "is-a" Animal. A Dog "has-a" Collar.

And the code would look like this:

```
Public class Animal { }
Public class Dog extends Animal {
 Protected Collar myCollar;
}
```

In the previous code, the Dog class has an instance variable of type Collar, so you can say that the Dog "has-a" Collar. In other words, the Dog has a reference to a Collar which it can use to invoke methods on the Collar and get Collar behavior without having Collar code (methods) inside the Dog class.

Has-a relationships allow you to design classes which follow strong OO guidelines by not having big monolithic classes that do a zillion different things. Classes (and the objects instantiated from those classes) should be specialists. The more specialized the class, the more likely it is that you can reuse that class in other applications. If you put all the Collar-related code into the Dog class, you'll end up duplicating that code in the Cat class and any other class that might use a Collar. By keeping the Collar code in a separate specialized Collar class, you have the chance to reuse that one Collar class in multiple ways (at the very least, both the Dog and Cat class can use it).

To the outside world—users of the Dog class—(that is, code that calls methods on a Dog instance), the Dog class has Collar behavior. The Dog class might have a `tie(Leash theLeash)` method, for example. Users of the Dog class should never have to know that the Dog class is simply *delegating* the tie code to its Collar variable by invoking `myCollar.tie(theLeash)`. In OO, we don't want the callers to have to worry about which class or which object is actually doing the work. Those are implementation details that the Dog class will hide from Dog users. Dog users ask the Dog object to do things, and the Dog will either do it or ask someone else (some other object) to do it. To the caller, it always appears that the Dog takes care of itself. Callers should not know, or care, how the Dog chooses to do it.

Objective 3.02

Write Code to Invoke Overridden or Overloaded Methods and Parental or Overloaded Constructors

Methods can be both overloaded and overridden, while constructors can only be overloaded. Overloaded methods and constructors let you define the same method (or constructor) using different signatures. Overriding methods let you redefine a method in a subclass to add subclass-specific behavior.

Overridden Methods

Anytime you have a class that inherits a method, you have the opportunity to override the method (unless, as you learned in Chapter 2, the method is marked final). The key benefit of overriding methods is to get behavior specific to a particular subclass type. The following example demonstrates a Dog subclass of Animal overriding the Animal version of the `eat()` method:

```
public class Animal {
   public void eat() { }
}
public class Dog {
   public void eat() {
     // insert dog-specific eat functionality
   }
}
```

In the case of abstract methods, you have no choice: you *must* override the method unless the parent class is also abstract. The first concrete (that is, nonabstract) subclass must implement all inherited abstract methods.

The Animal class creator might have decided that for the purposes of polymorphism, all Animal subtypes should have an `eat()` method defined in a unique, specific way. Marking the `eat()` method as abstract is the Animal developers' way of saying to all subclass developers, "It doesn't make any sense to have a generic, abstract `eat()` method, so you all have to come up with your own. But you must have it in your code, since people will write code using Animal references to actual Animal subclass objects, and they'll want to compile code that calls `eat()` on Animal types, even though the actual objects are not Animals but some subtype of Animal."

The rules for overriding were partially covered in Chapter 2, but they are covered here in more detail:

* The argument list must match exactly.
* The return type must match exactly.
* The overriding method cannot have a more restrictive access modifier than the method being overridden (for example, you can't override a public method and make it protected). Think about it: if the Dog's `eat()` method were marked protected, a Dog would no longer be an Animal because everyone can call `Animal.eat()` but not everyone would be able to call `Dog.eat()`. The is-a relationship would be violated, and those holding a reference to an Animal would be shocked to discover that the object at the other end of the Animal reference isn't behaving as an Animal is supposed to.
* Overriding methods can have less restrictive access modifiers (for example, a protected method can be overridden with a method using a public access modifier).
* Overriding methods cannot throw new or broader exceptions than those declared by the overridden method (for example, a method that throws

FileNotFoundException can't be overridden by a method that throws Exception or SQLException or any other nonruntime exception that is not a subclass of FileNotFoundException).

- Overriding methods can throw narrower or fewer exceptions. Just because an overridden method "takes risks" doesn't mean that the overriding subclass's exception has to take those same risks. *An overriding method doesn't have to declare any exceptions that it will never throw, regardless of what the overridden method declares.*

- You can't override a method marked `final()`.

- You can't override a method that can't be inherited. So if the subclass does not have access to the superclass method because of access modifier restrictions, the method can't be overridden. For example, the following code is not legal:

```
public class Animal {
 private void doStuff() { }
}
public class Dog extends Animal {
}
pblic class TestDog {
  public static void main (String args[]) {
  Dog d = new Dog();
  d.doStuff(); // not legal because Dog didn't inherit doStuff()
  }
}
```

Invoking a Superclass Version of an Overridden Method

Often, you'll want to take advantage of some of the code in the superclass version of a method, yet still override it to provide some additional specific behavior. It's like saying, "Run the parent version of the method, then come back down here and finish with my child's additional method code." (Although there is no restriction that the parent's version run before the child's).

It's easy to do in code; you use the keyword `super` to invoke the superclass version of a particular method, as follows:

```
public class Animal {
 public void printYourself() {
```

```
 //… all sorts of cool generic printing code
 }
}
public class Dog extends Animal {
 public void printYourself() {
 // first go take advantage of the generic print-related work in
Animal
 super.printYourself();
 // now come back and do additional work here
 …
 }
}
```

Examples of Legal and Illegal Overridding Methods

Given the following class, Animal, the code examples that follow demonstrate legal and illegal ways to override the eat() method:

```
public class Animal {
public void eat() { }
}

public class Dog extends Animal {
 private void eat() { } // won't compile; can't make it more restric-
tive
 }
public class Dog extends Animal {
 public void eat() { } // legal
}
public class Dog extends Animal {
 public void eat() throws IOException { } // won't compile because of
exception
}
public class Dog extends Animal {
 public void eat(int howMuch) { } // legal, but not an override!
}
```

The previous code is not a valid override of the eat() method, but it is a legal example of overloading the eat() method. This is covered in the next section. The argument list is the clue that this is not an overriding method.

```
public class Dog extends Animal {
 public int eat() { } // won't compile because of the return type
}
```

The previous code is neither a valid overloaded nor overriding method. Changing only the return type does not constitute an overloaded method, and overriding methods *must* keep the same return type as the method they're overriding.

Overloaded Methods

Overloaded methods are a way to reuse the same method name in a class but use different arguments. Overloading can be a way to be nicer to those who call your code because your code takes on the burden of coping with different arguments rather than forcing the caller to have all the information needed for the method and having it in a particular format.

The rules are simple:

- Overloaded methods must change the argument list (by order, number, and/or type). Note that you can't just change the names of the arguments; the compiler won't let you do the following, because it wouldn't have any way to tell which method to invoke:

```
void doStuff(String a, String b) { }
    void doStuff(String b, String a) { }
```

- Overloaded methods can vary the return type.

The following code demonstrates overloaded methods:

```
public class Dog {
 int size;
 String name;
 int numOfSpots;
 public void change(int size, String name) {
 this.size = size;
```

```
 this.name = name;
 }


public void change(int size, String name, int numOfSpots) {
 this.size = size;
 this.name = name;
 this.numOfSpots = numOfSpots;
}
}
```

What makes `change()` an overloaded method is the fact that both methods are named `change()`, but the argument lists are different.

But you can also vary the return type, and that's what you'll need to know for the exam. It's perfectly legal to do the following:

```
class Adder {
 public int addNums(int x, int y) {
 return x + y;
 }
 public double addNums(double x, double y) {
 return x + y;
 }
}
```

Examples of Invoking Overloaded Methods

```
public class UseAdder {
 public static void main (String [] args) {
 Adder a = new Adder();
 int x = 27;
 int y = 3;
 int intResult = a.addNums(x,y); // invokes first addNums method
 double dx = 343;
 double dy = 1.8;
 double doubleResult = a.addNums(dx, dy); // invokes second addNums
 }
}
```

Invoking overloaded methods that have object references as arguments is a little more interesting. If you have an overloaded method such that one version takes an Animal and one takes a Dog (subclass of Animal), if you pass a Dog object in the method invocation, you'll invoke the overloaded version that takes a Dog rather than the method that takes an Animal. Or so it looks at first glance:

```
Class Animal {}
Class Dog extends Animal { }
Class UseAnimals {
 public void doStuff(Animal a) {
 System.out.println("in the Animal version");
 }

 public void doStuff(Dog d) {
 System.out.println("in the Dog version");
 }
public static void main (String [] args) {
 UseAnimals use = new UseAnimals();
 Animal animalObject = new Animal();
 Dog dogObject = new Dog();
 use.doStuff(animalObject);
 use.doStuff(dogObject);
 }
}
```

The output is what you'd expect:

```
in the Animal version
in the Dog version
```

But what if you use an Animal reference to a Dog object?

```
Animal dogObjectAnimalRef = new Dog();
use.doStuff(dogObjectAnimalRef);
```

Which of the overloaded methods gets invoked?

You might be tempted to say, "The one that takes a Dog, since it's a Dog object on the heap at runtime." But that's not how it works. The previous code would cause the output:

```
in the Animal version
```

Even though the actual object at runtime is still a Dog. So polymorphism does not apply to dynamic binding to the arguments of an overloaded method. Just remember, *it is the reference type, not the object type, that determines which overloaded method will be invoked.*

Overloaded and Parental Constructors

So far, we've covered overridden methods and overloaded methods; now we'll switch to constructors and cover overloaded constructors and instructor chaining. Constructors are never overridden, so overriding does not apply to the topic of constructors.

What's a Constructor For?

Constructors are not methods, but they work something like methods in that they contain code that runs with all local variables and arguments on the stack, just like normal methods. Constructors are invoked whenever you say new. The constructor's main purpose is to let you initialize the object's instance variables.

But remember that any object being created is made up of not just the instance variables from the class you're doing a new on, but all the instance variables from all the superclass/parental parts of the object you're creating.

For example, if the Animal class has two protected instance variables and the Dog class adds two more, the Dog object has at least four instance variables that must be allocated on the heap by the JVM. (It has more, of course, since Animal implicitly extends from class java.lang.Object, which is covered in Chapter 5.)

```
class Animal {
 protected String name;
 protected in size;
}
class Dog extends Animal {
 protected String breed;
 protected int numOfSpots;
}
```

If you create a Dog object (Dog d = new Dog()), the JVM must build out the Dog portion of the Dog object, as well as the Animal portion of the Dog and any other parts of the Dog's inheritance tree. As you'll learn in Chapter 5, every class in Java has `java.lang.Object` at the top of its inheritance tree, so even though Animal doesn't appear to extend anything, any class not extending another automatically extends the Object class.

If you remember that all the facets of a Dog must be created when a Dog is instantiated using `new`, the way constructors work should become easier to remember.

At Least One Constructor from Each Class in an Object's Inheritance Tree Must Run for an Object to Be Created

1. This is known as "constructor chaining," and it works by having each constructor invoke the constructor of its immediate superclass/parent. The Dog constructor, which runs when you run `new Dog()`, invokes the constructor of class Animal, which in turn invokes the constructor of class Object. The constructor order for creating/instantiating a new Dog is as follows: Dog constructor is invoked
2. Animal constructor is invoked
3. Object constructor is invoked
3. Object constructor runs to completion
4. Animal constructor runs to completion
5. Dog constructor (at last!) runs to completion

As you can see, the Dog constructor is invoked first, but it will be the last constructor to run to completion, since *the first statement of each constructor (except the top of the chain, Object) is a call to* `super()`.

Rules for Constructors

- If you don't type a constructor, a *default* constructor will be automatically inserted by the compiler.
- The default constructor has no arguments and makes a call to the superclass constructor with no arguments.
- A constructor's name must exactly match the name of the class.
- Constructors must not have a return type.
- It's legal (although not recommended) to have a method with the same name as your class, which makes the method *look* like a constructor, but it's still just a method that happens to have the same name as the class. The difference is that the method will have a return type, whereas constructors won't. The following legal code demonstrates this:

```
Class Dog {
Dog() { }
void Dog() { } // just a method that happens to use the class name
}
```

- Constructors can use any access modifier.
- The default constructor is always a no-arg constructor. It does not matter what the superclass constructor looks like.
- If you type any constructors at all, the default constructor will not be put in. If you want a no-arg constructor and you've typed in other constructors, you'll have to type in the no-arg constructor yourself.
- Every constructor must have as its first statement a call to either an overloaded constructor in the same class or to the super constructor.
- A call to a super constructor can be no-arg or include arguments passed to the super constructor.

```
Class Dog {
 Dog() {
 super("Fido"); // pass a String to Dog's super constructor
 }
 }
```

How Do You Know If a Default Constructor Will Be Created?

Because *you* didn't write any constructors in your class.

How Do You Know What That Constructor Will Look Like?

It will have the same access modifier as your class (public or default) and it will be no-arg with a no-arg call to super.

Given the following class:

```
public class Dog {
}
```

The compiler will put in a constructor that looks like this:

```
public Dog() {
 super();
 }
```

What Happens If Your Super Constructor Has Arguments?

Constructors can have arguments just as methods can, and if you try to invoke a method that takes, say, an int, but you don't pass it anything, you won't be able to compile. The compiler will complain that it can't find a matching method.

```
class Foo {
 public void doStuff(int i) {}
}
class TestFoo {
 public static void main (String [] args) {
 Foo f = new Foo();
 f.doStuff(); // won't compile since doStuff takes an int
 }
}
```

Constructors work exactly the same way. So if your super constructor (that is, the constructor or your immediate superclass/parent) has arguments, you need to write the call to super, supplying the appropriate arguments. There's a crucial implication here: *if your superclass does not have a no-arg constructor, you must type a constructor in your class because you must have a place to write the appropriate call to super(someArgs).*

Even if you don't need anything but the default constructor in your class, if your superclass only contains constructors with arguments, you won't be able to use the compiler-provided default constructor, because it always—and only—puts in a no-arg call to super.

The following example shows the problem:

```
class Animal {
 // the Animal constructor takes a String
 // the compiler will not build in the default no-arg constructor
 Animal(String name) { }
}
class Dog extends Animal {
 // the default constructor would look like this:
 Dog() {
 super(); // problem! No matching constructor in Animal
 }
}
```

Overloaded Constructors

Just as Java lets you overload methods by reusing the method name with different argument lists, Java also lets you overload constructors. Overloading a constructor means typing in multiple versions of the constructor, each having different argument lists, as the following examples show:

```
class Cow {
 Cow(String name) { }
 Cow() { }
}
```

The previous code for the Cow class has two overloaded constructors, one that takes a String and one that is a no-arg.

Why Would You Overload a Constructor?

To be nice to those who want to instantiate objects from your class, you might want to provide several different ways to construct a class. In the previous Cow example, one piece of code might want to make a cow with a specific name, while another piece of code might need a cow but doesn't care about a name. It's more convenient to the calling code if the code doesn't always have to be sure to pass null, or some made-up value, into a constructor. For that reason, good coding practice encourages you to try to have a no-arg constructor in your class, even if you have overloaded constructors with a wide range of argument types. That way, you make it easy for someone to make an object of your type without having to have a bunch of information up front.

Of course, not all objects can be made without arguments. For example, it makes no sense to make a Color object without passing something to the constructor: what Color would it be if you don't give it one? Immutable objects such as those from the Float and Integer classes must have constructor arguments because once they're instantiated, the object's state cannot be changed. Nonetheless, if you look through the J2SE API, you'll find that most classes do include a no-arg constructor.

Code duplication is a potential concern with overloaded constructors, so most programmers will invoke one overloaded constructor from another to avoid code duplication, as the following example demonstrates:

```
class Animal {
 protected String name;
```

```
// constructor that takes a String for the name
Animal (String name) {
this.name = name;
}
// a constructor for making an animal without a known name
Animal() {
this(Animal.makeRandomName());
}
static String makeRandomName() {
… // code that generates a name
return theName;
}
}
```

Notice that the no-arg constructor has, for its first line, a call to `this`. *Every constructor must have, as its first statement, either a call to* `this` (which invokes an overloaded constructor) *or a call to* `super` (which invokes the constructor of the immediate superclass). *There are no exceptions to this rule.*

But notice also that neither of the constructors in the code example above has a call to `super`. That's because the compiler will insert a call to `super()` in any constructor that does not already have a call to either `super` or `this`, even in constructors you've typed in your class code.

Objective 3.03 — Write Code to Construct Instances of Any Concrete Class

Y ou already know how to construct instances of a "normal" class; using the new keyword:

```
Dog d = new Dog();
```

Or, if the constructor has arguments:

```
Dog = new Dog("Aiko");
```

But if the class you're instantiating is an inner class, things get a bit more interesting. In this section, we'll look at inner classes and how you instantiate them.

Inner Classes

Inner classes let you define one class within another. They provide a type of scoping for your classes since you can make one class a member of another class. Just as classes have member variables and methods, a class can also have member classes. They come in several flavors, depending on how and where you define the inner class. There's a special kind of inner class known as a "top-level nested class" (some also call it a "static inner class"). For the purposes of this book, the term "inner class" will refer to all inner class variations except top-level nested classes, which will be covered in a separate section.

The three inner class flavors are as follows:

- Inner class
- Method-local inner class
- Anonymous inner class

One of the key benefits of an inner class is the "special relationship" an inner class instance shares with an instance of the outer class. Inner class objects have special access to even private variables of instances of the outer class. They can be particularly useful in situations where you want the benefits of a separate class (better OO, encapsulation, and the ability to inherit from something different from the outer class) but still maintain the benefits of being a member of the outer class (private data is directly accessible). You'll find examples of inner classes in most Java books by looking at the sections on GUI event listeners, a situation where inner classes come in very handy.

Regular Inner Classes

An inner class is defined inside another class. In other words, the inner class is written within the curly braces of the outer class.

```
class MyOuter {
 class MyInner {
 }
}
```

How Do You Instantiate a Regular Inner Class?

How do you create an instance from a class written within another class? *You must have an instance of the outer class as well.* There is no way to have an instance of a regular inner class without also having an instance of the outer/enclosing class.

Often, an instance of the outer class creates the inner object, so the code might look like this:

```
class MyOuter {
 void makeInner() {
 // from within the outer class' methods, an instance
 // is created just like any other object
 MyInner mi = new MyInner();
 }
 class MyInner {
 }
}
```

Creating an Inner Class Object from Outside the Outer Class's Instance Methods

From within a method (nonstatic) of the outer class, the code is easy:

```
MyInner mi = new MyInner();
```

But what if you're inside a static method of the outer class (so no implicit reference to a current object is available) or you're inside a completely different class? *You must have an instance of the outer class to construct an instance of the inner class.* Inner class instances always hold an implicit reference to an instance of the outer class; that's how the inner instance is able to access the other members of the outer class.

The code to make an instance of an inner class from somewhere other than an instance method of the outer class looks like this:

```
public class TestInner {
 public static void main (String [] args) {
 // we want the inner class instance, but we must start with the
outer class
 MyOuter out = new MyOuter();
 // then use that instance to create the inner class instance
 MyOuter.MyInner inner = out.new MyInner();
 }
}
```

You can also do this all in one line (create the outer object and inner object) as follows:

```
public class TestInner {
 public static void main (String [] args) {
 // we want the inner class instance, but we still need an outer
instance
 MyOuter.MyInner inner = new MyOuter().new MyInner();
 }
}
```

Method-Local Inner Class

A regular inner class is scoped inside another class's curly braces, but outside any method code. But you can also define an inner class within a method:

```
class MyOuter {
 void doStuff() {
 class MyInner {
 // do important inner class stuff
 } // close inner class definition
 // now instantiate the MyInner class,
 // which must come after the code which declares the inner class
 MyInner mi = new MyInner();
 } // close doStuff method
} // close outer class
```

What a Method-Local Inner Object Can and Can't Do

A method-local inner class can only be instantiated within the method where the class is defined. Like regular inner class objects, the method-local inner class object shares a special relationship with the enclosing class object and can access its private (or any other) instance variables and methods. However, the inner object cannot use the local variables of the method the inner class is in. The reason is simple: the inner class object on the heap might be, for example, passed to some other object and thus have a life long after the method is blown off the stack (in other words, the object can live even after the method has completed). So if the inner instance were to access one of the local variables inside the method (including arguments to the method), and the method had already completed, the arguments and local variables would no longer exist since the stack frame they lived in would be gone. History. Not there.

If the arguments or local variables are declared as final, however, the inner class object can access them:

```
class MyOuter {
 void doStuff(final String s, int i) {
 int x = 23;
 final int y = 45;
 class MyInner {
 // do important inner class stuff
 // can use s and y, but not i and x
 } // close inner class definition
 // now instantiate the MyInner class,
 // which must come after the code which declares the inner class
 MyInner mi = new MyInner();
 } // close doStuff method
} // close outer class
```

Anonymous Inner Class

So far we've looked at defining a class within an enclosing class (a regular inner class) and within a method (a method-local inner class). Finally, we're going to cover the most unusual place for declaring an inner class: inside an argument to a method invocation! Anonymous inner class code looks quite strange the first (and second and third) time you see it:

```
public interface Vet {
   public void innoculate();
}
class Unusual {
 public void doStuff() {
 Dog d = new Dog();
 d.giveShot(new Vet() {
 public void innoculate() {
 System.out.println("vet giving a shot");
```

```
  }
  });
  }
}
```

The following code duplicates the Unusual class above but adds comments to help explain the situation:

```
class Unusual {
 public void doStuff() {
 // make a Dog instance because we're going to invoke a method on it
 Dog d = new Dog();
 // here's where it gets strange…
 // the giveShot method takes an instance of Vet, but we don't
 // have one, so we'll make one - except for one problem
 // we need a Vet subclass because we need to override a method
 // but we don't have that Vet subclass
 // so not only must we make a Vet instance,
 // but we must also make a Vet implementation class
 d.giveShot(new Vet() {
 // new Vet() actually creates an instance of a new implementation of
Vet
 // the new Vet class is defined below
 // first we override the Vet method we care about
 public void innoculate() {
 System.out.println("vet giving a shot");
 } // close the overridden innoculate method
 }); // close the new class, method argument, and giveShot statement
 } // close the doStuff method
} // close the Unusual class
```

A key feature of anonymous inner class syntax is that when you say new Vet(), if Vet is a class, it's as though you are saying to the compiler, "Create me a new instance of a class which I'm about to define, and *that class will be a subclass of Vet*." But if Vet is an interface, you're saying to the compiler, "Create me a new instance of a class which I'm about to define, and *that class will implement the Vet interface*."

Don't forget that since anonymous inner classes are defined within a method, they are still subject to all the restrictions of method-local inner classes.

Top-Level Nested Classes

Like regular inner classes, a top-level nested class is a class defined within another. Also as with inner classes, this nesting provides a type of scoping for your nested class. But unlike an inner class, a top-level nested class (also known as a "static inner class") *can be instantiated without having an instance of the outer class.* The top-level nested class is declared like a normal inner class, except it is marked with the `static` modifier. Unlike the situation for normal inner classes, an instance of a top-level nested class does not share a "special" relationship with an outer instance, and in fact behaves just as any other normal Java class. Thus, top-level nested classes are much closer to regular old Java classes than they are to inner classes.

The benefit of a top-level nested class (as opposed to a normal Java class) is that you get to organize a namespace for your nested class so that it still belongs to the outer class, even though it is not technically a member of that outer class. Once an instance of a top-level nested class is running, that instance does not have any other relationship with any instances of the outer class.

For the purposes of the exam, you must be able to recognize that a top-level nested class can be instantiated as long as you have access to the outer class without needing any references to outer instances. The code is simple:

```
TheInner ti = new TheOuter.TheInner();
```

In the previous example, TheInner is a top-level nested class, while TheOuter is the enclosing class as follows:

```
public class TheOuter {
   public static class TheInner { } // note the keyword static
}
```

Travel Assistance

For more information about methods and constructors in Java, please see: The JavaTM 2 Platform, Standard Edition, v 1.3.1 API Specification at **http://java.sun.com/j2se/1.3/docs/api/index.html;** *The Java Class Libraries, Second Edition, Volume 1* by Patrick Chan, Rosanna Lee, and Douglas Kramer, Addison-Wesley, 1998; and *The Java Programming Language, Second Edition* by Ken Arnold and James Gosling, Addison-Wesley, 7th printing, February 2000.

✔ **Objective 3.01** State the benefits of encapsulation in object-oriented design and write code that implements tightly encapsulated classes and the relationships "is-a" and "has-a." A class is tightly encapsulated if it protects the object's data by forcing calling code to use methods instead of directly accessing instance variables. The "is-a" relationship is defined when one class extends another. The "has-a" relationship is defined when one class has an instance variable that holds a reference to an instance of another class.

✔ **Objective 3.02** Write code to invoke overridden or overloaded methods and parental or overloaded constructors; and describe the effect of invoking these methods. Overloaded methods and constructors reuse the same name but use different argument lists. Overridden methods redefine a method in a subclass to add subclass-specific behavior not described by the superclass version of the method.

✔ **Objective 3.03** Write code to construct instances of any concrete class including normal top-level classes, inner classes, and anonymous inner classes. Inner class instances have a special relationship to an instance of an outer/enclosing class, unless the inner class is marked static.

REVIEW QUESTIONS

1. In OO terms, if you read "A Pancake is a Food", which of the following are true of the code implementing that statement?

   A. Class Pancake extends class Food
   B. Class Food extends class Pancake
   C. Class Pancake is in the package Food
   D. Class Pancake has a reference to a Food
   E. Class Food has a reference to a Pancake
   F. Class Food is in the package Pancake

2. In OO terms, if you read "A Car is a Vehicle that has a Motor", which of the following are true of the code implementing that statement?

   A. Class Vehicle extends class Car
   B. Class Car extends class Vehicle

   C. Class Car extends class Motor

   D. Class Motor extends class Vehicle

3. Does the following code demonstrate encapsulation?

```
class Foo {
public int x;
protected void setX(int i) {
x = i;
}
}
```

   A. Yes

   B. No

4. Given the following class, which of the following methods would be legal in a subclass of Foo?

```
class Foo {
String doStuff(int x) { }
}
```

   A. String doStuff(int x) { }

   B. int doStuff(int x) { }

   C. public String doStuff(int x) { }

   D. protected String doStuff(int x) { }

   E. String doStuff(String s) { }

5. Given the following class, which of the following methods would be legal in a subclass of Foo? (Select two.)

```
class Foo {
public String doStuff(int x) { }
}
```

   A. String doStuff(int x) { }

   B. int doStuff(int x) { }

   C. public String doStuff(int x) { }

   D. protected String doStuff(int x) { }

   E. String doStuff(String s) { }

6. Given the following class, which of the following are legal constructors you can add to a Beagle subclass of Dog?

```
Class Dog {
 Dog(String name) { }
 }
```

    A. No constructor, allow the compiler default

    B. Beagle() {super();}

    C. Beagle() {super("fido");}

    D. Beagle() { }

7. Would the following code compile?

```
public class Animal {
 private Animal() { }
}
public class Dog extends Animal { }
```

    A. Yes

    B. No

8. Which of the following statements are true about constructors?

    A. Constructors must not have arguments if the superclass constructor does not have arguments.

    B. Constructors are not inherited.

    C. Constructors cannot be overloaded.

    D. The first statement of every constructor is a call to super or this.

9. Which of these statements are true about method overriding?

    A. Overriding methods must have the same return type as the overridden method.

    B. Overriding methods are allowed to change the return type.

    C. Overriding methods are allowed to change the argument list.

    D. Overriding methods can be defined in the same class as the overridden method.

10. Which of these statements are true about method overloading?

    A. Overloaded methods must have the same return type.

B. Overloaded methods are allowed to change the return type.

C. Overloaded methods must have different argument lists.

D. Overloaded methods can be defined in the same class.

REVIEW ANSWERS

1. **A** D and E are wrong because they describe the "has-a" relationship rather than "is-a". C and F are wrong because "is-a" does not define package relationships.

2. **B** The "has-a" relationship is not reflected in any of the answers.

3. **B** Encapsulation requires restricted access to the object's data; public instance variables violate encapsulation.

4. **A** **C** **D** **E** A, C, and D are legal overrides. E is a legal overload; putting overloaded methods in a subclass is legal. B is not a legal override because the return type is different and not a legal overload because the argument list is the same.

5. **C** **E** C is a legal override, E is a legal overload. A and D are not legal because the access modifier is more restrictive than the overridden method. B is not legal because the return type is different (and the access modifier is more restrictive).

6. **C** Only C is correct because the Dog class does not have a no-arg constructor, therefore you must explicitly make the call to super, passing in a String.

7. **B** The compiler will put in the default constructor, which includes a no-arg call to super(). But since the Animal constructor is private, the Dog object does not have access to it. This example demonstrates that marking a constructor as private (which is legal) prevents a class from ever being subclassed.

8. **B** **D** A is wrong because subclass constructors do not have to match the arguments of the superclass constructor. Only the call to super must match.

9. **A** B and C are wrong because overriding methods must exactly match the overridden method of the superclass. D is wrong because overriding methods must be defined in a subclass.

10. **B** **C** **D** A is wrong because overloaded methods are allowed to change the return type.

Garbage Collection

ITINERARY

○ **Objective 4.01** State the behavior that is guaranteed by the garbage collection system, and write code that explicitly makes objects eligible for collection.

	NEWBIE	SOME EXPERIENCE	EXPERT
ETA	6 hours	3 hours	1 hour

We use the term *garbage collection* to describe Java's *automatic storage management system*. Usually programmers are responsible for managing the memory their applications use. The developers of Java chose to delegate this task to the *Java Virtual Machine* (JVM), the software engine that executes the Java class files when an application is started.

Local Lingo

Garbage collection is often referred to as *gc*.

Exam Tip

The exam is not likely to have more than one or two questions directly related to garbage collection; however, the knowledge you gain studying the garbage collector will improve your overall understanding of the language and assist you in deciphering code examples, especially those involving method invocations.

Objective 4.01

Guaranteed Garbage Collector Behaviors

To understand the behavior that is guaranteed by the garbage collector, you need to know how the JVM utilizes system memory: how it creates objects in memory and how it handles *parameter variables*, a.k.a. method arguments.

The Java Memory Model

When a Java application is started, the JVM establishes a number of runtime data areas:

- **The JVM stack**   Shared by all processes and used to store local variables and temporary results. Also utilized during method invocation.

- **The heap**   Used to allocate memory space for newly created objects and arrays. Also shared by all processes. *This is the only memory area which is subject to garbage collection.*
- **The method area**   Stores the runtime constant pools, field data, and the code for method, constructor, and initialization blocks. Logically, the method area is part of the heap; however, the JVM is not required to garbage collect or compact this area of memory. The method area also contains a special *string constant pool* that is used to store literal string objects of the type `java.lang.String`. Each JVM maintains one, and only one, string constant pool.
- **Runtime constant pools**   Allocated memory from the method area. One exists for each class or interface used by the application. The runtime constant pool contains values that are known at compile time and field references that are evaluated at runtime.

Travel Advisory

While the JVM specifications do not require the garbage collection of string literals, a majority of the mock exams available on the World Wide Web have code examples that require you to choose the point at which string literals become eligible for garbage collection. For the purpose of answering such questions, assume that garbage collection is valid for string literals.

You have some control over the size of the heap via the `java.exe` command-line options. By default, the initial size of the heap is 2MB and the maximum size is 64MB. To increase the initial heap size, use the `java.exe` command-line option −Xms. The required size must be expressed in kilobytes, as multiples of 1,024, or megabytes. For example, to set the initial heap size to 6MB, start an application, on a Win32 system, using:

```
java –Xms6144k ClassName or java –Xms6m ClassName
```

To increase or decrease the heap's maximum size at startup, use the command-line option −Xmx. For example, to decrease the heap's maximum size to 32MB on a Win32 system, start your application using the command: `java  –Xmx32m ClassName`.

The Garbage Collector

The automatic storage management system, or garbage collector, monitors the heap for the JVM. The garbage collector is a runtime service that is automatically executed as a low priority background process when the JVM is started. The process reclaims heap memory allocated to objects no longer being used by the application.

> **Travel Advisory**
>
> The JVM specification does not define a garbage collection algorithm. As a result, implementation details vary from one operating system and JVM to the next.

To see the garbage collector in action, use the `java.exe -verbose:gc` option. On a Win32 system, start the following example from the command line using these options:

```
java -Xms1m -Xmx1m -verbose:gc GCInAction
```

This instructs the JVM to set both the initial and maximum heap size to 1MB and print statements to the screen when garbage collection occurs. The following example can be used to demonstrate the behavior.

```
package ch36604;

public class GCInAction {
    public static void main(String[] args) {
        int i = 0;

        while( true ) {
            String str = new String("Welcome to Java!");
            i++;
            if( i % 1000 == 0 ) {
                System.out.println(str);
            }
        }
    }
}
```

On a Win32 system, you should see something similar to the following:

```
Welcome to Java!
[GC 634K->122K(960K), 0.0004006 secs]
Welcome to Java!
Welcome to Java!
Welcome to Java!
Welcome to Java!
Welcome to Java!
Welcome to Java!
Welcome to Java!
[GC 634K->122K(960K), 0.0004107 secs]
```

The statements in square brackets are generated by the JVM when a garbage collection event occurs.

If you want to disable the garbage collector at startup, use the -Xnoclassgc option; or, to turn off incremental garbage collection, use the -Xincgc option. This option will prevent occasional pauses, which may occur during program execution while the garbage collector is reclaiming memory. However, according to the Tool documentation pages on Sun's website, it will also reduce the overall efficiency of the garbage collector by approximately 10 percent.

Objects in Memory

Every time an application creates a new object, it occupies space in the heap. While Java has a new() method for object creation, there is no corresponding delete() method. You cannot explicitly destroy an object. Instead, Java programmers rely on the garbage collector to manage memory and delete unused objects for them.

Exam Tip
You cannot explicitly destroy an object once it has been created.

The garbage collector *does not guarantee* an application will never run out of memory. Memory leaks are still possible. For example, you can create a list that contains references to objects. The objects will not be eligible for garbage collection until the list itself is eligible. Eventually, if you create enough objects, the application will run out of memory.

The following example uses a continuous loop to create new string objects, adding them to a `java.util.Vector` object. When executed on a Win32 platform, an `OutOf Memory` error is generated after 2,000+ string objects are created.

```
package ch36604;
import java.util.Vector;

public class GCOutOfMemory {
    public static void main(String[] args){
        Vector v = new Vector();
        int i = 0;
        String str = new String("Use up memory.");
        String str1 = " ";

        while(true) {
            str1 = str + str1;
            v.addElement(str1);
            System.out.println("Object #: " + i++);
        }
    }
}
```

While you cannot force the garbage collector to reclaim memory, you can *suggest* that it do so by calling the `java.lang.System.gc()` method or the `java.lang.Runtime.getRuntime().gc()` method. Both these methods send a request to the garbage collector asking it to reclaim memory. The garbage collector can honor or ignore the request at its whim.

Travel Advisory

The accepted convention is to invoke `System.gc()`, which is equivalent to `Runtime.getRuntime().gc()`.

Exam Tip

You cannot force the garbage collector to reclaim memory.

When Objects Become Eligible for Garbage Collection

In the normal course of program execution, objects become eligible for garbage collection as follows:

Declaration	Eligible for Garbage Collection
Static field	When the class is unloaded
Instance field	When the instance (object) becomes eligible for collection
Array components	When the array is no longer referenced
Constructor parameters	When constructor execution ends
Method parameters	When method execution ends
Objects created in methods	When method execution ends
Exception handling parameters	When the catch clause completes execution

---

Exam Tip

Objects become eligible for garbage collection when no references to them exist.

The preceding table applies as long as *no other references to the object exist.* In the following code, a reference to the object `oref`, created in the method `createObject()` is passed to `main()`. The object oref will not be eligible for garbage collection when the method `createObject()` completes because a reference to the object still exists in the `main()` method.

```
package ch36604;

public class GCObjectRef {
```

```
public static Object createObject() {
    // create a new object and return it's reference
    Object oref = new Object();
    return oref;
}
public static void main( String[] args ) {
    Object obj = createObject();
}
}
```

Travel Assistance

You can learn more about garbage collection and the JVM by going to **http://www.artima.com/insidejvm/ed2/ch09Garbage CollectionPrint.html.**

Parameter Variables Are Passed as Copies

An understanding of how Java passes arguments to methods is crucial to understanding how method operations affect objects and to recognizing exactly when an object is eligible for garbage collection.

When a method is invoked, the JVM creates new, temporary *parameter variables*; one for each parameter. It then *copies* the argument values to the corresponding parameter variables.

The value of a primitive type is its *data*. Within the method, any change made to a primitive type parameter variable does not affect the data contained in the original primitive type argument variable.

The following example demonstrates that the original value of a primitive type variable passed as an argument to a method is not altered.

```
package ch36604;

public class GCPassAPrimitive {
    public static void tryToChangeMe( int num ){
        num = 5;     // change the value
        System.out.println("'num' in tryToChangeMe(): " + num );
    }
```

```
    public static void main(String[] args) {
        int num = 10;
        System.out.println();
        System.out.println("'num' before tryToChangeMe(): " + num );
        tryToChangeMe( num );
        System.out.println("'num' after tryToChangeMe(): " + num );
    }
 }
Output:
'num' before tryToChangeMe(): 10
'num' in tryToChangeMe(): 5
'num' after tryToChangeMe(): 10
```

The value of a reference type variable is the *memory address* of the object it references or points to. Within the method, any change made to the object referenced by the parameter variable affects the object pointed to by the corresponding argument variable.

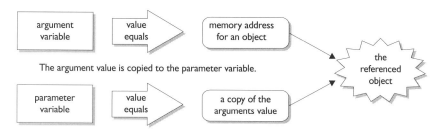

Both the argument variable and the parameter variable point to the same object.

However, if the reference type parameter variable is assigned to a *different* object, the corresponding argument variable is not affected; it will continue to point to the original object.

The following code example demonstrates what can happen when a reference type variable is passed as an argument to a method.

```
package ch36604;

public class GCPassAnObject {
    public static void tryToChangeMe( StringBuffer buf ){
        // the original object will be changed
        buf.append(" Goodbye World!");
```

```
        System.out.println("'buf' modified by tryToChangeMe(): " +
buf );

        //point the parameter variable at a different object
        StringBuffer sb = new StringBuffer("I'm a new String!");
        buf = sb;
        System.out.println("'buf' assigned to new object in
tryToChangeMe(): " + buf );
    }

    public static void main(String[] args) {
        StringBuffer buf = new StringBuffer("Hello World!");
        System.out.println();
        tryToChangeMe( buf );
        System.out.println("'buf' in main() after tryToChangeMe(): "
+ buf);
    }
}
```

```
Output:
'buf' modified by tryToChangeMe(): Hello World! Goodbye World!
'buf' assigned to new object in tryToChangeMe(): I'm a new String!
'buf' in main() after tryToChangeMe(): Hello World! Goodbye World!
```

When an object's reference is passed to a method, *the original object can be modified within the method.* The method, however, cannot change the reference value of the variable originally passed in as an argument. The original reference type argument variable cannot be made to reference a new object or any other area of memory.

Travel Assistance

You can learn more about setting object references to null by going to **http://developer.java.sun.com/developer/TechTips/1997/ tt0903.html#tip2.**

Explicitly Making an Object Eligible for Garbage Collection

You can't force the garbage collector to reclaim an object's memory, but by setting all of an object's references to null you can let the garbage collector know the application no longer requires the object:

```
myObj = null;     // de-references the object
```

The preceding in no way *guarantees* that the object will be garbage collected. You are just notifying the garbage collector that the application no longer needs the object, and the garbage collector decides when—or if—the object's memory will be reclaimed.

Travel Assistance

You can learn more about reference objects by going to **http://developer.java.sun.com/developer/TechTips/1999/tt0511.html#tip2.**

The Role of `finalize()` in Garbage Collection

Every object inherits a `finalize()` method from the `java.lang.Object` class. The garbage collector is guaranteed to invoke this method once prior to reclaiming the object's memory.

The method, as defined, does nothing. You may override the method to release system resources being used that are not subject to garbage collection. For example, if you have an object that handles I/O transactions, you may want to ensure any connections are closed before the object's memory is reclaimed.

If an exception is raised during the execution of `finalize()`, the finalization is halted, but the exception itself is ignored.

It is possible to reassign an object's reference during the finalization process, that is, you can assign the reference to an active thread or static variable. The object will then no longer be eligible for garbage collection; however, the next time the object becomes eligible for garbage collection, the `finalize()` method will *not* be invoked by the garbage collector. The Java Language Specification (JLS) guarantees that `finalize()` will be called *once and only once* by the automatic storage collection system. This does not prohibit you from calling `finalize()` from other parts of your application. Your application can call `finalize()` on any object at any time, but the garbage collector will invoke it once and once only.

You may also request to have the `finalize()` method executed on all objects that are eligible for collection but that have not yet been finalized, by invoking either `Runtime.getRuntime().runFinalization()` or the equivalent, but more convenient, `System.runFinalization()`.

Travel Advisory

The developers of Java recommend calling `super.final-ize()` when overriding `finalize()`. This will ensure the proper finalization of superclasses.

There are no guarantees as to the order in which objects are finalized. Your application cannot assume that the `finalize()` method of another object has occurred simply because its references were set to null before the current object became eligible for garbage collection. The order in which two or more objects become eligible for garbage collection has no bearing on the order in which the garbage collector invokes their `finalize()` method.

Travel Assistance

You can learn more about object finalization by going to **http://www.javaworld.com/javaworld/jw-06-1998/jw-06-techniques_p.html**.

CHECKPOINT

✔ **Objective 4.01: Garbage Collection**

- **Guaranteed Garbage Collection Behavior**   The Java Language Specification guarantees that

a. The nonmethod area of heap memory will be monitored by the garbage collector.

b. An object's `finalize()` method will be invoked, by the garbage collector, once and only once prior to an object's memory being reclaimed, regardless of the number of times it becomes eligible for collection.

You cannot force the garbage collector to reclaim memory. You can *request* that the garbage collector reclaim memory by invoking the `Runtime.getRuntime().gc()` or `System.gc()` methods but there is *no guarantee* the garbage collector will actually reclaim memory.

- **Explicitly Make an Object Eligible for Garbage Collection**   You can explicitly make an object eligible for garbage collection by setting all of its references to `null`. This *does not guarantee* the object's memory will be reclaimed. You cannot explicitly delete objects once they have been created.

REVIEW QUESTIONS

1. An object can be deleted by invoking its `delete()` method. True or False?

2. You can turn off the garbage collection process by using the `–Xnoclassgc` command-line option when starting `java.exe`. True or False?

3. The garbage collection process ensures your application will never run out of memory. True or False?

4. Your program can explicitly reclaim unused memory by invoking `System.gc()`. True or False?

5. The `finalize()` method is guaranteed to be invoked by the garbage collector only once before an object's memory is reclaimed. True or False?

6. Setting all of an object's references to `null` guarantees it will be garbage collected. True or False?

7. At what point in the following example code does the object passed to `method()` become eligible for garbage collection?

   A. After line 10
   B. When the method finishes executing
   C. After line 5
   D. Never within this example

```
1  public class Q36604_7 {
2    public static void main(String[] args) {
3        String str = new String("An Object");
4        String str1 = (String) method(str);
5        str = null;
6        System.out.println( str1 );
7    }
8    public static Object method(Object anObject) {
9        Object objB = anObject;
10        anObject = null;
11       return objB;
12   }
13 }
```

8. How many objects are eligible for garbage collection once line 10 is reached?

    A. 1
    B. 5
    C. 4
    D. 3

```
1 public class Q36604_8 {
2    public static void main(String[] args) {
3        String s1 = new String("John");
4        String s2 = new String("Paul");
5        String s3 = new String("Ringo");
6        String s4 = new String("George");
7        String s5 = new String("Beatles");
8        s1 = s2 = s3 = s4 = s5;
9        s1 = null;
10   }
11 }
```

9. The garbage collector will always execute an object's `finalize()` method immediately before reclaiming its memory. True or False?

10. Objects are finalized in the same order in which they became eligible for garbage collection. True or False?

REVIEW ANSWERS

1. **False** There is no `delete()` method and there is no way to explicitly delete an object once it has been created.

2. **True** It is possible to turn off the garbage collection process for a single Java session by starting the session using the `java.exe` command-line option `-Xnoclassgc`.

3. **False** Java's automatic storage collection mechanism handles basic memory management chores but does not guarantee an application will never run out of memory.

4. **False** Your application can invoke `System.gc()` at any time; however, the JVM treats this as a request to reclaim unused memory, and it may heed the request or ignore it.

5. **True** The garbage collector will invoke an object's `finalize()` method prior to reclaiming the object's memory. The method is guaranteed to be run once and once only.

6. **False** Setting all of an object's references to `null` lets the garbage collector know the object's memory can be garbage collected but does not guarantee that its memory will be reclaimed.

7. **D** The object does not become eligible for garbage collection during the life of the application. The reference variable created in line 9 holds a reference to the object, so it is not eligible for garbage collection. The method passes a reference to the object back to the `main()` method, so it is not eligible for garbage collection. The reference variable created on line 4 still holds a reference to the object.

8. **C** Line 8 sets the references `s1` through `s4` to the `String` object "Beatles" referenced by `s5`. The objects "John", "Paul", "Ringo", and "George" are no longer being referenced. Line 9 sets the reference `s1` to `null`, and it no longer points to the `String` object "Beatles"; however, the references `s2`, `s3`, `s4`, and `s5` continue to point to the `String` object "Beatles". That leaves the four `String` objects ("John", "Paul", "Ringo", and "George") eligible for garbage collection.

9. **False** The garbage collector will run an object's `finalize()` method once and only once.

10. **False** The order in which objects are finalized is not guaranteed.

The java.lang Package

NEWBIE	SOME EXPERIENCE	EXPERT
16 hours	8 hours	2 hours

ETA

The classes in the `java.lang` package form the heart and soul of the Java language. In Chapter 1, it was stated that the JDK API extend the Java language, and so they do; however, there are some classes (`Object`, `Class`, `String`, `Thread`, and `Throwable`) whose behavior is constrained by the *Java Language Specification* (JLS). Many of the language features and behaviors discussed in the other chapters are implemented through and rely on the existence of the aforementioned classes, which is why *every* JRE is guaranteed to implicitly include the `java.lang` package.

The exam objectives *explicitly* focus on the `Math` and `String` classes; however, they *implicitly* require an understanding of the Object, Wrapper, and StringBuffer classes and a basic familiarity with the System class, so these will be the primary focus of this chapter. For an understanding of the `Thread` class and `Runnable` interface, see Chapter 8. For more on the Throwable, Error, and Exception classes, see Chapter 7. The remaining classes are not covered on the exam; for more information on their use see the JDK API.

Package Overview

The defined types in the `java.lang` package may be grouped into ten general categories, as shown in Table 5.1.

TABLE 5.1	Overview of the `java.lang` Package

Category	Defined Type
Basic classes	`Class, Object, Throwable`
Interfaces	`Cloneable, Comparable, Runnable`
Strings	`String, StringBuffer`
Wrapper classes	`Boolean, Byte, Character, Double, Float, Integer, Long, Number, Short, Long, Void`
Mathematics	`Math`
Threads	`Thread, ThreadGroup, ThreadLocal, InheritableThreadLocal`

(Continued)

TABLE 5.1 *CONTINUED*	
Method Name	**Description**
Errors and Exceptions	Error, Exception, RuntimeException
System	ClassLoader, Package, Process, Runtime, System
Security	RuntimePermission, SecurityException, SecurityManager
Miscellaneous	Character.Subset, Character.UnicodeBlock, Compiler

Travel Assistance

For more information on the java.lang package, go to **http://java.sun.com/j2se/1.3/docs/api/index.html.**

Objective 5.01

Write Code Using Methods of the `java.lang.Math` Class

The Math class is a public final class which contains two static final fields, E and PI, as well as a number of static methods to handle standard mathematical operations such as logarithms, square roots, and trigonometric functions. The class has a private constructor and may not be instantiated. Before diving into the specifics of the Math class you need to be familiar with the "wrapper" classes.

The Wrapper Classes

The primitive data types described in Chapter 1, boolean, byte, char, short, int, float, double, and long, are not objects; however, Java provides *wrapper classes*, Boolean, Byte, Character, Short, Integer, Float, Double, and Long, that allow you to create an object that mimics its corresponding primitive type. They essentially "wrap" a primitive type within an object.

Each of the classes have two constructors: one that takes a primitive value of the wrapper primitive type and one that takes a value of the corresponding type passed in as a string. The exceptions are the `Character` class, which has only one constructor and takes a single character value, and the `Float` class, which has a third constructor to take a `double` value that it converts to a float.

The integral and floating-point classes are subclasses of the abstract class `Number`. The `Number` class is generic and may be used to represent any number.

There is one additional wrapper class: `Void`. This class has no constructors and is a placeholder class used to hold a reference to a `Class` object representing the primitive type `void`. It cannot be instantiated.

All the classes are declared `final` and have at least one `public static final` field: `TYPE`, which references the runtime `Class` object for the type. All but `Boolean` and `Void` contain two additional `public static final` fields: `MIN_VALUE` and `MAX_VALUE`, representing the minimum and maximum values the class can represent or contain.

The floating-point classes contain three additional `public static final` fields: `NaN` (not a number), `NEGATIVE_INFINITY`, and `POSITIVE_INFINITY`.

All but the `Boolean` and `Void` classes implement the `Comparable` and `Serializable` interfaces. Objects of classes implementing the `Comparable` interface can be sorted and compared (see Chapter 12 for more information on the `Comparable` interface). Objects of classes implementing the `Serializable` interface can be saved as persistent objects (see Chapter 11 for more information on the `Serializable` interface). `Boolean` implements `Serializable`; `Void` implements neither interface.

Exam Tip

Once a wrapper object has been created, its value cannot be modified; they are *immutable*.

`java.lang.Math` Fields
Covered by the Objectives

The Math class has two fields: E and PI. The field E represents *e*, the base of natural logarithms, as the `double` number 2.7182818284590452354.

The field PI represents π as the `double` value 3.14159265358979323846.

java.lang.Math Methods
Covered by the Objectives

You are expected to understand the workings of the Math methods discussed in the following sections.

abs()

The abs() method is overloaded to take an int, long, float, or double as an argument and return values of the argument type. As a general rule, if the argument is positive, the argument is returned. If the argument is negative, its negation is returned.

```
public class TestAbsolute {
    public static void main(String[] args) {
        long lpos = 9810;
        long lneg = -9810;
        float fpos = 0.3456f;
        float fneg = -0.3456f;

        System.out.println("Math.abs(10) \t" + Math.abs(10));
        System.out.println("Math.abs -10) \t" + Math.abs(-10));
        System.out.println("Math.abs(lpos) \t" + Math.abs(lpos));
        System.out.println("Math.abs(lneg) \t" + Math.abs(lneg));
        System.out.println("Math.abs(21.53) \t" + Math.abs(21.53));
        System.out.println("Math.abs(-21.53) \t" + Math.abs(-21.53));
        System.out.println("Math.abs(fpos) \t" + Math.abs(fpos));
        System.out.println("Math.abs(fneg) \t" + Math.abs(fneg));
    }
}
Output:
Math.abs(   10   )      10
Math.abs(  -10   )      10
Math.abs(  lpos  )      9810
Math.abs(  lneg  )      9810
Math.abs(  21.53 )      21.53
```

```
Math.abs( -21.53 )       21.53
Math.abs(  fpos )        0.3456
Math.abs(  fneg )        0.3456
```

The only time `abs()` will return a negative value is if the argument is equal to the `MIN_VALUE` of either the `Long` or `Integer` type. This is because the negation of `MIN_VALUE` cannot be represented in the same data type. In fact, `MIN_VALUE` == `-MAX_VALUE - 1`. The following statements:

```
System.out.println( "Math.abs( Integer.MIN_VALUE )\t" +
                    Math.abs(Integer.MIN_VALUE));

System.out.println( "Math.abs( Long.MIN_VALUE ) \t" +
                    Math.abs(Long.MIN_VALUE) );
```

will produce the following output:

```
Math.abs( Integer.MIN_VALUE )   -2147483648
Math.abs( Long.MIN_VALUE )      -9223372036854775808
```

In addition, there are three special cases which apply to floating-point numbers:

1. If the argument is 0 or –0, positive zero is returned.
2. If the argument is an infinity, either negative or positive, `Infinity` is returned.
3. If the argument is not a number, `NaN` is returned.

The following statements:

```
System.out.println("Math.abs( -0.0 ) \t\t\t" + Math.abs( -0.0 ) );
System.out.println("Math.abs( Float.NEGATIVE_INFINITY ) \t" +
                    Math.abs( Float.NEGATIVE_INFINITY) );
```

produce

```
Math.abs( -0.0 )                         0.0
Math.abs( Float.NEGATIVE_INFINITY )      Infinity
```

ceil()

The `ceil()` method returns a `double` that is the smallest whole number greater than or equal to its argument. It has three special cases:

1. If the argument is an int, it returns the argument widened to a Double.
2. If the argument is NaN, 0, -0, or positive or negative infinity, it returns the argument widened to a Double.
3. If the argument is less than zero but greater than -1.0, it returns -0.0.

```
public class TestCeil {
    public static void main(String[] args){
        float nan = Float.NaN;
        double pos = Double.POSITIVE_INFINITY;
        double neg = Double.NEGATIVE_INFINITY;
        System.out.println("Math.ceil( 12.321 ) \t" +
                            Math.ceil( 12.321 ) );
        System.out.println("Math.ceil( -12.321 ) \t" +
                            Math.ceil( -12.321 ) );
        System.out.println("Math.ceil( 10 ) \t" + Math.ceil( 10 ) );
        System.out.println("Math.ceil( nan ) \t" +
                            Math.ceil( nan ) );
        System.out.println("Math.ceil(pos) \t" + Math.ceil( pos ) );
        System.out.println("Math.ceil(neg) \t" + Math.ceil( neg ) );
        System.out.println("Math.ceil(-0.5) \t" + Math.ceil( -0.5 )
);
    }
}
Output:
Math.ccil( 12.321 )     13.0
Math.ceil( -12.321 )    -12.0
Math.ceil( 10 )         10.0
Math.ceil( nan )        NaN
Math.ceil( pos )        Infinity
Math.ceil( neg )        -Infinity
Math.ceil( -0.5 )       -0.0
```

Exam Tip

If the argument is negative, ceil() moves *toward* zero (-12.321 has a ceiling of -12); if the argument is positive, it moves *away* from zero (12.321 has a ceiling of 13).

floor()

The floor() method returns a double that is the smallest whole number less than or equal to the argument. It has the two special cases:

1. If the argument is an integer, the argument is returned widened to a Double.
2. If the argument is not a number, positive or negative infinity, or negative or positive zero, the argument is returned widened to a Double.

```
public class TestFloor {
    public static void main(String[] args){
        float nan = Float.NaN;
        double pos = Double.POSITIVE_INFINITY;
        double neg = Double.NEGATIVE_INFINITY;
        System.out.println("Math.floor( 12.321 ) \t" +
                            Math.floor( 12.321 ) );
        System.out.println("Math.floor( -12.321 ) \t" +
                            Math.floor( -12.321 ) );
        System.out.println("Math.floor(10) \t" + Math.floor(10) );
        System.out.println("Math.floor(nan) \t" + Math.floor(nan) );
        System.out.println("Math.floor(pos) \t" + Math.floor(pos) );
        System.out.println("Math.floor(neg) \t" + Math.floor(neg) );
        System.out.println("Math.floor(-0.0) \t" + Math.floor(-0.0));
        System.out.println("Math.floor(-0.5) \t" + Math.floor(-0.5))
    }
}
Output:
Math.floor( 12.321 )     12.0
Math.floor( -12.321 )    -13.0
Math.floor( 10 )         10.0
Math.floor( nan )        NaN
Math.floor( pos )        Infinity
Math.floor( neg )        -Infinity
Math.floor( -0.0 )       -0.0
Math.floor( -0.5 )       -1.0
```

> ### Exam Tip
>
> If the argument is negative, *floor()* moves *away from* zero
> (-12.321 has a floor of -13); if the argument is positive, it moves
> *toward* zero (12.321 has a floor of 12).

max() and min()

The max() method returns the larger of two arguments, while the min() method returns the smaller of two arguments. Both methods are overloaded to take pairs of arguments as int, long, float, or double values. The value returned has the same type as the widest argument type. They have two special cases:

1. If the arguments have the same value, the argument is returned.
2. For floating-point values, if one of the arguments is NaN, NaN is returned.

```java
public class TestMinMax {
    public static void main(String[] args){
        float nan = Float.NaN;
        double pos = Double.POSITIVE_INFINITY;
        double neg = Double.NEGATIVE_INFINITY;
        System.out.println("Math.max( 12.32, 12.12 ) \t" +
                            Math.max( 12.32, 12.12 ) );
        System.out.println("Math.min( -12.32, -12.12 ) \t" +
                            Math.min( -12.32, -12.12 ) );
        System.out.println("Math.max( 12,12 ) \t\t" +
                            Math.max( 12, 12 ) );
        System.out.println("Math.min( nan, 10 ) \t\t" +
                            Math.min( nan, 10 ) );
        System.out.println("Math.max( pos, neg ) \t\t" +
                            Math.max( pos, neg ) );
        System.out.println("Math.min( 0.0, -0.0 ) \t\t" +
                            Math.min( 0.0, -0.0 ) );
    }
}
```

```
Output:
Math.max( 12.32, 12.12 )        12.32
Math.min( -12.32, -12.12 )      -12.32
Math.max( 12,12 )               12
Math.min( nan, 10 )             NaN
Math.max( pos, neg )            Infinity
Math.min( 0.0, -0.0 )           -0.0
```

Exam Tip

The `Math` methods distinguish between -0.0 and 0.0; however, if the argument is a nonfloating-point value no distinction is made. For example, an argument of -0 will be returned as 0.0.

random()

The `random()` method generates a pseudo-random number between 0.0 and 1.0 exclusively. It takes no arguments and always returns a *positive* `double` value. It is pseudo-random because the returned numbers tend to repeat themselves after a very large number of continuous calls.

```
public class TestRandom{
    public static void main(String[] args){
        System.out.println("Math.random() \t" + Math.random() );
    }
}
Output:
Math.random()   0.2564935323077401
```

round()

The `round()` method takes either a `float` or `double` value as an argument, adds `0.5` to the value, takes the *floor* of the result and returns it as an `int` or `long`. The method has three special cases:

1. If the argument is not a number, it returns zero (*not* NaN, which cannot be represented by an `int` or `long` data type).

2. If the argument is a float and is less than negative infinity or
   Integer.MIN_VALUE, Integer.MIN_VALUE is returned (*not*
   Float.MIN_VALUE). The same is true if the argument is greater than
   positive infinity or Integer.MAX_VALUE; Integer.MAX_VALUE is
   returned (*not* Float.MAX_VALUE).
3. If the argument is a double and greater than or equal to
   Long.MAX_VALUE, Long.MAX_VALUE is returned (*not*
   Double.MAX_VALUE). The same is true if the argument is less than neg-
   ative infinity or Long.MIN_VALUE; Long.MIN_VALUE is returned (*not*
   Double.MIN_VALUE).

If you forget that round() adds 0.5 and returns the *floor* of the result, you
may be surprised by the returned value. In the following example, round
(12.321) returns 12, *not* 13! 12.321 + 0.5 gives 12.821, which you might
expect would round to 13, but the use of floor(12.821) causes 12 to be
returned.

```
public class TestRound {
    public static void main(String[] args){
        float nan = Float.NaN;
        float pos = Float.POSITIVE_INFINITY;
        double neg = Double.NEGATIVE_INFINITY;
        System.out.println("Math.round( 12.321 ) \t" +
                            Math.round( 12.321 ) );
        System.out.println("Math.round( -12.321 ) \t" +
                            Math.round( -12.321 ) );
        System.out.println("Math.round( 10 ) \t" +
                            Math.round( 10 ) );
        System.out.println("Math.round( nan ) \t" +
                            Math.round( nan ) );
        System.out.println("Math.round( pos ) \t" +
                            Math.round( pos ) );
        System.out.println("Math.round( neg ) \t" +
                            Math.round( neg ) );
    }
}
Output:
Math.round( 12.321 )        12
Math.round( -12.321 )       -12
```

```
Math.round( 10 )          10
Math.round( nan )         0
Math.round( pos )         2147483647
Math.round( neg )         -9223372036854775808
```

Exam Tip

round() is the only Math method that will not return a double or float value when given a double or float argument.

sin(), cos(), and tan()

The three main trigonometric functions, sin(), cos(), and tan(), all return a double value in *radians*, not degrees. You can use the method toDegrees() to convert the result. There are two special cases:

1. If the result is not a number or an infinity, NaN is returned.
2. The methods differentiate between positive and negative zero. For example, if the result is –0.0, then –0.0 is returned.

```
public class TestTrig {
    public static void main(String[] args){
        double angle = Math.PI / 3 ;
        System.out.println("Math.sin(angle) \t" + Math.sin(angle) );
        System.out.println("Math.cos(angle) \t" + Math.cos(angle) );
        System.out.println("Math.tan(angle) \t" + Math.tan(angle) );
    }
}
Output:
Math.sin(angle)       0.8660254037844386
Math.cos(angle)       0.5000000000000001
Math.tan(angle)       1.7320508075688767
```

sqrt()

The sqrt() method returns the mathematically correct square root of the argument as a double value. It has four special cases:

1. If the argument is not a number or is a negative number, NaN is returned.
2. If the argument is positive infinity, the argument is returned.
3. If the argument is negative infinity, NaN is returned.
4. If the argument is 0.0 or –0.0, the argument is returned.

```java
public class TestSqrt {
    public static void main(String[] args) {
        float nan = Float.NaN;
        double pos = Double.POSITIVE_INFINITY;
        double neg = Double.NEGATIVE_INFINITY;
        System.out.println("Math.sqrt( 9 ) \t\t" + Math.sqrt(9) );
        System.out.println("Math.sqrt(nan) \t" + Math.sqrt(nan));
        System.out.println("Math.sqrt(pos) \t" + Math.sqrt(pos));
        System.out.println("Math.sqrt(neg) \t" + Math.sqrt(neg) );
        System.out.println("Math.sqrt(-0.0) \t" + Math.sqrt(-0.0));
    }
}
Output:
Math.sqrt( 9 )         3.0
Math.sqrt( nan )       NaN
Math.sqrt( pos )       Infinity
Math.sqrt( neg )       NaN
Math.sqrt( -0.0 )      -0.0
```

Exam Tip

The exam tends to test for knowledge of how NaN, positive and negative infinity, and 0.0/-0.0 values are handled by the various Math methods.

The Math class also includes the trigonometric functions acos(), asin(), atan(), and atan2() and the methods toRadians(), exp(), IEEERemainder(), log(), pow(), and rint(). These are not specifically included in the objectives; check the JDK API for details.

The `System` Class

The `System` class provides a number of useful properties and methods that can be used to examine or interact with the underlying system. It is defined as `final` and cannot be extended. All fields and methods are `static`.

The `System` class contains three fields: `err`, `in`, and `out`, which are initialized when the JVM starts and provide an interface to the standard system error, input and output. These standard streams are normally opened by and available from the host operating system. The `in` stream typically corresponds to keyboard input, and `out` corresponds to the standard display console. The `err` stream can correspond to the standard display console or not, depending on the host system. Often, system errors are redirected to log files. The `err` and `out` fields are of type `PrintStream`, and `in` is an `InputStream`. (See Chapter 11 for more information on stream classes.) The statement `System.out.println()` invokes the `println` method of the `PrintStream out` object to display output on the standard console.

The other two commonly mentioned methods are `System.exit()`, which forces an application to exit to the system, and `System.gc()`, which asks the garbage collector to reclaim memory (see Chapter 4).

The `Object` Class

The `Object` class is the *root* class for all objects in Java. Every array and API class, as well as every user-defined class, implicitly inherits the behaviors of `java.lang.Object`. These behaviors are summarized in Table 5.2.

`equals()` and `hashCode()`

The `Object.equals()` method compares objects based on the equality of some *value*. The default behavior is based on the value of the objects' reference. The method is defined as:

```
public boolean equals(Object obj) {
    return (this == obj);
}
```

The method returns the result of `this == obj` which returns `true` if both object references refer to *the same object in memory*. For example, if `objA == objB` is true, then `objA.equals(objB)` is true.

TABLE 5.2	Summary of **Object** Methods

Method	Description
public boolean equals(Object obj)	Compares two objects for value equality.
public int hashCode()	Returns an object's hashcode.
public String toString()	Returns the string representation of an object.
public final Class getClass()	Returns the runtime Class object for the object's type.
public final void notify()	Wakes up a thread waiting on the object.
public final void notifyAll()	Wakes up all threads waiting on the object.
public final void wait() throws InterruptedException	Causes a thread to wait for a notify on the object.
protected Object clone() throws CloneNotSupportedException	Copies every field in the object to a new object of the same type. If a field is a reference variable, the reference, *not* the object referenced, is copied.
protected void finalize() throws Throwable	Called by the garbage collector before the objects memory is reclaimed.

The general contract for the Object.hashCode() method requires that any two objects that are equal according to equals(Object) must return the same integer value for hashCode(). The Object.hashCode() method uses an algorithm that converts the objects' address in memory to an int. The following example code demonstrates this behavior:

```
public class TestEquals {
    public static void main(String[] args) {
        Object objA = new Object();
        Object objB = objA;

        System.out.println("objA.hashCode(): " + objA.hashCode() );
        System.out.println("objB.hashCode(): " + objB.hashCode() );

        System.out.println("objA.equals(objB): " + objA.equals(objB) );
        System.out.println("objA == objB: " + ( objA == objB ) );
    }
}
Output:
    objA.hashCode()    -> 306121
    objB.hashCode()    -> 306121
    objA.equals(objB) -> true
    objA == objB       -> true
```

The preceding demonstrates the *default* behavior of the two methods. Any class can choose to override the equals() and hashcode() methods in Object to provide their own definition of equality.

Travel Advisory

If equals() is overridden, hashCode() should always be over-ridden and vice versa. Regardless of the definition of equality, objects that are equal should always return the same hashcode.

The developers of the Java API chose to override Object.equals() in all the wrapper classes: Boolean, Character, Byte, Short, Long, Double, and Float. In each instance, hashCode() was also overridden. The following example demonstrates the behavior of the overridden equals() and hashCode() methods in wrapper classes:

```
public class TestWrapperEquals {
public static void main(String[] args){
  Character charA = new Character('A');
```

```
    Character charB = new Character('A');
    System.out.print("charA.equals(charB): " +
                        charA.equals(charB) );
    System.out.println("\tcharA == charB: " +
                        ( charA == charB));
    Integer intA = new Integer( 100 );
    Integer intB = new Integer( 100 );
    System.out.print("intA.equals(intB): " +
                        intA.equals(intB));
    System.out.println("\tintA == intB: " +
                        ( intA == intB ));
    System.out.print("\ncharA hashcode: " +
                        charA.hashCode() );
    System.out.println("\t\tcharB hashcode: " +
                        charB.hashCode());
    System.out.print("intA hashcode: " +
                        intA.hashCode() );
    System.out.println("\t\tintB hashcode: " +
                        intB.hashCode() );
  }
}
Output:
charA.equals(charB) : true charA == charB : false
intA.equals(intB) : true intA == intB : false
charA hashcode: 65 charB hashcode: 65
intA hashcode: 100 intB hashcode: 100
```

Equality is no longer based on the value of the objects referenced; it is based on the value of the class and the data contained within the object. Two Integer objects are equal if they both are of the same class (Integer) and contain the same numeric value. Two Character objects are equal if they are both of the same class (Character) and contain the same Unicode character. In both cases, equal objects return the same hashcode value. The same holds true for the other wrapper classes; objects are equal if they are of the same class and contain the same data.

The Java API developers also overrode the equals method in the String class *but not in the* StringBuffer *class*:

```
public class TestStringEquals {

    public static void main(String[] args){
        String strA = new String("Java");
        String strB = new String("Java");
        System.out.print("strA.equals(strB): " + strA.equals(strB) );
        System.out.println("\tstrA == strB: " + ( strA == strB ) );

        StringBuffer sbA = new StringBuffer("Java");
        StringBuffer sbB = new StringBuffer("Java");
        System.out.print("sbA.equals(sbB): " + sbA.equals(sbB) );
        System.out.println("\tsbA == sbB: " + ( sbA == sbB ) );

        System.out.print("\nstrA hashcode:" + strA.hashCode() );
        System.out.println("\t\tstrB hashcode:" + strB.hashCode() );
        System.out.print("sbA hashcode:   " + sbA.hashCode() );
        System.out.println("\t\tsbB hashcode:   " + sbB.hashCode() );
    }
}
Output:
strA.equals(strB)    : true     strA == strB    : false
sbA.equals(sbB)      : false    sbA == sbB      : false

strA hashcode:   2301506        strB hashcode:   2301506
sbA hashcode:    306121         sbB hashcode:    2765838
```

Exam Tip

It is important to remember that String.equals() overrides
Object.equals() to return true if the string objects contain the same
characters. StringBuffer.equals() is *not* overridden and will
only return true if both objects reference the same object in memory:
the behavior defined in Object.equals().

Travel Assistance

See the Java API documentation for a full description of the general contracts of both methods. For a more complete discussion of the equals() and hashCode() methods see *Effective Java: Programming Language Guide* by Joshua Bloch.

toString()

The toString() method returns a textual description of an object. The default implementation in java.lang.Object returns the object's class, an at symbol (@) and the object's hashcode as one string. Whenever you invoke System.out. println to display a nontext object, toString() is called behind the scenes:

```
public class TestToString {
    public static void main(String[] args){
        System.out.println( new Object() );
    }
}
Output:
    java.lang.Object@4abc9
```

The toString method can be overridden to provide a more informative text, and the API recommends that every class should override toString():

```
public class OverrideToString {
    public String toString(){
        return "The result of overriding Object.toString()";
    }
    public static void main(String[] args){
        System.out.println( new OverrideToString() );
    }
}
Output:
    The result of overriding Object.toString()
```

getClass()

Class objects are created automatically by the JVM at runtime. One exists for each class being used in the application. getClass() returns the runtime class of an object as a Class object, not the name of the class. You can, however, use the Class.getName() method to return the class name. Note that this will also work on arrays.

```
public class TestGetClass {
    public static void main(String[] args){
        Object obj = new Object();
        int[] arr = { 1, 2, 3 };
        double[] d = { 10.0, 5.5 };

        System.out.println("The class of obj is " +
                               obj.getClass().getName() );

        System.out.println("The class of arr is " +
                               arr.getClass().getName() );
        System.out.println("The class of arr is " +
                               d.getClass().getName() );
    }
}
Output:
The class of obj is java.lang.Object
The class of arr is [I
The class of arr is [[D
```

In the preceding, [I and [[D represent the internal class names for an int array and a multidimensional double array.

notify(), notifyAll(), and wait()

These three methods are discussed in detail in Chapter 8. Keep in mind that as the methods are all defined in the Object class, every object can have a monitor (lock) and can thus be accessed in a thread-safe manner.

clone()

The Object class provides a full implementation of the clone method that may be utilized by any class implementing the Cloneable interface. The Object. clone() method creates a *shallow* copy of an object. It will create a new object of the same class and copy the existing object's field values to the new object. It *will not* create new objects for objects referenced by the fields. In other words, if a field is a reference variable, the value of the reference variable is copied and *both* the original object and the new clone will point to the same object. The following code demonstrates the default behavior:

```
public class TestClone {
    public static void main(String[] args) {
        Copy c = new Copy();
        Copy c1;
        try {
            c1 = (Copy)c.clone();
            System.out.println( "sb in c: " + c.sb );
            // change the string in the clone.
            c1.sb.append(" plus clone");
        }catch(CloneNotSupportedException e){}
        System.out.println( "sb in c after clone operation: " + c.sb
);
    }
}


class Copy implements Cloneable {
    StringBuffer sb = new StringBuffer("Original field");
        public Object clone() throws CloneNotSupportedException {
        return super.clone();
    }
}
Output:
  sb in c: Original field
  sb in c after clone operation: Original field plus clone
```

In the preceding example, the `Copy.clone()` method creates a new object of class Copy and copies the value of the reference field `sb` to the `sb` field in the new object. That value is the memory address of the `StringBuffer` object, so both the cloned object and the original point to the same `StringBuffer` object. Any change made in the cloned object affects the original `StringBuffer` object. To create a *deep* copy using `clone()`, you must override it and include statements that will create new copies of any referenced objects. A class that does not support cloning will throw a `CloneNotSupportedException`.

Exam Tip
You may only clone an object if the class implements the `Cloneable` interface. The `Cloneable` interface is a marker interface and defines no methods.

`finalize()`

The default implementation of the `finalize()` method does nothing. It can be overridden to allow objects to release system resources or perform other clean up chores. For more information on `finalize()`, see Chapter 4.

Objective 5.02
Describe the Significance of the Immutability of `String` Objects

The objectives state that you should be able to *"describe the significance of the immutability of String objects."* Implicit in this statement is the need to understand the following:

- That a `String` object, once created, can never be modified
- What happens when you invoke a `String` method that *appears* to modify a String object

Strings

Chapter 1 describes String literals and their creation in the string constant pool. This is Java's means of optimizing strings to conserve memory. If it is to work correctly, the language must ensure that the contents of a String object cannot be altered. The language ensures this in the following ways:

- By defining the String class as final, making it nonextensible—that is, there is no way you can subclass String and override its behavior.
- By utilizing the StringBuffer class behind the scenes to make it *appear* as if strings are being modified.

The StringBuffer class is the key that unlocks the mystery of immutable strings! It is the magic behind the String concatenation operators (+ , +=).

When we write a statement such as

```
String str = "Hello" + "Java" ;
```

the compiler replaces our code with the equivalent of

```
String str = new StringBuffer().append("Hello").append("Java").
toString();
```

In the preceding example, the StringBuffer constructor creates a memory buffer that initially holds 16 characters (the buffer expands automatically as needed). The first append places the characters H, e, l, l, and o into the buffer. The second append adds in the characters for "Java." The toString() method in StringBuffer overrides Object.toString() to create a *new* String whose contents equal the characters in the buffer. The following illustrates this point.

```
public class TestString {
    public static void main(String[] args){
        String strA = "Hello ";
        String strB = strA.trim();
        System.out.println( "strA default hashcode: " +
            System.identityHashCode( strA ) );

        System.out.println( "strB default hashcode: " +
            System.identityHashCode( strB ) );
```

```
        System.out.println( "strA == strB          " +
            ( strA == strB ) );
        System.out.println( "strA.equals(strB)       " +
            strA.equals(strB) );
    }
}
Output:
strA default hashcode: 306121
strB default hashcode: 2765838
strA == strB           false
strA.equals(strB)      false
```

The `System.identityHashCode()` method invoked in the preceding example returns the same hashcode an object would have been given by the default `Object.hashCode()` method, regardless of whether or not the actual class of the object overrides the behavior. An earlier section discussing `hashCode()` stated that the default hashcode of any object was its memory address expressed as an `int`. From the preceding output we can see that the original `strA` object was not modified; instead, an entirely new `String` object, having a different location in memory, was created. The comparison operator (`==`) returns `false` as the two reference variables do not point to the same object, and the `equals()` method returns `false` as `strA` contains the original characters -> "Hello" and `strB` contains the characters resulting from the `trim()` operation: -> "Hello".

String Methods

There is one side effect that can occur, and it often confuses those new to the Java language. If a new `String` is always created behind the scenes, why does the following example return `true` instead of `false`?

```
public class TestNoTrim {
    public static void main(String[] args){
        String strA = "Hello";
        String strB = strA.trim();
        System.out.println( strA.equals( strB) );
    }
}
Output:
true
```

If the methods do not actually require an alteration of the string, the original `String` object is returned! In the previous example, `strA` has no empty spaces that need to be trimmed, so a reference to the original `strA` object is returned and no new `String` object is created. We can assure ourselves of this by checking the object's hashcode values and the results of the comparison operator:

```
System.out.println( "strA hashcode: " +
    System.identityHashCode( strA ) );
System.out.println( "strB hashcode: " +
    System.identityHashCode( strB ) );
System.out.println( "strA == strB   " + ( strA == strB ) );


Output:
strA hashcode: 306121
strB hashcode: 306121
strA == strB   true
```

As the preceding output shows, no new `String` object was created. The `trim()` method was redundant. The object referenced by `strA` had no leading or trailing spaces, the JVM saw no need to create an entirely new object when the existing one sufficed. The same is true for other `String` methods which manipulate strings.

```
public class TestStringMethods {
    public static void main(String[] args){
        String strA = "HELLO";
        String strB = "world";
        String strC = "Goodbye";

        String strA1 = strA.toUpperCase();
        String strB1 = strB.toLowerCase();
        String strC1 = strC.concat("");

        System.out.println("strA == strA1   " + ( strA == strA1 ) );
        System.out.println("strB == strB1   " + ( strB == strB1 ) );
        System.out.println("strC == strC1   " + ( strC == strC1 ) );
    }
}
```

```
Output:
strA == strA1  true
strB == strB1  true
strC == strC1  true
```

In the preceding, none of the method operations resulted in the creation of a new `String`. In each case, the original string was in the form requested by the method, so the original string reference was returned; the net result is that memory is conserved.

Exam Tip

The `delete()`, `deleterCharAt()`, `insert()`, and `reverse()` methods are part of the StringBuffer class, *not* the `String` class.

There are a few other `String` methods not directly related to the immutable nature of strings that may appear in exam questions.

equalsIgnoreCase()

The `equalsIgnoreCase()` method will return equal if two strings are the same length and have the same sequence of characters, regardless of their case. The characters are compared using their Unicode values.

```
public class TestEqualsIgnoreCase {
    public static void main(String[] args){
        String strA = "tomorrow";
        String strB = "Tomorrow";
        boolean eq = strA.equals( strB );
        boolean eic = strA.equalsIgnoreCase( strB );
        System.out.println("strA.equals(strB):          " + eq );
        System.out.println("strA.equalsIgnoreCase(strB): " + eic );
    }
}
Output:
strA.equals(strB):          false
strA.equalsIgnoreCase(strB): true
```

In the preceding example, strA.equals(strB) returns false as the lower-case letter *t* has a different Unicode value than an uppercase letter *T*. The equalsIgnoreCase() method does not make this distinction. It converts both the strings to the same case and then does the comparison.

substring()

The substring() method returns a section of the string as a new string. It has two constructors, one takes a starting index: public String substring(int offset). The second takes both a beginning and ending index: public String substring(int offset, int endIndex). The indices are zero-based and the number of characters returned is equivalent to the endIndex value minus the offset:

string	i	n	a	n	u	t	s	h	e	l	l
indices	0	1	2	3	4	5	6	7	8	9	10

To return the letter *a* in the string represented in the illustration, use a start index of 2 and an end index of 3. The JVM interprets this to mean "Start at the second indice and extract one character (3–2 = 1)." To extract the word *nut*, use a start index of 3 and an end index of 6, which the JVM interprets as "'Start at the third index and extract '3' characters (6–3 = 3)." The following example code illustrates the behavior:

```
public class TestSubString{
    public static void main(String[] args){
        String str = "inanutshell";
        System.out.println( str.substring( 0,2 ) );
        System.out.println( str.substring( 2, 3 ) );
        System.out.println( str.substring( 3, 6 ) );
        System.out.println( str.substring( 6 ) );
    }
}
Output:
  in
  a
  nut
  shell
```

indexOf and lastIndexOf()

The `indexOf()` method returns the index of the first matching character or substring in a string. `lastIndexOf()` returns the index of the last matching character or substring in a string. Both methods are overloaded to take a single character, a string, a single character and a starting index, or a single string and a starting index.

The `lastIndexOf()` method searches *backward* from the end of the string if no start position is supplied. If a starting position is given, it will search backward *starting from the stated position.*

```java
public class TestIndexOf{
    public static void main(String[] args){
        String str = "inanutshelloutofanutshell";

        System.out.println("indexOf 'a' and 'nut'");
        System.out.println("'a'   -> " + str.indexOf('a') );
        System.out.println("'nut' -> " + str.indexOf("nut") );

        System.out.println("indexOf 'a' and 'nut' starting at index
6");
        System.out.println("'a'   -> " + str.indexOf('a', 6) );
        System.out.println("'nut' -> " + str.indexOf("nut", 6) );

        System.out.println("\nlastIndexOf 'a' and 'nut'");
        System.out.println("'a'   -> " + str.lastIndexOf('a') );
        System.out.println("'nut' -> " + str.lastIndexOf("nut") );

        System.out.println(
                "\nlastIndexOf 'a' and 'nut' starting at index 6");
        System.out.println("'a'   -> " + str.lastIndexOf('a', 6) );
        System.out.println("'nut' -> " + str.lastIndexOf("nut", 6) );
    }
```

```
indexOf 'a' and 'nut'
'a'    -> 2
'nut' -> 3


indexOf 'a' and 'nut' starting at index 6
'a'    -> 16
'nut' -> 17


lastIndexOf 'a' and 'nut'
'a'    -> 16
'nut' -> 17


lastIndexOf 'a' and 'nut' starting at index 6
'a'    -> 2
'nut' -> 3
```

In the preceding example, the JVM evaluates str.lastIndexOf('a', 6) by extracting the first six characters *inanut* and then locating 'a' at indice 2.

charAt()

The charAt() method returns the character positioned at the stated indice.

```
public class TestCharAt {
    public static void main(String[] args){
        String str = "inanutshell";
        System.out.println("str.charAt(2) -> " + str.charAt(2) );
    }
}
Output:
str.charAt(2) -> a
```

length()

The length() method returns the number of characters in a string, which is always one more than the last indice value.

```
public class TestLength{
    public static void main(String[] args){
        String str = "inanutshell";
        System.out.println("str.length() -> " + str.length() );
    }
}
Output:
str.length() -> 11
```

The object `str` holds 11 characters, but its last indice value is 10 as string indexes are zero-based.

Exam Tip

Watch out for questions using `String.length` instead of `String. length()`. Don't confuse the method with a property such as the one available to arrays.

The `String` class has 11 constructors, 2 of which are deprecated. A `String` object may be created using a string literal, a character, an array of characters, or an array of bytes. It also contains a *copy constructor* which will take a `String` argument and return an exact copy.

Travel Assistance

For more information on all the Java class packages, see *The Java Class Libraries, Second Edition, Volume 1* by Patrick Chan, Rosanna Lee, and Douglas Kramer, Addison-Wesley, 1998.

CHECKPOINT

✔ **Objective 5.01** Write code using methods in the `java.lang.Math` class

- The `java.lang` package is guaranteed to be included in every JRE.
- One wrapper class, Boolean, Byte, Character, Short, Integer, Float, Double, or Long, exists for each primitive data type: `boolean`, `byte`,

char, short, int, float, double, or long and can be used to create an object whose characteristics mimic the primitive type. All the primitive type wrapper classes are declared final and implement the Comparable and Serializable interfaces except Boolean, which only implements Serializable. All wrapper classes, like strings, are immutable. All the primitive wrapper classes contain the static final fields TYPE, MIN_VALUE, and MAX_VALUE, except Boolean, which contains the TYPE, TRUE, and FALSE fields. The floating-point wrapper classes, Float and Double, contain three additional public static final fields: NaN, NEGATIVE_INFINITY, and POSITIVE_INFINITY.

- The Object class is the root class of all Java defined types and arrays and is implicitly extended by all user-defined types. As a result, every class in Java inherits the nine methods defined in the object class: equals(), hashCode(), toString(), getClass(), notify(), notifyAll(), wait(), clone(), and finalize().
- The Object.equals() method's default behavior returns true if the compared object references point to the same object. Object.equals() is overridden by the String class and all the wrapper classes but *not* the StringBuffer class.
- The Object.hashCode() method's default behavior returns the memory address of the object converted to an int. The hashCode() method should be overridden whenever equals() is overridden to ensure two objects that are equal will always return the same hashcode.
- The Object.toString() method's default behavior returns a description of the object based on its class name, the at symbol (@), and its address in memory. The method is overridden by the String class and all the wrapper classes to return a string representation of their data. The StringBuffer class overrides toString() to return a new String object whose characters match the characters in its buffer.
- The definition of the notify(), notifyAll(), and wait() methods in the Object class ensures that every object in Java has a *lock* and may be used in a thread-safe manner.
- Any class overriding the clone() method must implement the marker interface Cloneable. The Cloneable interface does not define any methods.
- The Math class is a final public class containing static methods that handle standard logarithmic, square root, and trigonometric functions. It cannot be instantiated.
- The Math.abs() method returns its argument as a positive double value unless the argument is equivalent to Integer.MIN_VALUE or

Long.MIN_VALUE, in which case it returns a negative value equal to the appropriate MIN_VALUE.

- The Math.ceil() method returns a double value that is the smallest whole number *greater than or equal* to its argument. If the argument is an int, NaN, 0, -0, or positive or negative infinity, the argument is returned.

- The Math.floor() method returns a double value that is the smallest whole number *less than or equal* its argument. If the argument is an integer, NaN, negative or positive zero, or negative or positive infinity, the argument is returned.

- The Math.min() and Math.max() methods return a value that is the smaller or larger of two arguments. The value returned has the same type as the widest argument type. If both arguments have the same value, the argument is returned. If one of the arguments is NaN, NaN is returned.

- The Math.random() method returns a pseudo-random number between 0.0 and 1.0 exclusively. It takes no arguments and always returns a positive double value.

- The Math.round() method takes a float or double as an argument and returns an int or long value, which is equivalent to Math.floor(arg + 0.5). If the argument is a NaN, zero is returned.

- The sin(), cos(), and tan() methods of the Math class all return a double value in radians. The Math.toDegrees() method may be used to convert the radians to degrees. If the result is a NaN or an infinity, NaN is returned. If the result is -0.0, -0.0 is returned.

- The Math.sqrt() method returns the mathematically correct square root of a number. If the result is a NaN, negative infinity, or a negative number, NaN is returned. If the argument is 0, -0, or positive infinity, the argument is returned.

✔ Objective 5.02 Describe the significance of the immutability of String objects

- All objects of the String class are *immutable*; they may not be modified. Java utilizes the StringBuffer class to implement the string concatenation operators + and +=.

- String methods that appear to modify strings (concat(), toLowerCase(), toUpperCase(), replace(), and trim()) return a *new* String object unless the original String fulfills the requirements of the methods contract, in which case the original String is returned by the method. In any event, the original String object remains unchanged.

- The String.substring() method returns a section of a string. If a starting index is given, all characters from the index to the end of the string are returned. If both a start and end index are supplied, the method returns the number of characters equal to the end index minus the start index, beginning the extraction at the start index.
- The String.indexOf() method returns the position of the first matching character or substring in a string. The String.lastIndexOf() method returns the index of the last matching character or substring in a string. If a start index is supplied, indexOf() counts positions *forward* from the start index; lastIndexOf() counts positions *backward* from the start index.
- The String.charAt() method returns the character located at the supplied index.
- The String.length() method returns the number of characters in a string. Do not confuse it with the length property supplied by arrays.

REVIEW QUESTIONS

1. Which class is implicitly extended by all classes in Java?

   A. Class
   B. Object
   C. ClassLoader
   D. Runtime

2. Which of the following are wrapper classes? (Select two.)

   A. Integer
   B. String
   C. Double
   D. character

3. What would be the output of the following code?

```
public class Q36605_4 {
    public static void main(String[] args){
        String strA = new String("hello");
        String strB = "Hello";
        System.out.println( strA.equals(strB) );
    }
}
```

A. False

B. True

4. What would be the output of the following code?

```
public class Q36605_5 {
    public static void main(String[] args){
        String strA = "Hello";
        String strB = strA.concat(" world!");
        System.out.println( strA.equals("Hello world!") );
    }
}
```

A. True

B. False

5. What would be the output of the following code?

```
public class Q36605_6 {

    public static void main(String[] args){
        StringBuffer sbA = new StringBuffer("Inagodadavida");
        StringBuffer sbB = new StringBuffer("Inagodadavida");
        System.out.println( sbA.equals( sbB ) );
    }
}
```

A. True

B. False

6. What would `abs(-0)` return?

A. The value -0

B. NaN

C. The value 0

D. NEGATIVE_INFINITY

7. Which `Math` method would return -10.0 if given the argument -9.75?

A. floor()

B. ceil()

C. abs()

D. None of the above

8. Which Math method would return -0.0 given the argument -0?

    A. `floor()`
    B. `ceil()`
    C. Both A and B
    D. Neither A nor B

9. What will be returned by the `Math.round()` method if the argument it is passed is not a number?

    A. `NaN`
    B. 0
    C. 0.0
    D. Infinity

10. Given the statement `String str = "jawbreaker"`; which of the following `substring()` versions will return the word "break"?

    A. str.substring(3, 5)
    B. str.substring(4, 6)
    C. str.substring(3, 8)
    D. str.substring(4, 8)

REVIEW ANSWERS

1. **B** Object is the root class of all Java types and arrays and is implicitly extended by all user defined types.

2. **A** **C** Integer and Double are both wrapper classes; String is not. Character, not character, is.

3. **A** The "h" in "hello" is capitalized in the strB object. equalsIgnore Case() would return true.

4. **B** strB is assigned "Hello world!", strA is unchanged and contains the original characters "Hello", so strA.equals("Hello world!") would return false.

5. **B** StringBuffer.equals() does not override the Object.equals() method to compare the values it contains. It will only return true if both string references point to the same object.

6. **C** The Math.abs() method returns a positive value unless the argument is equal to Integer.MIN_VALUE or Long.MIN_VALUE, in which case it returns a negative value equal to the appropriate MIN_VALUE.

7. **A** The `Math.floor()` method rounds to the closest whole number equal to or smaller than the argument. For negative numbers, it moves away from zero.

8. **D** When Math methods are passed 0 or -0 as an argument, they are treated as an `int`. Nonfloating-point primitive types do not distinguish between negative and positive zero.

9. **B** `Math.round()` returns an `int` or `long` value. `NaN`, infinities, or 0.0 would only be returned by methods returning a floating-point type.

10. **C** The index values (4,5) would return 'br', (4,6), 're' and (4,8) 'reak'.

PART

II

Java in Practice

Operators and Assignments

CHAPTER 6

	NEWBIE	SOME EXPERIENCE	EXPERT
ETA	10 hours	5 hours	3 hours

Here's the part you've been waiting for! The ever-necessary and ever-boring operators and expressions. Look, before you dive in, there's one thing you need to know: most of this stuff is pretty much the same as most other popular languages. That's good, in that you'll find most of these obvious. That's bad, in that you may be tempted to take them for granted and ignore this chapter, resulting in you missing some critical aspects of Java language. So, unless you want to bet on your instincts and risk missing easy questions in the test, read on!

Determine the Result of Applying Any Operator to Operands

For this objective, you'll determine the result of applying any operator, including assignment operators, instanceof, and casts, to operands of any type, class, scope, or accessibility, or any combination of these.

Like in any other programming language, arithmetic operators in Java are used in expressions that yield a numeric result. The + operator is an exception to this rule and can be used with string expressions that are covered later in this chapter.

Travel Advisory

In Java, it is illegal to use `boolean` types or values in arithmetic expressions.

Since many of these operators are common across different languages, it is easy to overlook some of the finer aspects of Java language. Let's look at some interesting expressions that can help us understand language-specific facets of these operators.

```
public class ArithmeticOperators {
    public static void main( String s[] ) {
        byte byteVar1 = 1 + 9 ;
        //byteVar1 = 128 ;
        //byteVar1 = byteVar1 + 1 ;
        System.out.println("byteVar1 = " + byteVar1 );

        int intVar1 = 3 + '4' - 0x12 ;
```

```java
        System.out.println("intVar1 = " + intVar1  );

        int intVar2 = intVar1 + byteVar1 ;
        System.out.println("intVar2  = " + intVar2 );

        int intVar3 = intVar2/10 ;
        System.out.println("intVar3  = " + intVar3 );

        int bigInt1 = Integer.MAX_VALUE ;
        int bigInt2 = bigInt1 + 1 ;
        System.out.println("bigInt2( Integer.MAXVALUE + 1) = " +
bigInt2 );

        long longVar1 = 30 ;
        long longVar2 = longVar1/4 ;
        System.out.println("longVar2 = " + longVar2 );

        double doubleVar1 = longVar1/4 ;
        System.out.println("doubleVar1 = " + doubleVar1 );

        float floatVar1 = (float)longVar1/4 ;
        System.out.println("floatVar1 = " + floatVar1 );

        double doubleVar2 = 9.9 ;
        int intVar4 = (int)doubleVar2 ;
        System.out.println("intVar4  = " +  intVar4 );

        long longVar3 = longVar1/longVar1-longVar1 ;
        System.out.println( "longVar3 = " + longVar3 );
        //long longVar4 = longVar1 / (longVar1-longVar1) ;

        int intVar5 = 11%3 ;
        System.out.println( "intVar5  = " + intVar5 );

        double doubleVar3 = -43.75%5 ;
        System.out.println( "doubleVar3 = " + doubleVar3 );
    }
}
```

This program offers an insight into Java's not-so-intuitive operator behavior. We suggest that you try running the program as is and then remove some of the commented lines and run it again. Before we jump into explaining the how's and why's of this program, let's look at the output generated:

```
byteVar1 = 10
intVar1 = 37
intVar2  = 47
intVar3  = 4
bigInt2( Integer.MAXVALUE + 1) = -2147483648
longVar2 = 7
doubleVar1 = 7.0
floatVar1 = 7.5
intVar4  = 9
longVar3 = -29
intVar5  = 2
doubleVar3 = -3.75
```

Now let's look closely at each line of the program.

```
1.    byte byteVar1 = 1 + 9 ;
2.    //byteVar1 = 128 ;
3.    //byteVar1 = byteVar1 + 1 ;
4.    System.out.println("byteVar1 = " + byteVar1 );
```

Line 1 demonstrates the use of a constant expression. According to the rules of expression evaluation, Java treats the operands 1 and 9 as integers. The result of an integer addition is also an integer. We are trying to assign an integer value to a byte variable. So why doesn't this line generate a compiler error? Well, since constants are evaluated at compile time, byteVar1 actually contains the value 10 even before the program is run. Since a byte variable can store the value 10 without any loss of magnitude, no errors are reported. The compiler does check, however, the magnitude of the value being assigned to see if it can be stored in the variable it is being assigned to. If the value exceeds the maximum range for the declared type, then an explicit down cast is required to satisfy the compiler. To validate this argument, simply uncomment line 2 and try compiling the program. The following error is generated by the compiler:

```
Incompatible type for =. Explicit cast needed to convert int to byte.
       byteVar1 = 128 ;
```

The expression in line 3 is a popular interview question! Many programmers are often caught off-guard with this seemingly sane expression. The compiler generates the following error:

```
Incompatible type for =. Explicit cast needed to convert int to byte.
    byteVar1 = byteVar1 + 1 ;
```

The reason is quite simple. Since all expressions in Java produce a result that is at least as wide as an integer, the type of the expression `byteVar1 + 1` is actually an integer. Since the assignment to a byte variable is treated as a narrowing conversion that can result in loss of value, compiler demands an explicit narrowing cast. Since this is not a constant expression, `byteVar` can indeed assume any legal value at runtime. This justifies the stronger type checking as a way of telling the compiler, "I know what I am doing!"

Travel Advisory

It's worth mentioning here that `byteVar1 += 1` does not need the cast. This is somewhat counterintuitive for those who think that `x += 1` is completely identical to `x = x + 1`.

Consider the next two lines:

```
5.    int intVar1 = 3 + '4' - 0x12 ;
6.    System.out.println("intVar1 = " + intVar1  );
```

The expression in line 5 is an example of mixing constant literals. Just as the number 3 is a constant integer literal, '4' is a constant character literal, and 0x12 is a hexadecimal literal. They all represent integer values but in different ways. During evaluation, the char '4' gets promoted to `int` and hence assumes its ASCII value of 53. Interestingly, Java considers the `char` type as an unsigned integral type and hence no explicit casting is necessary to convert a character literal to an integer literal. The hex number 0x12 evaluates to 18 in base 10. It is important to remember that the actual operation is being performed on binary numbers. Whether the constant literal is expressed in decimal, octal, or hexadecimal representation, all are treated as binary bit patterns.

Travel Advisory

Character literals are enclosed in single quotes. If you use double quotes, they become string literals.

So far so good. By now you should understand basics of compile-time type checking and operand type promotions performed by Java. Now let's go further by looking at arithmetic promotions:

```
7.    int intVar2 = intVar1 + byteVar1 ;
8.    System.out.println("intVar2  = " + intVar2 );
```

The expression in line 7 is quite simple to understand. Here, the `byteVar1` undergoes arithmetic promotion to type int.

What comes next:

```
9.      int intVar3 = intVar2/10 ;
10.  System.out.println("intVar3  = " + intVar3 );
```

Integer divisions sometime result in loss of precision—don't expect the compiler to warn you about them! In line 9, the value of `intVar2` is 47 and, when divided by 4, both the operands and hence the resulting type are treated as integers. The result undergoes truncation, causing the fractional part to be completely ignored. Note that the type of the expression `intvar2/10` is also an int since there are no other wider types.

Moving on, we have one of my favorite gotchas.

```
11.  int bigInt1 = Integer.MAX_VALUE ;
12.  int bigInt2 = bigInt1 + 1 ;
13.  System.out.println("bigInt2( Integer.MAXVALUE + 1) = " +
bigInt2 );
```

While dealing with integer division, we just saw how loss of precision can occur due to truncation without any warnings. In an almost similar way, value of expression can overflow the maximum range for a type resulting in unexpected values. In our example, the overflow results in a negative number.

Exam Tip

`MAX_VALUE` is a constant defined in `java.lang.Integer` class. Several other wrapper classes such as `Float`, `Long`, `Short`, `Double`, and so on define minimum and maximum values for respective types.

The next few lines show the effects of widening conversion due to assignment and casting:

```
14.   long longVar1 = 30 ;
15.   long longVar2 = longVar1/4 ;
16.   System.out.println("longVar2 = " + longVar2 );
17.   double doubleVar1 = longVar1/4 ;
18.   System.out.println("doubleVar1 = " + doubleVar1 );
19.   float floatVar1 = (float)longVar1/4 ;
20.   System.out.println("floatVar1 = " + floatVar1 );
21.   double doubleVar2 = 9.9 ;
22.   int intVar4 = (int)doubleVar2 ;
23. System.out.println("intVar4  = " +  intVar4 );
```

The expression `longVar/4` is an example of integer division. However, in line 17, due to the assignment, the result undergoes automatic widening to type `double`. Since `double` has a higher precision than `long`, even the decimal portion of the result - that is, zero is displayed. This example also demonstrates what happens when operands of mixed type participate in an expression: the type of the resulting value is the type of the *widest* operand in the expression. That is, `float + double` results in a `double`; `int * long` results in a `long`.

Exam Tip

If an integral literal contains a decimal point, the compiler treats it as a `double` value. Such a value cannot be assigned to a narrower type; for example, an `int`, without explicit casting. The expression `int p = 7.0` results in a compiler error.

In line 19, using the explicit cast to `float`, we tell the compiler to perform a high precision division. Naturally, the resulting value is not truncated and hence, it produces the more accurate result of 7.5. It is important to remember the difference between simply assigning an expression to a wider type and making casting of the operands to a wider type. The assignment only changes the signature (a.k.a. the bit pattern) of the value being assigned, whereas the cast affects the way the operator is applied.

Narrowing casts result in truncation, not rounding. The assignment in line 22 ascertains this point. The `double` value when assigned to a narrower `int` type loses its fractional part due to truncation.

Effects of operator precedence are visible in the following lines:

```
24.  long longVar3 = longVar1/longVar1-longVar1 ;
25.  System.out.println( "longVar3 = " + longVar3 );
26.  //long longVar4 = longVar1 / (longVar1-longVar1) ;
```

In line 24, since the / has higher precedence than –, the expression is evaluated as

```
(longVar1/longVar1) -longVar1
```

In line 26, the parenthesis overrides the default operator precedence. When you uncomment this line and run the program, it results in an Arithmetic Exception due to division by zero:

```
"java.lang.ArithmeticException: / by zero"
at ArithmeticOperators.main(ArithmeticOperators.java:40) Exception
in thread "main"
```

ArithmeticException is a runtime exception so the compiler knows nothing about it when the bytecode is generated. In fact, even using a zero as a constant integer in the denominator will not generate a compile-time error. More on exceptions is covered in Chapter 7.

Exam Tip

Other than the integer division operator / and modulo operator %, no arithmetic operators throw exceptions. Use this fact to eliminate the wrong answers.

What comes next is an example showing typical usage of the modulo operator:

```
27.  int intVar5 = 11%3 ;
28.  System.out.println( "intVar5  = " + intVar5 );
29.  double doubleVar3 = -43.75%5 ;
30.  System.out.println( "doubleVar3 = " + doubleVar3 );
```

The modulo operator produces the remainder from an integer division. Therefore, the result produced is always less than the divisor; that is, the operand on the right side of the operator.

Exam Tip

Expect to see negative operands and operands with decimal points in the exam. For any expression of the format `op1 % op2` , use the following rules to evaluate the result:

- Negative operands: Calculate the result ignoring the sign, then apply the sign of the op1 to the result. The sign of op2 is insignificant and should be ignored.
- Operands with decimal points: If only one of the operand has a decimal point, calculate the result ignoring the fractional value, then apply the fractional value to the result. If both the operands have the decimal point, you will have to do it the hard way, that is, with careful division using paper and pencil!

Unary Arithmetic Operators

The unary + and – act on their single operand; the – changes the sign. The unary increment and decrement operators ++ and - - come in two flavors, the prefix and postfix form. In the prefix form, the operand is incremented or decremented before the value is obtained for use in the expression. In the postfix form, the existing value is obtained for use in the expression and then the operand is modified.

The result of the prefix or postfix expression must be a variable of a numeric type, or a compile-time error occurs. The evaluation of postfix and prefix expressions may involve binary numeric promotion of the operands. If necessary, the result of the expression is narrowed by a narrowing primitive conversion to the type of the variable before it is stored. Consider the following lines of code:

```
byte c = 10;
byte d = c++ ;
```

The `byte` variable c undergoes numeric promotion to `int`, and the expression produces an `int` result of value `10 + 1`. The `int` value 11 then is narrowed by a narrowing primitive conversion to the `byte` type. Hence, no compiler error is generated for this line of code. However, if you replace c++ with c + 1, Java treats the expression as `int` and you will get a compiler error.

Travel Advisory

Since `final` variables cannot be modified, they cannot be used as the operand of a postfix or prefix increment or decrement operator. However, it is okay to use the unary + or – with a `final` variable since the result of the unary plus or unary minus expression returns a value without changing the operand.

The following program illustrates the difference between prefix and postfix increment operators:

```
public class PrefixPostfixDemo {
    public static void main( String s[] ) {
        int a = 2;
        int b = a++ ;
        System.out.println( "a = " + a ) ;
        System.out.println( "b = " + b ) ;

        int c = 2 ;
        int d = ++c ;
        System.out.println( "c = " + c ) ;
        System.out.println( "d = " + d ) ;
    }
}
```

This program produces the following output:

```
a = 3
b = 2
c = 3
d = 3
```

The expression b = a++ is evaluated as

```
b = a ;
a = a + 1
```

Hence, the variable b gets the original value of variable a before a is incremented.

On the other hand, the expression d = ++c is evaluated as

```
c = c + 1;
d = c
```

Therefore, d gets the new value of c after c is incremented.

The Bitwise Operators

Java supports several operators that can be applied to bit patterns of integral types. The following table lists such operators grouped by their order of precedence.

~	Bitwise unary NOT
&	Bitwise AND
|	Bitwise OR
^	Bitwise XOR(Exclusive-OR)
>>	The right shift operator.
<<	The left shift operator.
>>>	The unsigned right shift operator.

Except the ~ operator, all of these are binary operators; that is, they take two operands. The valid types for these operands are long, int, short, char and byte. Since the bitwise operators manipulate the bit pattern of a number, it is important to understand what effects such manipulations may have on the value. Before we plunge into understanding the behavior of these operators, let us spend a moment to learn few important things about the wonderful world of binary numbers—specifically, how Java stores negative numbers.

Like many other languages, Java uses two's complement format to represent negative numbers. This means, negative numbers are represented by inverting (flipping 1's to 0's and vice-versa) all of the bits in the original value and then adding 1 to the result. For example, the number 23 is represented in binary as 10111; that is, the bit pattern will look like this:

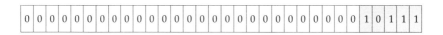

To get the bit pattern for –23, we simply flip all the bytes and then add 1 to it. Remember, when we say add, it is binary addition and not integral addition!

The first step, flipping the bits, will result in this:

Adding 1 to the previous binary number, which will yield the binary value for –23:

Because Java makes use of two's complement format to store negative numbers and because all integers are signed values in Java, applying the bitwise operators can sometime produce unexpected results. For instance, turning on the high-order bit (the leftmost bit also called Most Significant Bit [MSB]) will cause the resulting value to be interpreted as a negative number. Just remember that the MSB is the sign-bit and will always determine the sign of the resulting number. When MSB is set to 1, the number being represented is a negative number. When it is 0, the number being represented is a nonnegative number.

With that background, let's look at each of the binary operators in detail. Before we proceed, one last word about a convention that we will use in the forthcoming sections in this chapter. Since all the numbers in Java are at least as wide as an `int`, from a purist's point of view they all should be represented as 32-bit numbers. However, since trailing 0's have no effect on the value of the original number, we will use 16-bit patterns in our illustrations to reduce the visual clutter. On the other hand, whenever a negative number is involved, the full 32-bit pattern will be included to show the sign-bit to the readers. We will also shade the bits undergoing the transformations, as we did in the previous illustration, to draw the attention of the readers to specific details.

Exam Tip

While studying for the exam, use the standard Windows calculator in the Scientific mode to quickly generate the binary equivalent for any decimal number. Since Java always prints the values in decimal format, you can use the `toBinaryString()` method provided by most of the wrapper classes. This method returns the binary value of the argument as a `java.lang.String`.

The Bitwise Unary ~ Operator

The simplest of the all operators, the ~, simply inverts the bits of the operand, that is, it flips the 1's with 0's and vice-versa. If you have been reading all the sections carefully (and we hope you have), this is precisely what we did in the first step of computing the two's complement form for a number. Since all bits are switched, including the sign-bit (the MSB), this operator most certainly changes the sign of the original number.

For example, short a = 23 will be represented as

0	0	0	0	0	0	0	0	0	0	0	1	0	1	1	1

~a would change this bit pattern to

1	1	1	1	1	1	1	1	1	1	1	0	1	0	0	0

If you do the binary-to-decimal conversion of the above bit pattern, it yields the number –24. As you can see, the sign of the original number has changed. We assign you, the reader, the experiment of reverse scenario: what would have happened if the original number was –23?

> **Exam Tip**
>
> For any valid variable a, use the formula ~a = (-1)*(a) - 1. That is,
> flip the original sign of a and then subtract 1 from it. For example:
> if a = 14, ~a is (- (14) - 1) that is, -15.
> if a = -10, ~a is (-(-10) - 1) that is, (10 - 1) that is, 9

The Bitwise & (AND) Operator

The following table captures the result produced by the bitwise & operator for all possible values of the operands:

A	B	A & B
0	0	0
0	1	0
1	0	0
1	1	1

As you can see, the & operator produces a result of 1 only if both of the operands are 1. Consider the expression 7 & 2. The following diagram illustrates the evaluation of this expression

7 = :

| 0 | 0 | 0 | 0 | 0 | 0 | 0 | 0 | 0 | 0 | 0 | 0 | 0 | 1 | 1 | 1 |

2 =

| 0 | 0 | 0 | 0 | 0 | 0 | 0 | 0 | 0 | 0 | 0 | 0 | 0 | 0 | 1 | 0 |

7 & 2 =

| 0 | 0 | 0 | 0 | 0 | 0 | 0 | 0 | 0 | 0 | 0 | 0 | 0 | 0 | 1 | 0 |

If you do the math, the resulting number is 2.

The bitwise | (OR) operator

The following table captures the result produced by the bitwise | operator for all possible values of the operands:

A	B	A|B
0	0	0
0	1	1
1	0	1
1	1	1

The | operator is the opposite of the & operator: it produces a result of 1 if *any* one of the operands is 1.

Consider the expression 7 | 2. The following diagram illustrates the evaluation of this expression

7 = :

| 0 | 0 | 0 | 0 | 0 | 0 | 0 | 0 | 0 | 0 | 0 | 0 | 0 | 1 | 1 | 1 |

$2 =$

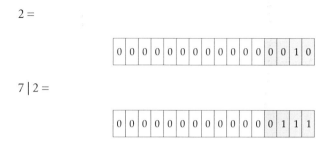

$7 \,|\, 2 =$

The resulting number is 7.

The Bitwise ^ (XOR, Exclusive Or) Operator

The following table captures the result produced by the bitwise ^ operator for all possible values of the operands:

A	B	A ^ B
0	0	0
0	1	1
1	0	1
1	1	0

Clearly the ^ operator returns 1 only if only one of the operands is 1.

Consider the expression $7 \wedge 2$. The following diagram illustrates the evaluation of this expression:

$7 =$

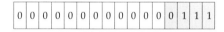

$2 =$

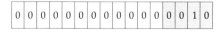

$7 \wedge 2 =$

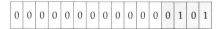

The resulting number is 5.

Travel Advisory

Be careful while evaluating expressions involving negative numbers. You will have to represent the number as an `int` for narrower types with the sign-bit set to 1 and pad with 1's all the way. Also, if one of the operands is not an `int`, widen it by padding leading 0's so that both the operands are of the same width before applying the operator.

The Binary Shift Operators >>, <<, >>>

The binary shift operators push the bit at the LSB (Least Significant Bit) position either to the left or to the right, thereby pushing all the other bits as well, padding the new bit slots thus created with a new bit. The number of bits to shift is supplied as the second argument to the operator and is often referred to as *shift magnitude* or *shift distance*. As you can imagine, this changes the bit pattern itself and hence the value represented by the bit pattern. The new bit pattern is returned as the result of the expression while the operands remain unchanged.

Typical of arithmetic expressions in Java, all the operands taking part in a bit shift expression undergo numeric promotions. This means if any operand is narrower than an `int`, it gets promoted to an `int`, or (in the case of a binary operator) the width of the second operand, whichever is the wider. Since `int` has 32 bits and `long` has 64, it would be meaningless to shift them beyond 32 and 64 positions respectively. This means number of bits to be shifted has to be less than or equal to 32 for integers and 64 for longs. For any expression involving shift positions greater than these values, the number of bits actually shifted will be equal to operand modulus 32 for integers and operand modulus for 64 for longs. That is, if l is a `long` variable:

```
l >> 67 is evaluated as l >> (67%64) i.e., l >> 3
```

Similarly, if m is an `int` variable:

```
m >> 40 is evaluated as m >> (40%32) is m >> 8
```

The binary right shift operator >> shifts the bits to the right by specified number of positions padding the new trailing bit positions with the sign bit. The sign bit is the MSB, the leftmost bit in the original bit pattern. For negative numbers, the padding bit will be 1 and for positive numbers it will be 0. This implies that the sign of the original number is retained despite the shifting; negative numbers result in negative results and positive numbers yield positive results.

Consider an example:

```
int someNumber = 21 ;
int afterShift  = someNumber >> 3 ;
```

Since 21 is a positive number, the MSB will have a value 0 which, will be used as the padding bit during shifting:

someNumber = 21

0	0	0	0	0	0	0	0	0	0	0	0	0	0	0	0	0	0	0	0	0	0	0	0	0	0	0	1	0	1	0	1

someNumber >> 3

0	0	0	0	0	0	0	0	0	0	0	0	0	0	0	0	0	0	0	0	0	0	0	0	0	0	0	0	0	0	1	0

The resulting number is 2. Note that the >> operator can actually push the last nonzero bit off the cliff and result in value 0. In the previous example, someNumber >> 4 would yield a result of 1, and someNumber >> 5 or anything above 5 results in zero.

Exam Tip

Every position n in a binary number actually represents a value of 2^n (two raised to the power n) or, for numbers that have a zero bit in the MSB, each bit shifted right is equivalent to dividing the original number by 2. In our example, someNumber >> 3 is equivalent to someNumber/ (2^3) that is, someNumber/8. Of course, we are talking about integer division here so we ignore the fractional remainders. You can use this formula to quickly arrive at a result without doing the actual shifting using paper and pencil.

When negative numbers participate in the shifting, 1's are used for padding the trailing bits instead of 0's.

Consider an example:

```
int someNumber = - 21 ;
int afterShift  = someNumber >> 3 ;
```

Since −21 is a negative number, the MSB will have a value 1, which will be used as the padding bit during shifting:

```
someNumber  = -21
```

| 1 | 1 | 1 | 1 | 1 | 1 | 1 | 1 | 1 | 1 | 1 | 1 | 1 | 1 | 1 | 1 | 1 | 1 | 1 | 1 | 1 | 1 | 1 | 1 | 1 | 1 | 1 | 0 | 1 | 0 | 1 | 1 |

```
someNumber >> 3
```

| 1 | 1 | 1 | 1 | 1 | 1 | 1 | 1 | 1 | 1 | 1 | 1 | 1 | 1 | 1 | 1 | 1 | 1 | 1 | 1 | 1 | 1 | 1 | 1 | 1 | 1 | 1 | 1 | 1 | 0 | 1 |

The bit pattern represents the number −3.

The binary unsigned right shift operator >>> offers a slight variation of the plain >> operator. When the bits are shifted, the >>> operator always uses 0's to fill the trailing bits irrespective of the sign bit. For positive numbers, the result of >> and >>> are the same. However for negative numbers, >>> results in the change of sign.

Consider an example:

```
int someNumber = -21 ;
int afterShift  = someNumber >>> 3 ;
```

Although -21 is a negative number, a zero bit will be used as the padding bit during shifting instead of the MSB:

```
someNumber  =  -21
```

| 1 | 1 | 1 | 1 | 1 | 1 | 1 | 1 | 1 | 1 | 1 | 1 | 1 | 1 | 1 | 1 | 1 | 1 | 1 | 1 | 1 | 1 | 1 | 1 | 1 | 1 | 1 | 0 | 1 | 0 | 1 | 1 |

```
someNumber >>> 3
```

| 0 | 0 | 0 | 1 | 1 | 1 | 1 | 1 | 1 | 1 | 1 | 1 | 1 | 1 | 1 | 1 | 1 | 1 | 1 | 1 | 1 | 1 | 1 | 1 | 1 | 1 | 1 | 1 | 1 | 1 | 0 | 1 |

As strange as it may look, the result is a very large number: 536870909

The last of the trio, the binary shift left operator <<, does the exact opposite of right shifting. When the bit at the LSB (the rightmost bit) is shifted *inwards*, leading bits are padded with 0's.

Consider an example:

```
int someNumber = 21 ;
int afterShift  = someNumber << 3 ;
```

someNumber = 21

| 0 | 0 | 0 | 0 | 0 | 0 | 0 | 0 | 0 | 0 | 0 | 0 | 0 | 0 | 0 | 0 | 0 | 0 | 0 | 0 | 0 | 0 | 0 | 0 | 0 | 0 | 0 | 1 | 0 | 1 | 0 | 1 |

someNumber << 3

| 0 | 0 | 0 | 0 | 0 | 0 | 0 | 0 | 0 | 0 | 0 | 0 | 0 | 0 | 0 | 0 | 0 | 0 | 0 | 0 | 0 | 0 | 0 | 0 | 1 | 0 | 1 | 0 | 1 | 0 | 0 | 0 |

The resulting number is 168.

Exam Tip

Since bits are shifted left, each shift is equivalent to multiplying the number by 2. Hence `someNumber << 3` is the same as `someNumber * 2^3` that is, `someNumber * 8`. Use this formula in the test to compute results of complex-looking bit shift expressions.

The Operators &, |, && , ||, and Variables of Known Values

Objective 6.02

For this objective, state which operands are evaluated and the value of an expression involving the operators &, |, &&, ||, and variables of known values.

The Boolean Logical Operators

Java provides various `boolean` operators that can be applied to `boolean` operands. It is interesting to note that three of these operators—| (`boolean` OR), & (`boolean` AND), and ^ (`boolean` XOR)—behave in a context-sensitive fashion. This means that when both the operands are `boolean`, they produce a `boolean` result that can be either true or false. On the other hand, if both of the operands are `non-boolean`, they behave as bitwise operators producing numeric results. This is a classic example of operator overloading built into the Java language!

Boolean operators can only be used with `boolean` operands. Java provides the `boolean` literals `true` and `false` and, unlike other languages, numbers are never interpreted as `boolean` values.

If a and b are `boolean` variables, then (`a & b`) is a valid `boolean` expression, whereas (`a & 20`) generates a compiler error since 20 is an integer and not a `boolean` type. Boolean and non-boolean types have their own identity and are non-interchangeable.

The following table summarizes the results produced by these three logical operators:

A	B	A & B	A | B	A ∧ B
true	true	true	true	false
true	false	false	true	true
false	true	false	true	true
false	false	false	false	false

The logical complement operator ! is the boolean negation operator that reverses the truth-value of a `boolean` constant or an expression. Hence, `!true` is `false` and `!false` is `true`.

The Boolean Logical Short-Circuit Operators

Java provides two interesting `boolean` operators not found in many other computer languages. These are optimized versions of `boolean` OR (|) and AND (&) operators and are known as *short-circuit* logical operators. If you observe carefully, the previous tables show that the | operator returns `true` when A is `true`, no matter what the value of B is. Similarly, the & operator returns `false` when A is `false`, irrespective of the value of B. If you use the short-circuit operators && and ||, Java will not bother to evaluate the right-hand operand when the outcome of the expression can be determined by the left operand alone. Use of these operators can avert potentially dangerous and hard to debug error conditions that can occur in very simple expressions.

As an illustration of this point, consider an example. Let's say you want to check if a `Vector` object (perhaps returned from a function) has any elements before you use it. You might unintentionally code it this way:

```
if  (( v != null) & ( v.size() > 0))
```

For beginners, this looks like a perfectly valid `boolean` expression, and the compiler accepts it, too. However, the code will still throw a `NullPointerException` if v is `null`. The use of & operator causes both operands to be evaluated. What you want, of course is the *short-circuit* && operator. Since evaluation of the first operand is sufficient to determine the result of the expression, the second operand (`v.size() > 0`) in our example will not be evaluated if (`v != null`) returns `false`. The same behavior holds true for the short-circuit OR || operator that are just as problematic. They are used in cases where you need the negated form of the previous example: `if (v==null ||` `v.size() = 0)`

The short-circuit operators are not only safe to use, but are also efficient, since fewer operands need to be evaluated to arrive at the result.

The Equality Operators == and !=

These operators check whether the operands being compared are equal and return a `boolean` result. The behavior of the equality operators depends mainly on the type of the operands. The operands can either be primitives or object types. For primitive operands, the value stored in the operand is used for comparison. For object type operands, the comparison is made on the reference (under the hood, it is the memory address) of the object. Let us paraphrase the rules in simple words:

- Two non-object operands are equal if they represent the same value.
- Two object references are equal if they are stored in the same memory location; that is, if they both refer to the same object.

Travel Advisory

In Java, it is illegal to compare primitive values with object references. The equality operators do not even inspect the content of the object being compared. They return `false` even if the object being compared has the same content as the value of the primitive.

Since these operators are often a great source of confusion, let us look at an example that demonstrates all the facets of such expressions:

```
public class EqualityOperatorsDemo {
    public static void main ( String s[] ) {
```

```
int x = 13 ;
int y = 015 ;
int z = 0xD ;

// Primitive comparisons.
System.out.println( x == y );
System.out.println( y == z );
System.out.println( x != 13.0000000f ) ;

// The following line will not compile. See the explanation.
// System.out.println( x == y == z );

// Object reference comparisons.
Integer i = new Integer(x);
Integer j = new Integer(y);

System.out.println( i == j );

Integer k = j ;
System.out.println( j == k );
    }
}
```

The primitive comparisons demonstrate how the actual contents are used for comparison, with no importance being given to the base in which the numbers are being expressed. The variables y and z are using octal and hexadecimal literals to represent the same value. The (x != 13.0000000f) comparison shows automatic numeric promotion of x. Since the constant x is being compared to has a higher precision than x, it gets promoted to the same width before the comparison is done.

As weird as it might look, the next line

```
System.out.println( x == y == z );
```

generates a compiler error. This can really catch you off guard if you have a C++ background. Here's why it happens: the equality operator is left associative and always return a boolean value. The expression (x == y == z) is evaluated as (x == y) == z. Since (x == y) returns a boolean, the second equality operator sees mixed operand types, one boolean and the other integer, which is not permitted in Java!

The correct way to write the same expression would be `(x == y) && (x == z)`.

The object reference comparison shows how `==` behaves with objects. Although the two `java.lang.Integer` objects have the same content, they are two different physical objects stored in two entirely different locations. This means their references are different and hence `==` returns `false`. Note how the `j == k` comparison returns `true` since `k` is not an object by itself, but just another reference to the same object held by `j`.

> ### Exam Tip
>
> The `==` operator raises a compiler error if object references are not compatible. For example, Longobj `==` DoublObj gives compiler error.

A Note about Zero and Special Numbers

`float` and `double` types have special values that may be the result of certain floating-point operations that cannot be represented as a number. The `java.lang.Float` and `java.lang.Double` classes define some of these values as constants: `POSITIVE_INFINITY`, `NEGATIVE_INFINITY`, and `NaN`.

NaN (Not-a-Number) is unordered. Comparing it to any other number, including itself, always yields `false`.

In Java, negative zero compares equal with regular (positive) zero Therefore, the comparison `-0.0==0.0` always returns `true`. However, two 0's may be distinguished by division: one divided by negative zero yields `NEGATIVE_INFINITY`; one divided by a positive zero yields `POSITIVE_INFINITY`.

The Shorthand Operators

Java provides several convenient operators that combine both expression evaluation and assignment as one operation. For example, the `+=` operator performs both addition and assignment, in that order. Using the shorthand operator `+=`, we can rewrite a statement

```
a = a + b ;
```

as

```
a += b ;
```

Java supports the following shorthand operators : `+=`, `-=`, `*=`, `/=`, `%=`, `&=`, `|=`, `^=`, `<<=`, `>>=` and `>>>=` .

The shorthand operators also implicitly narrow or widen the result of the expression to the type it is being assigned to, eliminating the necessity for an explicit cast. For example, consider the code fragment

```
byte c = 10;
c = c + 2 ;
```

Since `c + 2` evaluates to an integer expression, the compiler raises an error saying implicit cast is required to convert an integer type to a `byte` type. To make the code work, you can either use a messy explicit cast as in:

```
c = (byte)( c + 2) ;
```

or use the shorthand operator that automatically casts the result into a `byte` type, as in

```
c += 2 ;
```

Travel Advisory

Care should be taken while using the shorthand operator in situations where loss of magnitude can happen. The compiler will not raise any errors detecting the overflow. For example,

```
byte c = 127 ;
c += 20 ;
```

will result in an overflow . The same will happen when the shorthand operator isn't being used (for example, c = (byte)(c+20)). The danger is that there is no cast operator to make that fact explicit.

The Conditional Operator ?:

Java provides a special ternary (three-argument) operator that can replace certain types of simple if-then-else statements. This operator is the ?: conditional operator which has the general form

```
<Booleanexpression> ? <true-path> : <false-path>
```

If the `boolean` expression returns `true`, the statement in the true-path is executed, if not, the statement in the false-path is executed. The overall result of the ? expression is the result returned either by the `true` path or by the `false` path. This means both the `true` and `false` path statements must return the same type, which cannot be void. Here is a handy example:

```
int abs =  value > 0 ? value : (-1)*value ;
```

Note that the type of the `true/false` path statement is subjected to usual widening conversions and they do not need to have exactly the same type. The following statement demonstrates this point:

```
int reading = 200;
double temperature =  reading < 99 ? reading : 99.0 - reading;
```

The String Concatenation Operator +

Strings form a unique data type in Java. While they can be used as simple primitive types as here:

```
String s = "Hello World";
```

they can also be used as objects if one wishes to make use of a number of useful functions defined by the `java.lang.String` class, as shown here:

```
String s = "Hello World".toUpperCase() ;
```

Every string that the program creates is internally stored as an object of class `java.lang.String`. Even string constants are actually `String` objects that are maintained by the Java virtual machine. In this section, we will talk only about the string concatenation operator. Since knowledge of strings is very essential for the certification exam, we encourage the readers to revisit the section on strings in Chapter 1.

The string concatenation operator + returns a new string that is formed by adding the second string (operand2) to the end of the first string (operand1). Note that the returned string is a completely new object and the + operator will not modify the original value of the either of the operands. Consider an example:

```
String s1 = "Get" ;
String s2 = " Certified!"
String s3 = s1 + s2 ;
```

At the end, the variable s3 will have the value "Get Certified!" while s1 and s2 will remain unchanged.

You can also use string constants as operands along with String variables. For instance:

```
String s1 = "Get" ;
String s2 = s1 + " Certified!"
```

yields the same result as the previous example.

The string concatenation operator + behaves in a highly context-sensitive manner. If one of the two of its operands is a String type, the other operand is converted to its String representation. Consider the following line of code:

```
String s = "Mars is the " + 3 + "rd planet in our solar system" ;
```

Since the + operator is left associative, it always evaluates the left operand first. Since the left operand "Mars is the" is of type String, the right operand, the number 3, is automatically converted to its String representation "3". The result of first concatenation produces the "Mars is the 3". This intermediate String is then used in the second concatenation to produce the final string:

```
"Mars is the 3rd planet in our solar system"
```

This fact shouldn't come as a surprise to our readers since we use expressions such as:

```
System.out.println( " Value of a is " + a  );
```

countless number of times in our daily programming chores.

Travel Advisory

Java uses wrapper classes to generate string equivalents of non-String types. For example, the String equivalent of number 3 is generated using `Integer(3).toString()`. The `toString()` method is defined by the primordial `java.lang.Object` class and is inherited by all the other classes in the Java class library. Many classes override the `toString()` method to return meaningful String representations of the contents, notably the `Boolean, Character, Integer, Long, Float, Double` and `String` classes.

The automatic conversion of operands to String values by the + operator is often very weird and nonnutritive. This chapter would not be complete if we didn't quote one of our favorite examples. Try evaluating the simple expression:

```
System.out.println( 3 + 5 + " = " + 3 + 5  ) ;
```

If you answered "8 = 8", you are wrong! The output produced is "8 = 35"! Here's how the expression is evaluated:

$$3 + 5 + " = " + 3 + 5$$

Step 1 → (3+5)   + " = " + 3 + 5
Step 2 → 8 + " = " + 3 + 5
Step 3 → "8 = " + 3 + 5
Step 4 → "8 = 3 " + 5
Step 5 → "8 = 35 "

Since the + operator is left associative, all the operands are evaluated left to right. Till Step 2, it is pure numeric addition. The + operator in Step 1 behaves like a numeric addition operator since both the operands involved are numbers. However, at Step 3, when + operator realizes the right operand "=" is a String, it converts the left operand 8 from number to String and performs string concatenation. From Step 3 onwards, every operation is a pure String concatenation and results in the totally misleading final String "8 = 35".

Exam Tip

Except the +, +=, and = operators, none other may be used with String types.

The Type Comparison Operator — instanceof

Sometimes it is useful to know the type of a particular object during runtime. For instance, when you want to perform some special processing on subclasses of an object and polymorphism won't do the job. A simple thing such as an explicit type cast can fool the compiler and a potentially dangerous code can get through compilation error free. The instanceof operator provided by Java comes to the rescue. An expression whose type is a reference type may be tested using instanceof to find out whether the class of the object referenced by the run-time value of the expression is assignment compatible with some other reference type.

The instanceof operator takes two operands. The left-hand argument must be an expression that evaluates to a reference type and the right hand argument must be a *type*. The operator returns a `boolean` value indicating whether the left hand operand can be cast to the righthand operand at runtime. A compile-time error occurs if the second operand cannot be evaluated to a valid type. The table below summarizes various valid operands and return values for the `instanceof` operator.

op1 (reference)	Instance of Type	Returns
null	Any class or interface	Always `false`
Any type	null	Compile-time error
Obj1	Class	`true` if Obj extends Class directly or indirectly
Obj1	Interface1	`true` if Obj implements Interface
Array	`java.lang.Object`	Always `true`
Array	`java.lang.Cloneable`	Always `true`

The following program verifies each of the scenarios just stated:

```
interface Edible {  }

class Fruit implements Edible { }
class Apple extends Fruit{  }
class Orange extends Fruit{  }

class RedApple extends Apple{  }
class FloridaOrange extends Orange{  }

public class InstanceOfDemo {
    public static void main( String args[] ) {
        Object obj1 = new Object() ;
        System.out.println( "null instanceof Edible : " +
```

```
                                        ( null instanceof Edible ));

        // This line produces a compiler error since 'null' is not a
valid type.
        // System.out.println( "Object instanceof null : " +
        //                      ( obj1 instanceof null ));

        Fruit grapes     = new Fruit();
        Apple apple      = new Apple();
        Orange orange     = new Orange() ;

        System.out.println( "grapes instanceof Edible : " +
                        ( grapes instanceof Edible ));

        System.out.println( "grapes instanceof Fruit : " +
                        ( grapes instanceof Fruit ));

        System.out.println( "grapes instanceof Apple : " +
                        ( grapes instanceof Apple ));

        System.out.println( "apple instanceof Edible : " +
                        ( apple  instanceof Edible ));

         System.out.println( "apple  instanceof Fruit : " +
                        ( apple  instanceof Fruit ));

        // The following line can never be true and an error is
        // flagged at the compile time!
        /*
        System.out.println( "apple  instanceof Orange : " +
                        ( apple  instanceof Orange ));
        */

        RedApple redapple = new RedApple();
        FloridaOrange floridaOrange = new FloridaOrange();

        System.out.println( "redapple  instanceof Edible : " +
                        ( redapple  instanceof Edible ));
```

```
System.out.println( "redapple  instanceof Fruit : " +
                ( redapple  instanceof Fruit ));


System.out.println( "redapple  instanceof Apple : " +
                ( redapple  instanceof Apple ));


System.out.println( "floridaOrange  instanceof Orange : " +
                ( floridaOrange  instanceof Orange ));


Apple BagOfApples[] = new Apple[10];
System.out.println( "BagOfApples instanceof java.lang.Object
: " +

                ( BagOfApples instanceof Object ));


System.out.println( "BagOfApples instanceof
java.lang.Cloneable : " +
                ( BagOfApples instanceof Cloneable ));


System.out.println( "BagOfApples instanceof Edible[] : " +
                ( BagOfApples instanceof Edible[] ));


System.out.println( "BagOfApples instanceof Apple[] : " +
                ( BagOfApples instanceof Apple[] ));
    }
}
```

Objective 6.03

Apply `equals(Object)` to Objects of `java.lang.String`, `java.lang.Boolean`, and `java.lang.Object`

For this objective, you'll determine the result of applying the `equals(Object)` method to objects of any combination of the classes `java.lang.String`, `java.lang.Boolean`, and `java.lang.Object`.

The Ubiquitous equals() Method

Equality of two objects is defined as, at bare minimum, the two object references being the same, that is, they reference the same memory location. This definition is hardly useful in real life since equality is usually based on the *contents* of the entities being compared. To help programmers redefine equality of two objects, the designers of Java language created the equals() method in java.lang.Object class. Since all Java objects are subclasses of java.lang.Object class, any class can override the equals() method to perform more meaningful content-based comparisons.

The equals() method for java.lang.Object class implements the most discriminating possible equivalence relation on objects; that is, for any reference values x and y, this method returns true if and only if x and y refer to the same object (x==y has the value true).

Many classes in the JDK override the equals() method and perform equality checks in compliance with the following rules (these rules form the general contract for equals(), which all implementations must satisfy):

- It is *reflexive*: for any reference value x, x.equals(x) should return true.
- It is *symmetric*: for any reference values x and y, x.equals(y) should return true if and only if y.equals(x) returns true.
- It is *transitive*: for any reference values x, y, and z, if x.equals(y) returns true and y.equals(z) returns true, then x.equals(z) should return true.
- It is *consistent*: for any reference values x and y, multiple invocations of x.equals(y) consistently return true or consistently return false, provided no information used in **equals** comparisons on the object is modified.
- For any non-null reference value x, x.equals(null) should return false.

In addition to these rules, a special rule applies to wrapper classes: equals() returns false if the type of the objects being compared are different.

For the purpose of the certification, readers are expected to be familiar with the equals() method overridden by various wrapper classes and the String class.

All the wrapper classes—Boolean, Byte, Character, Integer, Long, Float and Double—override the equals() method to return the truth value based on the value being stored by the object. Consider the following lines of code:

```
Integer iObj1 = new Integer(10);
Integer iObj2 = new Integer(10);
Integer iObj3 = new Integer(20);
```

`iObj1.equals( iObj2 )` returns `true` since both the objects store the value 10.

`iObj2.equals( iObj3 )` returns `false` since the value stored by them are not the same.

Travel Advisory

The `equals()` method overridden by the wrapper classes always returns `false` if the object types are different, whether or not the contents are same.

The version of the `equals()` method defined in the `Boolean` class compares the two objects based on the truth value held by the object. For example:

```
Boolean b1 = new Boolean( true );
Boolean b2 = new Boolean( false );
Boolean b3 = new Boolean( true );
```

Here `b1.equals(b2)` returns `false` whereas `b1.equals(b3)` returns `true`.

The `String` class defines the `equals()` method that performs text-based comparison of the value held by the object. The comparisons are case sensitive. For example:

```
String s1 = "Hello Java" ;
String s2 = new String( "Hello world");
String s3 = "Hello " + "Java" ;
```

Here `s1.equals(s2)` returns `false`. However, `s1.equals( s3 )` returns `true`.

Exam Tip

While `String` overrides the `equals()` method, its mutable counterpart `StringBuffer` does not. This means calling the `equals()` method on two `StringBuffer` objects simply calls the `Object.equals()` method due to polymorphism and returns the result of *reference comparison*. Therefore, `StringBufferObj1.equals(StringBufferObj2)` is true only if they both are pointing to the same physical object, that is, , `StringBufferObj1 == StringBufferObj2` is true.

Pass Variables into Methods and Perform Assignments or Other Modifying Operations

For this objective, you'll determine the effect upon objects and primitive values of passing variables into methods and performing assignments or other modifying operations in that method.

Effects of Method Invocations on Objects and Primitives

Java passes all arguments by value, not by reference. However, this is one of the few places where the distinction between an object and a reference to an object becomes important. Object and array variables in Java are really references to the object or array.

When a primitive variable is passed to a method, a copy of the original value is used in the call to the method. Thus, any changes to the value done during the lifetime of the called method have no effect outside the method, especially in the calling code after the method returns. Consider the following example:

```
class PassingPrimitivesDemo {
    public static void main( String s[] ) {
        int MySalary - 4000 ;
        System.out.println("Salary before the increase : " + MySalary
);
        IncreaseSalary( MySalary );
        System.out.println("Salary after the increase : " + MySalary
);
    }

    public static void IncreaseSalary( int salary ) {
        salary += 2500;
        System.out.println( "Salary inside the method :" + salary );
    }
}
```

The program produces the following output:

```
Salary before the increase : 4000
Salary inside the method :6500
Salary after the increase : 4000
```

Since the variable being passed in to the `IncreaseSalary` method is a simple type, the changes have no effect after the method returns to the `main()` function. Let truth be told: `MySalary` remains the same!

When you pass an object to a method, the situation changes dramatically, because objects are passed by copy reference. Keep in mind that when you create an object, the name of the variable is the handle to the object reference. It is perfectly valid to have multiple references to the same object as long as you understand all of them are pointing to the same physical object.

In the following example, we modify the `PassingPrimitivesDemo` class to make use of a simple class to represent the salary instead of a primitive type:

```java
// Simple wrapper class to hold the salary.
class Salary  {
    int salary ;
    Salary() { salary = 4000; }
    public void add( int raise ) { salary += raise; }
}
class PassingObjectsDemo {
    public static void main( String s[] ) {
        Salary MySalaryObj = new Salary();
        System.out.println( "Salary before the increase : " +
MySalaryObj.salary );
        IncreaseSalary( MySalaryObj );
        System.out.println( "Salary after the increase : " +
MySalaryObj.salary );
    }
    public static void IncreaseSalary( Salary lSalaryObj ) {
        lSalaryObj.add( 2500 );
        System.out.println( "Salary inside the method :" +
lSalaryObj.salary );
    }
}
```

This program produces the following output:

```
Salary before the increase : 4000
```

```
Salary inside the method :6500
Salary after the increase : 6500
```

Since an object reference is being passed to the method, even the code inside the method refers to the original object through the copy of the reference passed. Hence, the effects of modification by the method are visible in the calling function.

Travel Advisory

For more information, check out these sources:

- The *Sun Java Tutorial* at **http://web2.java.sun.com/docs/books/ tutorial/**
- The *Java Language Specification* at **http://java.sun.com/docs/ books/jls/second_edition/html/j.title.doc.html**
- The *Java Virtual Machine Specification, 2ⁿᵈ Edition* at **http://java. sun.com/docs/books/vmspec/2nd-edition/html/VMSpecTOC. doc.html**
- The *Java 2 Platform Standard Edition* v 1.3 API **http://java. sun.com/j2se/1.3/docs/api/index.html**
- **Thinking in Java** by Bruce Eckel at **http://www. bruceeckel.com**
- *Java in a Nutshell* by David Flanagan by O'Reilly Associates.

CHECKPOINT

✔ **Objective 6.01** Determine the result of applying any operator, including assignment operators, instanceof, and casts, to operands of any type, class, scope, or accessibility, or any combination of these.

- Operands in an expression often undergo numeric promotion. Operands are converted to type `int`, or the type of the expression which ever is the widest. The result of a primitive expression is always at least as wide as an `int`.
- In every case, the type of each of the operands of the binary operator must be a primitive numeric type, or a compile-time error occurs.
- If an integer multiplication overflows, the result is the low-order bits of the mathematical product as represented in some sufficiently large

two's-complement format. Consequently, if overflow occurs, the sign of the result may not be the same as the sign of the mathematical product of the two-operand values.

- Multiplication of an infinity by a zero results in `NaN`.
- Integer division (/) by zero and integer remainder division (%) by zero always raise an `ArithmeticException`. Note noninteger division by zero (for example, a / 0.0) does not result in an exception, but the value of the expression will be infinity. The value infinity is represented by the characters "Infinity". Despite the fact that overflow, underflow, division by zero, or loss of information may occur, evaluation of a floating-point division operator / never throws a runtime exception.
- For any mathematical operation, if either of the operands is `NaN`, the result is `NaN`.
- Integer division rounds toward 0.
- If the type of either operand of a + operator is `String`, then the operation is equivalent to string concatenation. Otherwise, the type of each of the operands of the + operator must be a primitive numeric type, otherwise a compile-time error occurs.
- A variable that is declared `final` cannot be changed and hence cannot be used as the operand of a postfix/prefix increment/decrement operator.
- The assignment operator always checks for incompatible types and loss of magnitude. A compile-time error occurs if a value is being assigned to a variable of a narrower type.
- Explicit casting can result in loss of magnitude in primitive assignments.
- Shorthand assignment operators are one of *=, /=, %=, +=, -=, <<=, >>=, >>>=, &=, ^= and |= . Java performs automatic implicit conversion of the result to the type it is being assigned to, hence eliminating a need for cast.
- A literal with a decimal point is always treated as a `double`, for example, 7.0 is a `double` and not an `int` . However, use of a suffix can morph the variable into a different type; 'l' or 'L' would make it a `long` and 'f' or 'F' would make it a `float` type.
- The `toString()` method is defined by the primordial class `java.lang.Object`; many classes override it, notably `Boolean`, `Character`, `Integer`, `Long`, `Float`, `Double` and `String` .
- When both operands of a &, ^, or | operator are of type `boolean`, the type of the expression is `boolean` .
- The shift operators include left shift <<, signed right shift >>, and unsigned right shift >>>; they are syntactically left associative (they group left to right). The left operand of a shift operator is the value to be

shifted; the right operand specifies the shift distance. The type of each of the operands of a shift operator must be a primitive integral type. Binary numeric promotion is not performed on the operands; rather, unary numeric promotion is performed on each operand separately. The type of the shift expression is the promoted type of the left operand. When necessary, the operands undergo arithmetic promotion to either an `int` or a `long` type.

- Any value cannot be shifted further than the number of bits in the left argument. If the promoted type of the left operand is int, the shift distance actually used is therefore always in the range 0 to 31, inclusive. This means, for any bit shift expression of the form m (op) n where op is one of >>, << or >>>, if m is of type `int` and n>32 , the result of the expression is m (op) n%32. If m is of type `long` and n>64, the result of the expression is the same as m (op) n%64.

- The value of n<<s is n left-shifted s bit positions; this is equivalent (even if overflow occurs) to multiplication by two raised to the power s.

- The value of n>>s is n right-shifted s bit positions with sign-extension. The resulting value is $(n)/2^s$ e, n divided by two to the power of s. For nonnegative values of n, this is equivalent to truncating integer division, as computed by the integer division operator /, by two to the power s.

- For positive numbers, the result of >> and >>> are the same. However for negative numbers, >>> always results in the change of sign.

- The type of a relational expression is always `boolean`.

- For numerical comparison operators <, <=, >, and >=, if either operand is `NaN`, the result is always `false`. For numerical equality operators, if either operand is `NaN`, then the result of == is `false` but the result of != is `true`.

- Positive zero and negative zero are considered equal. Therefore, -0.0<0.0 is `false` and -0.0==0.0 is `true`. However, the methods `java.lang.Math.min` and `java.lang.Math.max` treat negative zero as being strictly smaller than positive zero.

- The equality operators == and != may be used to compare two operands of numeric type, two operands of type `boolean`, or two operands that are each of either reference type or the `null` type. All other cases result in a compile-time error. The type of an equality expression is always `boolean`.

- At runtime, the result of reference equality operator == is `true` if the both the operand values are either `null` or both refer to the same object or array; otherwise, the result is `false`.

- The operator == raises a compiler error if object references are not compatible. For example, LongType == DoubleType raises a compiler error.

- For `String` concatenation, if one of the operand is the `null` reference, it is converted to the string "null". Otherwise, the conversion is performed as if by an invocation of the `toString()` method of the referenced object with no arguments; but if the result of invoking the `toString()` method is null, then the string "null" is used instead.
- In all cases, ~x = (-x)-1.
- For the conditional operator ?:, the first expression must be of type `boolean`, or a compile-time error occurs. Note that it is not permitted for either the second or the third operand expression to be an invocation of a `void` method.
- Legal operands for instanceof operator are:
  - for the left operand, any expression or `null` value
  - for the right operand, class, interfaces, or array type

Objective 6.02 In an expression involving the operators &, |, &&, ||, and variables of known values state which operands are evaluated and the value of the expression.

- The `boolean` operators & and | always evaluate both operands. When conditional-and (&&) operator is used, the left operand is evaluated first. If its value is `false`, the value of the conditional-and expression is `false` and the right operand expression is not evaluated. If the value of the left operand is `true`, the right expression is evaluated. Likewise, the || operator is like | but evaluates its right operand only if the value of its left operand is `false`.

Objective 6.03 Determine the result of applying the `boolean` `equals(Object)` method to objects of any combination of the classes `java.lang.String`, `java.lang.Boolean`, and `java.lang.Object`.

- The `equals()` method is defined by the primordial `java.lang.Object` class. The default implementation returns the result of reference comparison. Many wrapper classes such as Integer, Long, Double, Float, Character, and String override `equals()` and perform content-based comparisons.
- For wrapper classes, the `equals()` returns `false` if the type of objects being compared is different, even if they store the same value.
- While == may be used to compare references of type `String`, such an equality test determines whether or not the two operands refer to the same `String` object. The result is `false` if the operands are distinct `String` objects, even if they contain the same sequence of characters. The contents of two strings s and t can be tested for equality by the method invocation s.equals(t).

✔ **Objective 6.04** **Determine the effect upon objects and primitive values of passing variables into methods and performing assignments or other modifying operations in that method.**

- Primitive variables are always passed by value. Any changes done to the variable inside the called method are not visible in the calling method after the method returns.
- Object references are always passed by value. This means the reference inside the method points to the original object and not a copy of the object. The changes made to the object inside the method will be apparent in the calling method after the call returns.

REVIEW QUESTIONS

1. What will be the output of following statements?

```
int myArray[] = null ;
System.out.println( myArray instanceof Object);
```

   A. true
   B. false
   C. Compiler error
   D. NullPointerException at runtime

2. Consider the following code block; after the statement in line 3 is executed, what will the values in array nSquares be?

```
1:  int nSquares[] = {1,4,9,16,25,36,49,81 };
2:  int j = 3 ;
3:  nSquares[j] = nSquares[++j] + j ;
```

   A. {1,4,6,16,25,36,49,81 }
   B. {1,4,9,19,25,36,49,81 }
   C. {1,4,9,16,6,36,49,81 }
   D. {1,4,12,16,29,36,49,81 }
   E. {1,4,12,16,28,36,49,81 }

3. What will be the output produced by the following statements

```
Boolean b = new Boolean (true);
System.out.println( b.equals("true"));
```

A. true
B. false
C. Compiler error reporting incompatible types
D. Compiler error since Boolean class doesn't define `equals()` method
E. TRUE

4. Consider the following statement; which of the following lines, when placed after this statement, will result in an error-free compilation? (Select two.)

```
Short s1 = new Short((short)2);
```

A. `short s2 = s1.intValue() + s1.shortValue();`
B. `int s2 = s1.intValue() + s1.shortValue();`
C. `short s2 = (short)s1.intValue() + s1.shortValue();`
D. `short s2 = (short)s1.intValue() + (short)`
   `s1.shortValue();`
E. `short s2 = (short) (s1.intValue() + s1.shortValue());`

5. Given the following simple statements, which of the statements is true? (Select two.)

```
1:        byte b = 2;
2:        b = b >> 2;
```

A. No compiler errors are generated.
B. After line 2, b will have the value 0.
C. Line 2 should be modified as b = `(byte)b>>2` in order for the code to compile.
D. Line 2 should be modified as b = `(byte)(b>>2)` in order for the code to compile.
E. Line 2 should be modified as b `>>= 2` in order for the code to compile.

6. What will be the result of compiling and running the following code snippet?

```
int nSquares[] = {1,4,9,16,25,36,49,81 };
int nIndex = 0 ;
if ( −nIndex > 0  && nSquares[ nIndex ] > 10)
    System.out.println("Ping");
else
    System.out.println("Pong");
```

    A. The string Ping will be printed.

    B. The string Pong will be printed.

    C. The code will not compile since && takes integer arguments.

    D. The code will compile fine but throws `ArrayIndexOutOfBounds Exception` at runtime.

    E. The code will not compile due to illegal array initialization statement.

7. Given the declaration int i = 9, the expression ~i returns the value

    A. -10

    B. 10

    C. -9

    D. 9

8. What will be the output of the following program?

```
public class ChangeTest {
    public static void main ( String s[] ) {
        final int Odds[] = {1,3} ;
        SwapThem( Odds );
        System.out.println( Odds[0] + "," + Odds[1] ) ;
    }
    static void SwapThem( int ar[] ) {
        int i = ar[0];
        ar[0] = ar[1] ;
        ar[1] = i ;
    }
}
```

    A. 1, 3

    B. A compiler error, since `SwapThem` attempts to modify a `final` array.

    C. 3, 1

    D. A compiler error: incompatible types in method invocation.

9. What will the following program print?

```
public class ChangeTest {
    public static void main ( String s[] ) {
        final int Odds[] = {1,3} ;
        SwapThem( Odds );
```

```
        System.out.println( Odds[0] + "," + Odds[1] ) ;
    }
    static void SwapThem( int ar[] ) {
        int newArray[] = new int[2];
        newArray[0] = ar[1] ;
        newArray[1] = ar[0] ;
        ar = newArray ;
    }
}
```

A. 1, 3

B. A compiler error, since SwapThem attempts to modify a final array.

C. 3, 1

D. A compiler error: incompatible types in method invocation.

REVIEW ANSWERS

1. **B** The instanceof operator always returns false for null references.

2. **D** Since the assignment operator is right associative, the expression nSquares[++j] + j is evaluated first. The pre-increment ++ increments j by one before applying the array index operator. Therefore, nSquares[++j] returns nSquares[4] which is 25 and j becomes 4. The final assignment will be nSquares[4] = 29.

3. **B** The string literal "true" is automatically converted to a reference to a String object. The equals() method returns false if the objects being compared are of different types. Since we are trying to compare a String object with a Boolean object, equals() returns false.

4. **B** **E** The result of the arithmetic expression is int by default, except when either operand is of type double, float or long. An int value can be assigned to an int variable without any cast, or to a short variable using an explicit downcast.

5. **D** **E** The expression b>>2 is of type int and hence the downcast is necessary to assign the result to a byte variable. The shorthand operand >>= automatically casts the result to byte type and no cast is necessary.

6. **B** The operator && will not evaluate the second expression nSquares [nIndex] since the first expression –nIndex > 0 returns false. Hence, the else part of the if statement is executed.

7. **A** For any value of i, ~i = -i-1.

8. **C** Just like objects, arrays are passed to methods as a copy reference. The method code accesses the original array using a different name and changes done in the method are durable and visible after the method returns. Note that the final modifier applies to the array reference itself and not the contents, so it doesn't produce a compiler error.

9. **A** Remember, what is passed to the method is only a copy of the reference. Although the method overwrites the argument array with a new array, it is the copy of the reference that is overwritten and not the original reference itself. The original array is still visible and accessible through its old reference Odds in the main() method. Hence, any changes done in the method affect only the copy of the array in the scope of the method.

Flow
Control

	NEWBIE	SOME EXPERIENCE	EXPERT
ETA	15 hours	5 hours	2 hours

If the behavior of algorithms was fixed during compilation and couldn't be modified at runtime, our programs would be very inflexible. The ability to analyze runtime information such as input parameters, user data, and an environment state and to choose an appropriate set of instructions is what makes programs so powerful. Flow control structures do exactly this.

How many flow control structures are enough? It has been proven that any arbitrary complex algorithm can be constructed using just three basic structures: sequence, repetition, and selection. How these basic structures are supported is left up to the language designers and reflects the language spirit.

The following flow control statements are provided in Java: selection statements (`if-else` and `switch`), iteration statements (`for`, `while`, and `do/while` loops), transfer statements (`break` and `continue`) and, finally, a statement to deal with exceptional situations (the `try-catch-finally` statement).

Objective 7.01

Write Code Using if and switch Statements and Identify Legal Argument Types

All flow control statements, in a sense, allow the program to modify its behavior during runtime. In particular, selection statements control which other statements should be executed or skipped.

Java provides two selection constructs: the `if-else` statement, which allows you to choose one of two alternatives, and the `switch` statement, which provides a choice between several alternatives.

if-else Statement

Syntax:

```
if (condition)
statement
```

or

```
if (condition)
```

```
    statement
else
    statement
```

The condition must evaluate to the `boolean` type, otherwise a compile-time error will be raised. Remember that there is no conversion to the `boolean` type from any other type. In particular, the integer values 0 and 1 will not be interpreted false and true.

The statement can be any of the following:

- A single Java statement ending with a semicolon (;)
- An empty statement (";")
- A compound statement (multiple Java statements each ending with a semicolon and enclosed in curly braces)

All three following forms are correct:

```
if (inputParam > 0) sum = sum + inputParam;
if (inputParam > 0) ;
if (inputParam > 0) {
    sum += inputParam;
    total += sum;
}
```

Exam Tip

`If` and `else` are Java keywords. Note that there is no "then" keyword in the `if-else` construct, and that "then" is not a reserved word in Java.

Travel Advisory

Even though Java syntax allows you to omit braces in the case of a single statement, it is good practice to always include them because it can help prevent programmers from adding more statements later and forgetting to add braces.

Nested `if` Statements

The `if-else` construct is simple by itself. Things get complicated when nested `if` structures appear. The `else` block that follows several `if`s can belong to each of them, introducing the so-called "dangling-else problem." The Java language designers made an arbitrary decision that an `else` block always belongs to the innermost `if` to which it may possibly belong.

The `switch` statement

The `switch` statement extends the `if` statement's functionality in one direction and restricts it in another. The choice can be made between more than two alternatives, but the condition is a subject for several restrictions.

In fact, the same effect can be achieved with a set of nested `if-else` statements. So why does Java introduce yet another structure? First, the `switch` structure is easier to understand than a conglomeration of `if-else` statements. Second, the compiler generates more efficient code for it. The JVM has two low-level instructions that directly support the `switch` structure. Both these instructions work with a set of integer constants. Here effectiveness is a consequence of specialization: the `switch` structure performs a choice between alternatives, each represented by a value, known at compile time and evaluated to one of integer types.

Syntax:

```
switch(expression) {
   case case-expression1 : statement break;
   case case-expression2 : statement break;
   ...
   default : statement
}
```

Expression

The expression must result in a value of `byte`, `char`, `short`, or `int` type.

Case-Expression

There are a few rules your case-expression should obey to make the compiler happy:

- The case-expression must be a constant expression whose value can be calculated at compile time. This means it can include only literals and variables defined as `final` and initialized using a compile-time constant expression.
- The case-expression must result in a value of `byte`, `char`, `short`, or `int` type.
- The result of case-expression must fit in the range of the `switch` type expression. For example, if the `switch` expression is represented by a `char` variable, no case-expression whose result is outside of the 0–65535 range will pass the compiler.
- If there are two or more case-expressions resulting in the same value, a compiler error will be raised.

Note that variables in case-expressions do not have to have a smaller integer type than the type of the `switch` expression. For example, it is possible to have a `char` variable in a `switch` expression and a variable declared as `final int` in a `case` clause, as long as the value of the last is within the `char` range and known at compile time. Since the value of the variable is known, the compiler can be sure it fits the expression range.

Statement

Statement can be a single Java statement ending with a semicolon (;), an empty statement (";"), or multiple Java statements each ending with a semicolon.

Default Clause

There can be either one `default` clause in a `switch` structure or none. If present, the `default` clause doesn't have to be the last and can be placed between `case` statements or even precede them.

Optional Parts

Note that `case`, `default`, `break`, and statement parts are all optional, so the next form is legal, although useless:

```
switch (expression) {
   case case-expression:
   default:
}
```

The shortest (and equally useless) form of the `switch` statement is as follows:

```
switch (expression) {}
```

Exam Tip

`Switch`, `case`, `break`, and `default` are Java keywords.

How It Works

First, the expression is evaluated. Next, the result is compared to each `case` value sequentially. If a match is found, all statements in the `switch` structure are executed beginning from the first in the matching `case` clause and continuing until `break` is found. Execution, thus, falls through all blocks, including `default`. As soon as `break` is found, control is transferred to the first statement after the `switch` structure. If no `break` is found, statements in all the subsequent `case` blocks are executed until the end of the `switch` structure.

If no `case` value matches the expression, the `default` statement, if any, is executed. If there is no `default`, the whole `switch` structure is skipped.

Exam Tip

Many languages have statements similar to `switch`. However, the idea of "falling through" is not that typical and may be unusual to you. In such a case, write small programs to test variants with `break` and `default` statements in different places and try to predict the output. It's very likely that you will get such questions on the exam. Experience shows that some results may not be what you expect!

Travel Assistance

For an in-depth look at JVM's bytecode instructions into which Java's flow control statements are translated, read Bill Venners' article "Control Flow in the Java Virtual Machine" at
http://www.artima.com/underthehood/flow.html.

Runtime vs. Compile-Time Information

The `switch` expression is the only part of the `switch` statement that may reflect runtime information: user input, data obtained from a database, and the like. The `switch` statement compares this runtime expression against a set of constant values, defined at the time of compilation.

Objective 7.02

Write Code Using All Forms of Loops

I teration statements (loops) are used to repeatedly execute a sequence of statements. There are three kinds of loops in Java: `for`, `while`, and `do/while` loops.

Definite Iteration: The `for` Loop

Typically, the `for` loop is used to execute a block of code repeatedly if the number of iterations is known in advance or can be calculated at runtime.

Syntax:

```
for (initialization; test; update)
    body statement
```

Optional Parts

Note that all parts in the loop are optional and can be omitted. In its minimal (and not particularly useful) form the `for` loop becomes

```
for ( ; ; ) {}
```

or

```
for ( ; ; ) ;
```

Both constructs cause an infinite cycle.

Initialization and Update

Initialization and update statements can be written as single expressions or as a series of expressions separated by commas. Multiple expressions will be evaluated sequentially.

An expression in the initialization section of the loop can both declare and initialize a variable:

```
for (int i = 0; ; ) {}
```

There can be only one such declaration, which, however, can be applied to several variables:

```
for (int i=0, j=1, k=2; ; ) {}
```

is correct. However,

```
for (int i=1, int j=0; ;) {}
```

will cause a compiler error.

Multiple expressions in the update section are less tricky. The following example is somewhat contrived but syntactically correct:

```
for ( ; ; i++, j++) {}
```

Test

Test must be a single expression that evaluates to the `boolean` type. The test section with multiple logical expressions separated by commas will cause a compiler error:

```
for (int i=0, j=0; i < 5, j < 5 ; ) {}
```

Test, however, can be represented by a compound logical expression: single logical expressions separated by logical operators such as && or || (for detailed information on logical operators see Chapter 6):

```
for (int i=0, j=0 ; i < 5 && j < 5 ; ) {}
```

The Body Statement

The body statement can be a single Java statement ending with a semicolon, an empty statement (";") or a compound statement (multiple Java statements ending with a semicolon and enclosed in curly braces).

All three following forms are correct:

```
for (int i=0, j=0; i<5; i++) j-;
for (int i=0, j=0; i<5; i++) ;
for (int i=0, j=0; i<5; i++) {
   j-;
   System.out.println (j);
}
```

> **Exam Tip**
>
> `For` is a Java keyword.

It's important to remember the following:

- If the test expression evaluates to `false` at the very beginning, the body statement and the update expression will never be executed.
- Java syntax doesn't prohibit you from using different variables in the initialization, test, and update sections, but typically the same variable controls the loop and appears in all the loop's expressions:

```
for (int i = 0; i < array.length; i++) {
   System.out.println (array[i]);
}
```

If a variable is declared in the initialization section of the loop, its scope is limited to the `for` statement itself and its body. An attempt to access such a variable outside the loop causes a compiler error.

Indefinite Iteration: `while` and `do/while` Loops

These indefinite iteration constructs are used when the number of iterations is impossible to count. In this case, iterations should continue until a certain condition is met. For example, a program may read file records in a cycle and terminate when the end of the file is reached.

Syntax:

```
while (test)
   statement
```

and

```
do
   statement
   while (test);
```

Test must be an expression that evaluates to a `boolean` type. If the test result evaluates to any other type, a compiler error will be raised. Unlike test in the `for` loop, the test expression in `while` and `while/do` loops cannot be omitted.

Statement can be a single Java statement ending with a semicolon, an empty statement (";"), or a compound statement (multiple Java statements, each ending with a semicolon and enclosed in curly braces).

All three of the following forms are syntactically correct:

```
1. while (true) ;
2. while (true)  i++;
3. while (true)  {
      i++;
      j-;
   }
```

Exam Tip
Do and while are Java keywords.

How It Works

With the `while` loop, the result of the test expression is first checked. If it yields `true`, the loop body is executed. Check-execute iterations are repeated until the test expression becomes false. If the first evaluation of the test expression yields `false`, the loop's body will never be executed.

The do loop works similarly and differs only in that the test expression is checked after the loop body is executed. This constitutes the main difference between the while and the do/while loops: the do/while loop body will be executed at least once.

Travel Advisory

Even though Java syntax allows you to blur the distinction between definite (for) and indefinite (while and do/while) iterations, by writing, for example:

```
for ( ; userInput == terminator ; ) {
...
}
```

doing so is not a good idea. The program should communicate the author's intentions as clearly as possible. That's why there are different forms of loops, each with its own mission.

The Transfer Statements: `break` and `continue`

These statements transfer control from the current point in the program to some other statement. The most powerful of all transfer statements, the infamous goto statement, was in an arsenal of first high-level computer languages. Later it was noticed that the arbitrary jumps of control goto introduces can easily tangle the program logic, and goto was considered harmful. A less radical point of view is that not goto by itself, but its overuse, is harmful. There are situations where programs struggling to avoid the stigmatic goto, become, in fact, less readable.

Java language designers made a palliative. There is no goto statement in Java. The most useful and least harmful part of its mission is granted to the break and continue statements. Sometimes it is handy to be able to break out of loops, and here break and continue come into play. Continue abandons the current iteration within a loop. Break abandons the whole loop. However, neither of them transfer control to an arbitrary point in the program because that could make the program flow hectic or even introduce implicit loops.

Break

Syntax:

```
break;
```

or

```
break label;
```

The first form of the `break` statement can appear inside the following statements: `switch`, `for`, `while`, and `do/while`. It immediately exits the loop or the `switch` structure and transfers control to the first statement following the enclosing structure.

The second form, `break` with a label, is used with nested loops when there is a need to abandon several layers of loops. It causes the control to abandon the current loop and all enclosing loops up to and including the one, denoted by the label. For example:

```
cycle1:for (int i=0; i < 3; i++) {
   cycle2:for (int k=0; k < 5; k++) {
      if (k==3) {
         break cycle1;
      }
      System.out.println ("i=" + i + " k=" + k);
   }
}
```

Here, `break cycle1` exits both loops. The output is as follows:

```
i=0 k=0
i=0 k=1
i=0 k=2
```

A labeled `break` can appear inside `for`, `while`, or `do/while` loops. It can appear inside a `switch`, if `switch` itself is enclosed in a loop statement.

It can also be legally placed inside a compound Java statement preceded by a label.

Continue

Syntax:

```
continue;
```

or

```
continue label;
```

The `continue` statement can appear inside of `for`, `while`, or `do/while` loops only.

The `continue` statement without a label stops the current iteration, skips the rest of the loop, and starts the next iteration within the same loop. If a label is supplied, the `continue` statement stops the current iteration and starts the next iteration of the loop denoted by the label. Note that in the case of nested loops the inner loop iterations do not continue from the point they were interrupted. After `continue` exits the inner loop, the loop's state is forgotten. When control reaches the inner loop again, the loop is executed from the beginning.

Exam Tip
Nested `for` loops with `break` and `continue` will very likely appear on the exam. Compose a few such nested loops yourself and make sure you can predict the output.

Exam Tip
`Break` and `continue` are Java keywords. In spite of the fact that Java does not have the goto statement, `goto` is also a keyword.

Labels

Labels are not statements; rather, they are identifiers that are used to designate other statements. There are a few points about label naming you should be aware of.

Label names are subject to the same rules as other identifiers. In particular, they cannot start with a number, and they cannot be Java reserved words.

Neither

```
4loop: for (int i=0; i < 5; i++) {
   break 4loop;
}
```

nor

```
while:while (true) {
   break while;
}
```

will pass the compiler.

Labels have their own namespace within the program. That means, for example, there is no collision (and no compiler error) if a label has the same name as a method.

There can be two or more labels with the same name, as long as they are not nested (otherwise the compiler would not know which loop to exit.).

Objective 7.03

Write Code That Makes Proper Use of Exceptions and Exception Handling Clauses

The golden rule of programming states that a program should produce either the correct result or no result at all. To write a correct program is a challenge in itself, but aside from errors in program logic there are a number of outside events that may cause the program to function incorrectly. In such a case, the program should stop and report an error.

Yet the first high-level computer languages had no support for this part of program behavior and programmers had to deal with exceptional situations on their own. One popular idiom was to return some unusual value indicating an error. Such a solution had a number of disadvantages:

- If a method is specified to return any, say, integer value, then to select one of integers to indicate an error would mean to break a method specifications.

- The problem is worse when there is more than one possible type of error.
- If there is a chain of calling methods, an error indicator may need to be passed through all of them.
- There is no guarantee that a calling method will do anything about an error or that it will interpret a returned value as an error at all.

In Java, the statements that deal with exceptional situations are included in the language itself and address all the preceding problems. In short, two main tasks need to be accomplished:

1. To transfer the control back through the calling method stack
2. To inform the calling method about the cause of the error

The JVM performs the control transfer, and the programmer is responsible for providing information in the form of an exception. So what is an exception?

You know that Java is an object-oriented language, so it should come as no surprise that exceptions are objects. All advantages of the object-oriented approach can be seen: one single object is transmitted and it carries as much information as needed. At a minimum, exceptions provide no extra information besides the type of the object. Often they include a string with a message. If that's still not enough, any number of extra fields can be provided. Finally, an inheritance mechanism allows you to build a hierarchy of exception classes from the generic to the specific.

The exception mechanism is so flexible and powerful that both the JVM and the Java API methods use nothing but exceptions to inform your program about any problem they encounter.

Java Statements Dealing with Exceptions

You can do the following with exceptions:

- Create
- Throw
- Catch
- Declare it in a method's header

The following example illustrates all of these:

```
public void someMethod() throws Exception {
   try {
      throw new IllegalArgumentException();
```

```
  }
  catch (RuntimeException re) { // some code here  }
  finally { //some other code here  }
}
```

Exceptions, like any other objects, are created with the new keyword.

After an exception object is created, it can appear as a parameter in the throw statement. When the throw statement is executed, an exception is said to be thrown. The JVM stops the current method and returns control back through all the calling methods consecutively, until the exception is caught by a catch clause in a try statement. If no method catches the exception, the thread will die. If it happens to be the main thread, the whole application terminates. If, however, the exception is caught, statements in the catch/finally block are executed and the program can proceed.

A list of possible exceptions is declared in the method's throws clause.

Exam Tip

Try, catch, finally, throw, and throws are Java keywords.

Let's examine each step in more detail.

Creating an Exception

To create an exception, you can either use a predefined class from the Java API, or create your own class by extending any one of the predefined classes.

The following shows the Java exception hierarchy:

```
Object
|
+-Throwable
  |
  +-Error
  |
  +-Exception
    |
    +-RuntimeException
```

At the root of the hierarchy is the `Throwable` class. All exceptions in Java must be objects of the `Throwable` class or one of its subclasses. The compiler is aware of this part of the API. If an object of any other class appears in a statement where an exception is expected, the compiler will raise an error.

Two other important classes inherit from the `Throwable` class: `Error` and `Exception`. The `Exception` class is extended by the `RuntimeException` class. These classes are extended by a variety of classes representing specific exceptions.

Errors

Throwable objects of this class are normally used by the JVM and, less often, by Java API methods, to report heavy, fatal errors. It means an application itself cannot perform its function in a reliable manner any more and should quit. As a programmer, you are supposed to neither throw `Error` objects nor catch them.

Exceptions

They represent problems, such as `InterruptedIOException`, that happen outside of your application and should not stop it. These problems can be foreseen and recovery from them is a part of program design. As a programmer, you will often deal with this branch of the exception hierarchy.

RuntimeExceptions

Objects of this class indicate a flaw in a program, such as `ArrayIndexOutOf BoundsException`, that can and should be eliminated during program debugging. Throwing `RuntimeException` can help debugging, but these exceptions should not appear in the final version of your application.

The `throw` Statement

Let's repeat it one more time: a program should return either the correct result or no result at all. If at some point a method determines that it cannot guarantee the correct result anymore, it must stop and return explanatory information. In Java, this is done with the `throw` statement.

Syntax:

```
throw ExceptionObject;
```

where `ExceptionObject` must be an object of the `Throwable` class or any of its subclasses; otherwise, the compiler will raise an error.

You can create and throw an exception within the same `throw` statement:

```
throw new MyException();
```

A method is free to throw any kind of `Throwable` object. The choice between creating a new exception class or using one provided by the Java API is a matter of design. However, there are serious limitations on possible exception types for methods participating in contract relationships: overriding methods and methods implementing an interface. We will talk about this in the section "Restrictions on Throwing Exceptions."

The `try-catch-finally` Construction

This construct is used to enclose a block of code that can potentially throw an exception, catch and stop the potential exception from being propagated, and perform any necessary recovery.

Syntax:

```
try {
   statements
}
catch (ExceptionClass variable) {
   statements
}
finally {
   statements
}
```

Syntax variations:

1. `Try`, `catch`, and `finally` blocks can be empty, for example:

```
try {}
catch (RuntimeException e) {}
finally {}
```

will not cause a compiler error.

2. `Try` is a mandatory part and cannot be omitted. Neither `catch` nor `finally` can appear without the corresponding `try`.

3. Both the `catch` and `finally` clauses are optional and can be omitted. However, they cannot both be omitted. Either a `catch` or `finally` block must be present, even if they are empty. For example:

```
try {}
catch (Exception e) {};
```

   and

```
try {}
finally {};
```

   are OK, but

```
try {};
```

   will not compile.

4. `Try-catch-finally` clauses, if present, must be in that order. The following code will not compile:

```
try {}
finally {}
catch (Exception e) {}
```

5. There can be more than one `catch` clause, but only one `finally` clause.

How It Works

If the code in a `try` block throws an exception, the program is stopped and the JVM starts to examine the `catch` clauses sequentially. The first `catch` block whose declared parameter type matches the class of a thrown exception, is executed. There need not be an absolute match, if the exception type in a `catch` clause is a superclass of a thrown exception, the match is found. For this reason, the `catch` clause with more specific exception types should be placed before those of a more generic nature. In fact, the compiler will not allow "superclass first" order; the following code

```
try {
    throw new NullPointerException ();
}
catch (RuntimeException r) {}
catch (NullPointerException n) {}
```

will make the compiler complain that the second catch is never reached.

After the statements in the matching catch block are executed, and if there is no finally block, execution resumes with the statements directly following the try-catch block. If there is a finally block, its code is executed, and the execution resumes after the try-catch block. Note that in neither case does control return to the interrupted try block; all statements in the try block following the one that caused the exception are skipped.

Special Mission of the `finally` Clause

There are some actions that have to be performed, regardless of how the try-catch block ends. If a resource is in use, it has to be released. The code performing such actions either has to be duplicated in each and every catch statement or to be written once, after the try-catch block. The latter decision, however, introduces another problem: your critical mission code could be bypassed with the help of some other unfortunately placed flow control statements, such as return in the catch block. Any exception you don't catch will result in the same effect.

The finally statement serves to enclose code that is guaranteed to be called once control enters a try statement. Statements in the finally block will be executed under any conceivable circumstance:

- If there was no exception in the try block
- If there was an exception caught by a catch block
- If there was an exception not caught by a catch block
- If there was an exception in the catch block itself
- If there was a return statement in the catch block

There is, however, one very special case when the finally block will not be executed. If there is System.exit() call in the catch block, your program will terminate immediately after the control reached it. In this case the finally block will not be executed.

Exception Complications

To complete (and complicate) the picture, let's consider what happens if an exception is thrown in a catch or finally block.

There are a few scenarios in which this may happen. It can be the result of calling another method. The code in a catch/finally block may throw an exception as an indicator of some other problem. In any case, the result is that the old exception is "forgotten," and the last one thrown propagates from a method. Particularly, if an exception is thrown in a `catch` block, the `catch` block is stopped and the `finally` block, if any, is executed. Note that other `catch` blocks will not catch an exception that occurred in one of them. `Catch` blocks in a `try-catch-finally` structure catch an exception only if it occurs in the `try` block, not in other `catch` blocks! After the `finally` block is finished, method execution stops, control is returned to the calling method, and the exception thrown in the `catch` block is propagated. If the `finally` block itself throws an exception, both previous exceptions are forgotten, and the last one is propagated.

Travel Advisory

Obscuring earlier exceptions is seldom useful. You can prevent this by enclosing problem code in the `finally` block in another `try-catch` block.

Checked and Unchecked Exceptions

```
Throwable              |
|                      | checked
+-Exception            |
|                      |
|  +-RuntimeException  |
|                      | unckecked
+-Error                |
```

Conceptually, all exceptions fall into two categories: "checked," represented by descendants of `Throwables` that are not subclasses of the `Error` and the `RuntimeException` classes, and unchecked, descendants of `Error` and `RuntimeException` classes. The compiler will treat code with exceptions of these two groups differently, and it will check if all checked exceptions (that's why they are called checked!) are properly handled; namely, they must be either caught in a method or declared in a method's `throws` clause. Unchecked exceptions are exempted from such control.

But why an exemption? Why does Java allow some exceptions to be ignored and possibly cause an application's death?

Exceptions are caught so an application can recover and continue its work. Therefore, an exception should be caught if it is either of the following:

1. Reasonable to expect an exception to be thrown
2. Reasonable and possible to recover from the exception

Instances of the classes in the `RuntimeException` branch are violators of the first rule. You remember that this hierarchy branch is designated to indicate flaws in a program that should be cleared out during debugging, for example "index out of bounds." Such exceptions are not supposed to appear in a final version. If they are, it means the program itself contains an error and its quit is quite reasonable.

Instances of the `Error` class and its descendants violate the second rule. They represent malfunctions in the environment an application relies on. It means that the application itself cannot be guaranteed to work reliably from this point on and should terminate. Mission-critical applications that are never supposed to crash may want to wrap `Errors`, but it is far from a typical approach.

In contrast, `Exceptions` meet both conditions and are checked. They represent problems that you as a programmer cannot prevent but can foresee and work out. An example is the `FileNotFoundException` exception.

If all exceptions were checked, the compiler would have to insist that almost every Java statement be enclosed in a `try` block, since `Errors` can occur at any time and `runtimeExceptions` can be thrown by many Java API methods. The "unchecked exceptions" concept saves a programmer's effort for more meaningful tasks than catching exceptions that either should not be caught or cannot occur.

Compile-Time vs. Runtime

The distinction between checked and unchecked exceptions exists during compilation only. It is the compiler that examines your code to check that certain exceptions are either caught or declared. At runtime, the JVM simply executes generated bytecode and doesn't care what class an exception belongs to for the very reason that the rules are already checked by the compiler.

The `throws` Clause

If a method doesn't have enough information to deal with an exception, it should not catch it—that would only hide the problem. The best approach is to allow an exception to be propagated into a calling method. However, in the case of a checked exception, Java wants to ensure that the programmers made such a decision deliberately, not that they simply forgot to deal with an exception. If a

Exam Tip

You do not need to memorize all classes in the exception hierarchy, but you should know the difference between checked and unchecked exceptions very well, especially that descendants of the `Exception` class are checked and that those of the `RuntimeException` class are not. Unfortunately, these class names are somewhat misleading and can cause confusion. Both `Exceptions` and `RuntimeExceptions` are exceptions, and indeed all exceptions are thrown at runtime! There are no exceptions thrown at compile time, only error messages. `RuntimeExceptions` are so called because they occur due to errors inside your application and, therefore, inside the Java runtime system (remember that your Java programs are executed in the JVM address pool). When your program violates the semantics of the Java language, the Java runtime system cannot perform its function and reports an error; for example, `ClassCastException` or `IndexOutOfBoundsException`. In contrast, `Exceptions` occur due to problems outside of your program (such as the above-mentioned "file not found" problem or `ServerNotActiveException`) or problems that don't prevent the runtime system from executing your program (for example, `InterruptedException`).

Travel Assistance

The questions of when to throw an exception and when not to and whether to throw a checked or unchecked exception are not exam objectives, but it is important for any Java programmer to know the answer. There is an excellent article on this subject, "Designing with Exceptions" by Bill Venners, on **http://www.artima.com/designtechniques/desexcept.html.**

checked exception is not caught in a `try-catch` block, it must be declared in the `throws` clause of the method. For example:

```
void someMethod () throws AWTException, IOException
```

Note:

- There can be more than one exception in a list, separated by commas.
- Although only checked exceptions need to be declared, it is not a compile-time error to declare an unchecked exception. The compiler will not insist that a calling method deal with an unchecked exception mentioned in the invoked method's `throws` clause.
- It is possible to declare an exception, checked or unchecked, which is not thrown in a method (this will allow overriding methods to throw extra exceptions not thrown in a super class's method (see the "Restrictions on Throwing Exceptions" section)). If a checked exception is declared but never thrown, the compiler will nevertheless insist that the calling method deal with such an exception.

Restrictions on Throwing Exceptions

Even though any `Throwable` object can legally appear in the `throw` statement, there are restrictions on the type of exceptions that can be thrown by a method participating in contract relationships: a method overriding another method and a method implementing a method in an interface. These methods can only throw checked exceptions specified in the `throws` clause of the overridden or implemented method or derived from those specified exceptions. More elaborately, such methods can throw the following:

- Any exception declared in the `throws` clause of an overridden or implemented method
- Any exception derived from these exceptions
- Any unchecked exception
- No exception at all

They cannot throw the following:

- A more generic checked exception
- A checked exception from another hierarchical branch

The explanation behind this rule is that these methods can substitute a method called by another method. The `catch` clause in a calling method will automatically catch all derived exceptions provided by your, say, overriding version. However, any other exceptions could sneak through as uncaught exception and cause an application death.

Conversely, overloaded methods cannot substitute each other, and there are no restrictions on the exception types overloaded methods can throw.

These restrictions are not applied to unchecked exceptions because unchecked exceptions represent either major `Errors` that stop the program and therefore break all contracts anyway, or `RuntimeExceptions` that are not supposed to be thrown in a correct program.

Exam Tip

The main point of this exam objective is the fact that overriding methods can throw only the same or more specific checked exceptions that an over-ridden method declares, whereas overloading methods are free to throw any exceptions.

Exceptions in Constructors, Initializers, and Finalizers

There are no restrictions on exceptions thrown by constructors. A constructor may throw any exception not thrown by a superclass's constructor. Of course, if it is a checked exception, it has to be declared in the constructor's `throws` clause.

However, there is another restriction. Unlike a method calling some other method, a subclass's constructor cannot catch an exception thrown by a super-class's constructor it calls. Remember, a call to a superclass's constructor must be the first statement in a subclass constructor; for this reason, it cannot be wrapped in a `try-catch` block. For example:

```
public subClass () { // subclass's constructor
   try {
      super();
   }
   catch (Exception e) {
      // some code here
   }
}
```

will raise a compiler error.

If you do not explicitly call any superclass constructor, the compiler will pro-vide such a call implicitly. Superclass's no-args constructor will be called and, of course, this call will not be wrapped in a `try-catch` block either. Thus, there is no way for a subclass constructor to catch an exception thrown by a superclass's constructor. This yields the rule that a subclass's constructor must declare all checked exceptions declared in the `throws` clause of a superclass's constructor it calls, whether explicitly or implicitly.

(Note: If a constructor terminates by throwing an exception, the object it attempted to create is immediately eligible for garbage collection. If you tried to assign a reference to it to some variable, such as:

```
try {
    someClass sc = new someClass();
} catch {...}
```

the assignment will fail and your variable's value will be left as is. From the programmer's point of view, no new object will be created.)

Regarding exceptions in initializers, the *Java Language Specification* states (section 8.6): "An instance initializer of a named class may not throw a checked exception unless that exception or one of its superclasses is explicitly declared in the `throws` clause of each constructor of its class and the class has at least one explicitly declared constructor. An instance initializer in an anonymous class can throw any exceptions."

However, this behavior is not implemented in JDK 1.2 or 1.3. If an initializer, instance, or static, throws a checked exception, the compiler will give an error message even if all constructors declare this exception in their `throws` clauses. This problem is listed by Sun as bug # 4409174 and is said to be corrected in JDK 1.4.

Like constructors, your `finalize()` methods are free to throw any exception but all exceptions will be trapped by GC mechanism and will not be reported to your program; neither will they prevent the object from being garbage collected.

CHECKPOINT

✔ **Objective 7.01** Write code using **if** and **switch** statements and identify legal argument types for these statements.

- The condition of the `if-else` statement must evaluate to the `boolean` type.
- In the `if-else` statement, an `else` block always belongs to the innermost `if` to which it may possibly belong.

- In the switch structure, an expression in the switch statement must be represented by a value of byte, char, short, or int type.
- In the switch structure, case-expression must be represented by a set of unique integer constant expressions whose values are known at compile time and fit in the range of the switch type expression.
- There can be one optional default clause in the switch structure, which doesn't have to be the last statement.

✔ **Objective 7.02** Write code using all forms of loops including labeled and unlabeled use of **break** and **continue**, and state the values taken by loop control variables during and after loop execution.

- All parts in the for loop are optional and can be omitted.
- Initialization and update sections of the for loop can be written as single expressions or as a series of expressions separated by commas. An argument in the while and do/while loops must be an expression that evaluates to a boolean type.
- The do/while loop body will be executed at least once.
- An unlabeled break can appear in switch, for, while, and do/while statements.
- A labeled break can appear inside for, while, do/while loops or inside a compound Java statement preceded by a label.
- The continue statement can appear inside of for, while, and do/while loops.
- Label names are subject to the same rules as other identifiers. In particular, they cannot start with a number, and they cannot be Java reserved words.

✔ **Objective 7.03** Write code that makes proper use of exceptions and exception handling clauses (**try, catch, finally**) and declares methods and overriding methods that throw exceptions.

- In the try-catch construct, try is a mandatory part and cannot be omitted.
- Both the catch and finally clauses are optional and can be omitted. However, they cannot both be omitted.
- Try-catch-finally clauses, if present, must be in that order.
- There can be more than one catch clause, but there can only be one finally clause.
- Statements in the finally block will be executed whether there was an exception in the try block or not and whether it was caught by the catch block or not.

- Neither the `return` statement nor an exception thrown in the `catch` block prevents the `finally` block from executing.
- A call to the `System.exit()` method in the `catch` block prevents the `finally` block from executing.
- Checked exceptions must be either caught in a `try-catch` block or declared in a method's `throws` clause.
- An overriding method can only throw checked exceptions specified in the `throws` clause of the overridden method or exceptions derived from those.
- Overloading methods can throw any exceptions.

REVIEW QUESTIONS

1. What will be the result of an attempt to compile and run the following code?

```
public class Demo {
   public static void main(String[] args) {
      int i = 1;
      if (i >= 0)
         if (i >= 2)
            if (i >= 4)
               System.out.println ("big number");
         else
            System.out.println ("not so big number");
      else
         System.out.println ("small number");
   }
}
```

    A. the compiler error "if without else"
    B. "not so big number" is printed
    C. "small number" is printed
    D. no output

2. What will be the output if you attempt to compile and run the following code?

```
public class Demo {
   public static void main(String[] args) {
      char test = 3;
```

```
    switch (test) {
      case 3 :
          System.out.println ("third case");
      default:
          System.out.println ("default");
      case 2 :
          System.out.println ("second case");
          break;
      case 1 :
          System.out.println ("first case");
    }
  }
}
```

A. the compiler error "incorrect order of case clauses in the switch statement"

B. third case

C. third case, default, second case,

D. third case, default, second case, first case

3. Given the following code, which of the following expressions as xxx will *not* cause a compiler error? (Select two.)

```
byte test = 32;
byte b = 32;
final byte fb=32;
final char c=32;
String s = "32";
switch (b) {
  case 31:
  case xxx:
      System.out.println(b);
}
```

A. b

B. fb

C. s

D. c

E. 132

F. fb − 1

4. Assuming that all variables not defined in `for` loops have already been properly defined, which `for` loops will compile? (Select three.)

   A. `for (int i=1, j=2; i< 5; i++, j++) {}`
   B. `for (int i, i< 5; i++) ;`
   C. `for (int i=0, int j=2; i< 5; i++, j++) {}`
   D. `for (i=1; k < 5; j++) {}`
   E. `for (i=1; j++) {}`
   F. `for (;;j++) {}`

5. Given the following code, predict the output.

```
public class Demo {
   public static void main(String[] args) {
      first:for (int i=1 ;  i < 3  ; i++) {
         System.out.print ("\n i= " + i);
         second:for (int j=0 ; j < 5 ; j++) {
            switch (j) {
               case 1:
               case 2:
                  continue first;
               case 3:
                  break first;
            }
            System.out.print (" j= " + j);
         }
      }
   }
}
```

   A. `i=1 j=0`
   B. `i=1 j=0`
   C. `i=2 j=0`
   D. `i=1 j=0 j=1`
   E. `i=2 j=0 j=1`
   F. `i=1 j=0 j=1 j=3`
       `i=2 j=0 j=1 j=3`

6. Which statements are true? (Select two.)

   A. If an exception is thrown in `try`, and the matching `catch` block is empty, the exception will not be considered caught and will be propagated from a method.

   B. If an exception is thrown in `try` and there is a `finally` block but no `catch`, the exception will not be considered caught and will be propagated from a method.

   C. Only checked exceptions can be caught by the `try-catch-finally` construct.

   D. If an exception is thrown in a `try` block, whether it is caught or not, the statement in the `try` block after one causing an exception will not be executed.

7. What will be the result of attempts to compile and run the following code?

```
public class Demo {
    public static void main(String[] args) {
        someMethod(0);
        System.out.println ("main");
    }


    public static void someMethod(int inputParam) {
        try {
            if (inputParam == 0) throw new RuntimeException();
                System.out.println ("try");
        }
        catch (RuntimeException r) {

            System.out.println ("catch");
        }
        finally {
            System.out.println ("finally");
        }
        System.out.println ("after try");
    }
}
```

A. `try catch finally after try main`
B. `catch finally`
C. `catch finally after try main`
D. `nothing is printed, a RuntimeException in main`

8. Given the following code, predict the output.

```
public class Demo {
   public static void main(String[] args) {
      someMethod(3);
   }
   public static void someMethod(int inputParam) {
      try {
         if (inputParam > 0 )
            throw new IllegalArgumentException();
         if (inputParam == 3)
            throw new IllegalArgumentException();
      }
      catch (RuntimeException r) {
         System.out.println ("catch");
      }
      finally {
         System.out.println ("finally");
      }
   }
}
```

A. `catch`
B. `catch finally`
C. `catch finally catch finally`
D. `catch catch finally`

9. Given the following exception class hierarchy, which method declarations can be legally substituted for xxxx? (Select two.)

```
Throwable
|
+-Exception
   |
```

```
   +-IOException
      |
      +-FileNotFoundException

import java.io.*;
public class Demo {
   xxxx {
      throw new IOException ();
   }
}
```

A. `void someMethod() throws Exception`
B. `void someMethod() throws IOException`
C. `void someMethod()`
D. `void someMethod() throws FileNotFoundException`

10. Given the following exception class hierarchy, which of the following method declarations can be legally substituted for xxxx? (Select four.)

```
Throwable
|
+-Exception
   |
   +-IOException
   |
   +-IllegalAccessException
   |
   +-RuntimeException
      |
      +— IllegalArgumentException
import java.io.*;
class A {
   void someMethod(short s) throws IOException {}
}

class B extends A {
   xxxx
}
```

A. `void someMethod (short s) throws Throwable {}`
B. `void someMethod (short s) {}`
C. `void someMethod (char c) throws Exception {}`
D. `void someMethod (short s) throws IOException,`
  `IllegalArgumentException {}`
E. `void someMethod (short s) throws IOException,`
  `FileNotFoundException {}`
F. `void someMethod (short s) throws`
  `IllegalAccessException {}`

REVIEW ANSWERS

1. **C** This `else` block belongs to the second `if`, whose condition is false, so it is executed. A is wrong because the `if` statement without `else` is legal. B is wrong because the `else` will not be reached since the `else` clause for the previous `if` is executed. D is wrong because there is output (see the explanation for the C option).

2. **C** There is a `break` in the second `case`, so control exits the `switch` structure. A is wrong because `case` clauses do not have to be placed in any specific order. B is wrong because there is no `break` in the first `case` block, so the execution falls through other `case` blocks. D is wrong because there is the `break` statement in the second `case`, so the statements in the last `case` block are not executed.

3. **B D** A is wrong because only literals and variables defined as `final` can appear in a `case` expression. C is wrong because `String` variables cannot be used in a `case` expression. E is wrong because the variable in the `switch` expression has the `byte` type. That means that all `case` expressions must fit in the `byte` range −128 through +127. F is wrong because the result of the expression is 31, which causes the compiler error "duplicate `case` label."

4. **A D** B is wrong because sections in the `for` loop must be separated by a semicolon, not a comma. C is wrong because there cannot be two declaration expressions in an initialization section of the `for` loop. E is wrong because any part of the `for` loop can be omitted, but separating semicolons must be present.

5. **B** A is wrong because there are no statements that could stop the first loop after the first iteration. C is wrong because `case 1` falls through, and the `continue` statement in the second `case` is executed, starting the next iteration of the outer loop. The line "`j=1`" will never be printed. D is wrong for the same reason: statement that prints "`j=1`" and "`j=3`" will never be executed.

6. **B** **D**   A is wrong because if a catch expression declares a class or a superclass of an exception thrown in a `try` block, the exception will be caught
   even if the `catch` block is empty. C is wrong because any exception, checked
   or unchecked, can be caught by a `catch` clause with proper declaration.

7. **C**   A is wrong because after an exception is thrown, all other statements in
   a `try` block are skipped, so "`try`" will not be printed. B is wrong because
   after an exception is caught in a `try-catch-finally` structure, the next
   statement after `try-catch-finally` is executed, so "`after try`" will be
   printed. Control is then transferred into the main method, so "`main`" will
   be printed. D is wrong because `RuntimeException` is caught in
   `someMethod` and is not propagated in the main method.

8. **B**   A is wrong because the `finally` block is executed whether an exception was thrown or not and whether it was caught or not; "`finally`" will
   be in the output. C is wrong because after `RuntimeException` is thrown,
   control will not be returned in the try block, so the second
   `RuntimeException` will not be thrown. There cannot be two "`catch`"
   and two "`finally`" in the output. D is wrong because at most one `catch`
   block in a `try-catch-finally` structure will be executed; there is no way
   to execute two of them.

9. **A** **B**   C is wrong because the checked exception `IOException` is thrown
   and not caught in `someMethod`. In such a case, it must be specified in the
   method's `throws` clause. D is wrong because `FileNotFoundException`
   is a subclass of `IOException` and specifying it in the `throws` clause will
   not help. Either the exact class of a thrown checked exception or its superclass must be specified to make a method compile.

10. **B** **C** **D** **E**   A is wrong because an overriding method cannot throw a
    more generic checked exception than the overridden method. B is correct
    because nn overriding method may not throw any exception at all. C is cor-
    rect because `someMethod` doesn't override `someMethod` from the parent
    class because it has a different signature. Therefore, it can legally throw any
    exception. D is correct because `IllegalArgumentException` is an
    unchecked exception and can be thrown in an overriding method. E is cor-
    rect because `FileNotFoundException` is a subclass of `IOException`
    declared in a overridden method. F is wrong because `IllegalAccess`
    `Exception` is a checked exception that is not a subclass of `IOException`
    and therefore cannot be thrown in an overriding method.

Threads

	NEWBIE	SOME EXPERIENCE	EXPERT
ETA	20 hours	10 hours	4 hours

Support for the multithreading is one of the Java language's most important features. Put simply, a *thread*, which is short for *thread of control*, is an asynchronous path of execution. It is a lightweight process that runs in the context of a program sharing the same process space and hence all the data and common resources. Programs that can run more than one thread at once are said to be *multithreaded*.

Every thread in Java is represented by an instance of the `java.lang.Thread` class. This class defines methods to create, run, and manage threads. Any class can support multithreading by simply extending the `Thread` class and overriding the `run()` method that has the signature `public void run()`.

Since most computers do not have multiple processors, the Java Virtual Machine (JVM) uses a mechanism in which each thread gets a chance to run for a little while, then activates another thread. The part of the Virtual Machine that manages threads is called the *thread scheduler*. New threads that are created by a program are handed over to the scheduler using the `start()` method that indicates to the scheduler that the thread is ready to run. The scheduler then calls the `run()` method directly.

Extending the `Thread` class may not be the best solution in some situations. Since Java doesn't support multiple inheritance, one can only extend or inherit from a single parent class. As a remedy to this problem, Java also provides the `java.lang.Runnable` interface, which also defines the `run()` method. A class can implement the `Runnable` interface and provide an implementation of the `public void run()` method. Another reason to use the `Runnable` interface is that you may need to run an object multiple times. As you will soon learn, once a thread has stopped, nothing will revive it. However, you can create as many threads as you want by using a `Runnable` instance.

Exam Tip	
Even the `Thread` class implements the `Runnable` interface.	

Objective 8.01

Instantiate and Start New Threads Using Both `java.lang.Thread` and `java.lang.Runnable`

The first method of creating a thread is to simply extend from the `Thread` class. The `Thread` class is defined in the `java.lang` package. Since this package is implicitly imported into every Java program by the compiler, an explicit import statement is not necessary.

```
class SimpleThread extends Thread {
    public void run() {
        // Include code here to get the work done by the thread.
    }
}
```

The second way of creating a thread involves implementing the Runnable interface. Implementing this interface lets you make an arbitrary object the target of a thread. The same class can be rewritten as the following:

```
class SimpleRunnable implements Runnable {
    public void run()  {
        // Include code here to get the work done by the thread.
    }
}
```

The only difference between the two methods is that by implementing the Runnable interface, there is greater flexibility in the creation of the class Simple Thread, since the opportunity still exists for the class to extend another class if need be.

Now that we have defined a thread-capable class, let's create the actual thread object. The java.lang.Thread class has the following overloaded constructors:

- Thread()
- Thread(Runnable target)
- Thread(Runnable target, String name)
- Thread(String name)
- Thread(ThreadGroup group, Runnable target)
- Thread(ThreadGroup group, Runnable target, String name)
- Thread(ThreadGroup group, String name)

For now, we'll look at only the first four and ignore the ones that take the ThreadGroup object as an argument. From the list of constructors, it is evident that a thread can also be initiated using a Runnable reference. The string argument *name* is a user-friendly name that can be assigned to a thread as an identifier. Using the definition of our SimpleThread and SimpleRunnable classes, we can instantiate a thread object in any of the following ways:

```
// No-arg constructor
Thread t1 = new SimpleThread();
```

```
// Using SimpleThread reference as a target
Thread t3 = new Thread( new SimpleThread());

// Using a name for the thread.
Thread t4 = new Thread( new SimpleThread(), "My first thread");

// Using SimpleRunnable as a target
Runnable target = new SimpleRunnable();
Thread t4 = new Thread( target );
```

Travel Advisory

Using a subclass of `Thread` as if it were a plain `Runnable` is bad programming style. For `t3` and `t4`, we could have used `SimpleRunnable` instead of `SimpleThread`. The example here only demonstrates the different approaches that are *plausible*. However, in real life, avoid using a subclass of `Thread` in place of a `Runnable` target.

After a thread is created, it needs to be started. A newly born thread remains idle until it is explicitly submitted to the thread scheduler by calling the `start()` method. Calling this method on a thread object indicates to the scheduler that the thread is ready to run. The scheduler then begins running the thread by executing the `run()` method defined by the target object. Once the `run()` method returns either normally or abnormally, the scheduler marks the thread execution as complete. Later in this chapter, we will look at some other methods you can use to control the thread's progress while it is running. Once a thread has completed running, it cannot be restarted with the `start()` method. You can however, create another `Thread` object with the same target if you must run the thread again.

Travel Advisory

It is perfectly valid to call the `run()` method directly on the target object. However, such a call is just a plain vanilla synchronous method call; that is, the control is transferred to the method, the method executes and the control returns to the next line in the program sequentially. Whereas if the `run()` method is called using the `start()` method, a new path of execution will be started for the `run()` method: the call to the `start()` method will return right away and the thread will start executing at the same time.

The following example captures all the concepts we have discussed so far—defining, instantiating, and running a simple thread:

```
// Approach 1 : Extending the java.lang.Thread class
class SimpleThread extends Thread {
    public void run() {
        System.out.println( "SimpleThread running ... ");
        // Include code here to get the work done by the thread.
    }
}

class SimpleRunnable implements Runnable {
    public void run() {
        System.out.println( "SimpleRunnable running ... ");
        // Include code here to get the work done by the thread.
    }
}

public class ThreadDemo {
    public static void main( String s[] ) {
        // No-arg constructor
        Thread t1 = new SimpleThread();

        // Using SimpleRunnable as a target
        Runnable target = new SimpleRunnable();
        Thread t2 = new Thread( target );

        // Using a name for the thread.
        Thread t3 = new Thread( new SimpleRunnable(), "My first
thread");
        t1.start();
        t2.start();
        t3.start();
    }
}
```

The following output is produced by this program:

```
SimpleThread running ...
SimpleRunnable running ...
SimpleRunnable running ...
```

Thread States

Each thread also has a state. The state of a thread specifies its condition with regard to its use of system resources and its ability to run. Before we proceed to looking at various methods that can be used to control a running thread, it is imperative that we understand the state transitions in a typical thread lifecycle.

New Thread

A new thread is just an empty thread object that has not been assigned any system resources. When a thread is new, you can only start it. A newly created thread represents the first stage in the thread lifecycle. It is important not to get confused between a Thread object and an actual thread. All threads created by Java applications have an associated underlying Thread object, but the converse may not be always true. For instance, threads that have not yet started or threads that have completed executing the run() method will not have an associated running thread.

Ready to Run or Runnable

Once the start() method is called on the thread, it is promoted to "ready to run" state. The scheduler will eventually pick this thread and execute its run() method. How soon the thread starts running depends on how many threads are currently running and how many more are in this state waiting to run. Scheduling is a complicated process and often depends on vendor implementation and the underlying operating system. However, it is guaranteed that once the start() method is called, the run() method will eventually be executed unless the Virtual Machine itself terminates.

In addition to the freshly started threads, a running thread can also revisit this state if one of the following conditions occur:

- If the current thread calls the yield() method on its Thread object to allow any other waiting threads to run. If no other threads are waiting, the thread may continue to run without being temporarily stopped.
- If the execution is temporarily stopped by the scheduler. This can happen if another thread of higher priority is ready to run and the scheduler honors thread priority. This can also happen if the scheduler uses a time-sliced algorithm and the current thread has exhausted its quota of CPU time. Details about thread scheduling and priority is covered in more detail later in this chapter.
- The thread just woke up from a sleep() method after the sleeping time expired or after being interrupted while sleeping.

Running

Running is the state of thread in action. While running, the thread is executing the statements in the `run()` method. In this state, the thread enjoys full access to all system resources and data. Note that on a multiprocessor system, more than one thread may be running at the same time.

Blocked

Often a running thread transitions to this state when it is waiting for an event to occur. Examples of such events include waiting for a monitor on an object, I/O operations, and network communication. Such methods may involve response latency, and the thread has to wait until the operation returns either normally or abnormally. The thread can become runnable again when the event occurs. While being blocked, the thread may or may not continue to utilize CPU cycles and any other system resources. This could depend a little on the resource being waited on and the hardware platform; some blocking operations on some platforms are implemented using polling. Nevertheless, blocks are generally very efficient. For instance, a thread blocked on a `ServerSocket` on Unix-based servers consumes virtually no CPU cycles, in the order of a few seconds per day! It is worth noting that a blocked thread can only be reactivated through the same route that blocked it. For instance, if a thread is blocked on input, it can start running again only when the input operation completes either normally or abnormally.

Waiting

When a running thread calls `wait()`, the thread enters a waiting state for a particular object on which `wait()` was called. A thread continues to wait until it gets notified about the specific event by another thread using `notify()` or `notifyAll()` calls. If a thread is waiting for an object lock that was owned by another thread, the other thread must have relinquished the lock. Smart thread schedulers can make use of this opportunity to run other threads. In a multithreaded application, there can be more than one waiting thread at any given time. You will see more on `wait()` and `notify()` interactions later in this chapter.

Sleeping

When the `sleep()` method is called on the thread, it remains idle for a specific duration or until it is awakened by an interrupt. When sleeping, the thread is not using any CPU time, but it can retain the ownership of any object locks it may be holding.

Dead

A thread dies when the `run()` method completes either normally or abnormally. Uncaught exceptions can terminate the `run()` method causing thread death. Either way, after the thread is dead, what remains is the `Thread` object. Once the thread has completed execution, the `start()` method cannot be called on the same object. However, you can create another thread using this object as the target. It is legal to access attributes and methods on this object.

A thread can be asked if it is alive. The `isAlive()` method will return `true` if the thread has been started and not stopped. It will return `false` if the thread has been stopped. You cannot find out if a live thread is runnable or blocked or if a runnable thread is actually running. In cases where the `isAlive()` returns `false`, you cannot differentiate between a thread that has not yet become runnable and one that has already died.

The different thread states and their state transitions are illustrated here.

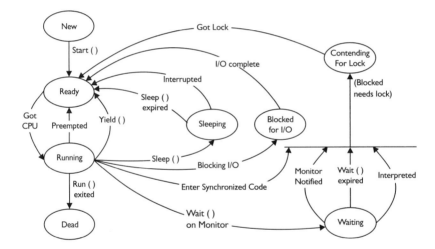

Recognize Conditions That Might Prevent a Thread From Executing

Objective 8.02

Several conditions can stop a running thread either temporarily or permanently. These can either be a system stimulus (like the scheduler preempting a running thread), an explicit method call on the thread object, or exiting the `run()` method. The `java.lang.Thread` class provides several methods that can be used to control the behavior of a running thread. Let's examine all such methods as well as the other conditions that can bring a running thread to a grinding halt.

Calling the `sleep()` Method

Java defines two overloaded `sleep()` methods that can be used to sedate a thread:

```
public static void sleep(long millis) throws InterruptedException
public static void sleep(long millis, int nanos) throws
InterruptedException
```

Both methods make the current thread (note the static modifier) sleep for the specified duration. A sleeping thread is ready to run once the specified period elapses or if it is interrupted in between, whichever happens first. When a thread goes to sleep it does not give up the ownership of any monitors (a.k.a. locks).

Interrupting Using the `interrupt()` Method

In a multithreaded environment, it may be desirable to have one thread control the other. The `Thread` class defines the method `public void interrupt()`, which sends a message to a particular thread disturbing its running sequence. An `InterruptedException` will be thrown when a thread is waiting or sleeping and another thread interrupts it using the `interrupt()` method. In fact, there is no language requirement that a thread that is interrupted should terminate; interrupting a thread only grabs its attention. For example, blocking I/O may throw an exception when it is interrupted. Interrupts are simply ignored until the operation unblocks.

Every thread has a status flag that indicates whether that thread has been interrupted by another thread. Calling the `interrupt()` method on a particular thread simply sets this status flag to true. The thread becomes ready for execution straightaway if it is sleeping or waiting when `interrupt()` is called. When it executes, the `wait()` or `sleep()` implementation checks the interrupt flag; if set, it is cleared and an `InterruptedException` is thrown.

Since the `InterruptedException` is a checked exception, the code has to handle the exception one way or the other. The interrupted thread can decide how to react to the interruption by placing appropriate actions into the `catch` clause that deals with the `InterruptedException`. The statements in the exception handler will be executed, and the interrupt status flag on the thread will be reset. If the target thread was sleeping, waiting, blocked for I/O, or busy doing some lengthy calculation, it will not even know that it was interrupted by another thread. In this case, the Java Virtual Machine will just set the interrupted flag of the target thread to be true.

The `Thread` class provides two very similar methods to check the interrupted state of a thread: `interrupted()` and `isInterrupted()`. The `interrupted()` method is a static method that checks whether the *current* thread has been interrupted. This method resets the interrupted flag on the thread. On the other hand, the isInterrupted() is an instance method that checks whether *any* thread has been interrupted. This method does not change the interrupted status of the thread on which it has been called.

Graceful Threads that `yield()` to Others

Calling the `yield()` method causes the currently executing thread (note the static modifier in the method signature: `static void yield()`) to temporarily pause and allow other threads to execute. The thread that yields moves back to "ready to run" state, relinquishing the CPU time. This will give a chance to the thread scheduler to attend to other threads. If no other threads are in the "ready to run" state, the yielded thread might start running immediately. An application that does not yield will appear to run fine on JVM with native, pre-emptive threads, but will fail miserably on a JVM with green threads. (The green threads package that is used by some versions Java on Solaris keeps a running thread active until a higher-priority thread awakes and takes control). This represents a bug that can easily catch out unwary developers.

A graceful thread always yields at regular intervals so that other "ready to run" threads get a chance to execute. The following example illustrates the effects of yielding:

```
class SelfishThread extends Thread {
    public void run() {
        for ( short i=1 ; i < 6 ; i++ ) {
            System.out.println( this.getName() + "..." + i);
            //if ( i%2 == 0 )
            //    yield();
        }
    }
}


class SelfishThreadDemo {
    public static void main( String s[] ) {
        SelfishThread t1 = new SelfishThread();
        t1.setName( "Ping" );

        SelfishThread t2 = new SelfishThread();
        t2.setName( "Bing" );
```

```
        t1.start();
        t2.start();
    }
}
```

When the program is compiled and run as is, it produces the output that clearly indicates thread t1 using up all the CPU time and not giving any chance to thread t2 to run until it finishes. The "Bing" thread gets to run only after the "Ping" thread completes all the iterations.

```
Ping...1
Ping...2
Ping...3
Ping...4
Ping...5
Bing...1
Bing...2
Bing...3
Bing...4
Bing...5
```

Now let's uncomment the two commented lines within the run() method. These two statements will cause the current thread to pause execution by calling yield(). Each thread runs for a while and yields to the other. When the revised code is compiled and run, the difference is hard to miss. Both the threads run with great friendship and goodwill as the output suggests:

```
Ping...1
Ping...2
Bing...1
Ping...3
Bing...2
Ping...4
Bing...3
Ping...5
Bing...4
Bing...5
```

Thread Priority and Scheduling

The Virtual Machine has a component called thread scheduler that manages all the threads of a program and decides which ones are to be run. The *Java Language Specification* leaves certain aspects of scheduling up to the JVM implementation. Popular scheduling algorithms can be broadly classified as follows:

- **Time slicing**   Each thread gets a quota of CPU time to run. Once a thread exhausts its quota, scheduler moves it out of CPU and allows the next thread to run. When all the threads have been run, the cycle repeats in round-robin fashion.
- **Non-time-sliced**   The priority of the thread is used to decide which one gets to run first. When a higher priority thread is ready to run, it pre-empts any lower priority thread that may be running.

Priority-based scheduling allows the programmers to control the order of thread execution. When selecting a new thread to run, the JVM generally picks the highest-priority thread from the ready to run pool. There is, however, no guarantee that the highest priority runnable thread is the one that is executing. Java defines three integer constants to represent ranges of thread priority: Thread.MIN_PRIORITY, Thread.NORM_PRIORITY, and Thread.MAX_PRIORITY. You set thread priorities with the setPriority() method, which takes an integer argument, and you examine them with the getPriority() method. When code running in some thread creates a new Thread object, the new thread has its priority initially set equal to the priority of the creating thread. When unspecified, all newly created threads will have their priority set equal to Thread.NORM_PRIORITY. On non-time-sliced systems, cooperating threads of equal priority should periodically call the yield() method to enable their peers to proceed smoothly.

Travel Advisory

Any attempt to set a priority value that is either less than Thread.MIN_PRIORITY or greater than Thread.MAX_PRIORITY results in IllegalArgumentException at runtime.

The following example program illustrates the effects of thread priority. Four thread objects are created in the main() method with different priorities. All the four threads are started sequentially in their order of creation. The output produced confirms that the scheduler executes the threads based on their priority value, starting with the highest, overriding any other order.

```
class PriorityThread extends Thread {
    private String myName;
    PriorityThread( String sName, int nPriority ) {
        myName = sName ;
        setPriority( nPriority );
    }

    public void run() {
        System.out.println( myName + " with priority " +
getPriority() +  " running..." );
    }
}


public class PriorityDemo  {
    public static void main( String s[] )  {
        PriorityThread t1 = new PriorityThread("Thread #1",
Thread.MIN_PRIORITY);
        PriorityThread t2 = new PriorityThread("Thread #2",
Thread.MAX_PRIORITY);
        PriorityThread t3 = new PriorityThread("Thread #3",
Thread.MAX_PRIORITY - 2 );
        PriorityThread t4 = new PriorityThread("Thread #4",
Thrcad.NORM_PRIORITY);

        t1.start();
        t2.start();
        t3.start();
        t4.start();
    }
}
```

The program produces the following output:

```
Thread #2 with priority 10 running...
Thread #3 with priority 8 running...
Thread #4 with priority 5 running...
Thread #1 with priority 1 running...
```

Write Code Using synchronized, wait, notify, or notifyAll

As you saw in the previous section, Java's promise of platform independence falls flat on its face in the threads arena because of the idiosyncratic difficulties introduced by platforms on which the Virtual Machine might run. Because the behavior of threaded programs is not predictable, you can run into some treacherous problems, and your program may not produce consistent result as you may expect on different platforms. In this section, we will examine what can go wrong with threaded behavior and how you can deal with this in the programs. A typical multithreaded application involves more than one thread concurrently accessing some shared data and resources. What happens if two threads have access to the same object and each calls a method that modifies the state of the object? As you can imagine, such a scenario can lead to corruption of object state and any shared data.

The following program demonstrates a typical scenario in which multiple concurrent threads are trying to modify a shared resource, the object of type Account:

```
class Account {
    private int nBalance ;
    public Account()    { nBalance = 100 ; }
    public int getBalance()  { return nBalance ; }

    public void deposit( int nAmount ) {
        nBalance += nAmount ;
        Thread.yield();
    }

    public void withdraw( int nAmount ) {
        nBalance -= nAmount ;
        Thread.yield();
    }
}
```

The AccountDemo is a sample application that uses the Account class. It defines a run() method that characterizes a typical account transaction, a deposit and a withdrawal. The run() method also checks the validity of a pair of deposit/withdrawal transactions by comparing the balance before and after the transactions. If the amount of transactions is the same, the balance check should pass the test. If the balance test fails, it is an indication of thread collision; that is, either the withdraw() or deposit() method is being executed twice successively by both the threads, throwing the balance out of sync.

The main() function in the AccountDemo class simply instantiates two threads using the same object as the target. This way we ensure all the threads created using the same target will execute the same run() method and hence access the same instance of Account object held by the AccountDemo class. On a JVM without time-sliced threads, this demo will fail. Because AccountDemo does not yield, only one thread will run. To fix this, we have added calls to the yield() method in Account.deposit() after the addition, in Account.withdraw() before the subtraction, and in AccountDemo.run() between calls to deposit() and withdraw(). A yield() method in any other place will fix the threading but fail to demonstrate the problem on such JVMs:

```
// Demonstrates the effect of concurrent threads accessing
// a shared resource without synchronization.
public class AccountDemo  implements Runnable {
    private Account myAccount = new Account();

    public static void main ( String s[] ) {
        AccountDemo a1 = new AccountDemo();

        // Start two threads using the same target.
        Thread t1 = new Thread( a1 ) ;
        Thread t2 = new Thread( a1 ) ;

        System.out.println( "Starting thread 1 ");
        t1.start();

        System.out.println( "Starting thread 2 ");
        t2.start();
    }

    public void run() {
        // Save the balance for cross-checking after transactions.
        int beginBalance = myAccount.getBalance();
```

```
        for ( long i=0 ; i < 500000 ; i++ ) {
            // These two operations typify a transaction.
            myAccount.deposit( 200 );
            Thread.yield();
            myAccount.withdraw( 200 );

            // Inspect if the result of the transaction is consis-
tent.
            if ( myAccount.getBalance() != beginBalance )
                System.out.println( "Iteration # " + i +
                                        " Begin balance = " + beginBalance
                                + " End balance = " +
myAccount.getBalance());
        }
    }
}
```

Here is an output from a sample run:

```
Starting thread 1
Starting thread 2
Iteration # 6 Begin balance = 100 End balance = 300
Iteration # 25901 Begin balance = 100 End balance = 300
```

Notice that the program printed two lines. One indicates that on the sixth iteration, the beginning balance was not the same as ending balance. Similarly, the second line shows that on the 25901st iteration, the balance mismatch occurred again.

Travel Advisory

This program might produce different results when run multiple times on a same machine. What will be consistent, however, is that at least once the balance test will fail, indicating a thread collision.

This output shows that Java threads can interrupt each other in as small an increment as a single instruction. While thread 1 was about to execute the `with-draw()` method, it lost the CPU time, and thread 2 was allowed to run, which executed the `deposit()` method again. Two `deposit()` methods were executed successively (which made the balance 400). When either thread 1 or thread 2 next executed the `withdraw()` method, a balance mismatch occurred.

One reason the number of iterations was set to 500,000 is that this behavior is hard to capture. This program might execute flawlessly hundreds of times before seeing such pernicious behavior. The `for` loop in the `run()` method enables us to repeat the deposit/withdrawal transaction cycle a large number of times, thereby increasing the odds for a thread collision. In the absence of such a large number of repetitions, the `run()` method would finish executing within no time on today's powerful computers.

If each thread contained all of the data and methods required for its execution, thread collisions would never occur. In our example, this is equivalent to starting t1 and t2 with different copies of the `AccountDemo` object.

Travel Advisory

An atomic operation cannot be interrupted by another thread. Java does define at least a few atomic operations. In particular, assignment to variables of any type except `long` or `double` is atomic. You don't have to worry about a thread preempting a method in the middle of the assignment, but the *result* of the assignment may not become visible to other threads until the code synchronizes on the object containing the modified data. In practice, this means that you need to be careful about concurrent access for a method that does nothing but assignment. Floating-point operations are not considered atomic and are vulnerable to overstepping by concurrent threads.

True to form, Java has provided a way to protect shared objects from corruption by preventing interference or interruption while executing critical sections of code. This concept is called synchronization. Synchronization can best be understood if you imagine that each object has it own copy of its class's code and that, within each object, the code is divided into two groups: normal and synchronized.

Normal code places no restrictions on thread access to the object. Every line of normal code can be simultaneously executed by different threads in order to operate on the object. The advantage of normal code is its low overhead and potentially high performance. The `run()` method we've previously demonstrated is in this normal group: many threads can simultaneously use this method to operate on the same `Account` object. Unfortunately, when `run()` is used in this way, it corrupts the shared `Account` object. On the other hand, an object's synchronized code may only be used by one thread at a time. If multiple threads attempt to execute synchronized code for the same object, only one will be permitted to begin. All the others will wait until the first one is done. At that point, only one of the waiting threads is permitted to start executing the synchronized code block again.

Synchronization is achieved using object locks (also called *monitors*). In Java, every object has a lock. When a thread enters a synchronized block, it takes the ownership of the lock on a particular object (for a `synchronized` method, the lock is obtained on the `this` object). Any other thread trying to execute the same method detects that the object has already been locked, and waits patiently for the lock to be released. Once the thread holding the lock completes the execution of `synchronized` block of code, it relinquishes the lock, and one of the contending threads will grab it. Therefore, it goes on, in a highly serialized and disciplined fashion.

You can create synchronized code in either of two ways. The first is to add the `synchronized` modifier to a method. This makes all the code in the method synchronized and ensures thread safety for the entire method.

To demonstrate the effect of synchronization, the `AccountDemo` class is modified as follows. The entire `run()` method is declared as `synchronized` in this revised version:

```
public class SyncAccountDemo  implements Runnable {
    private Account myAccount = new Account();

    public static void main ( String s[] ) {
        SyncAccountDemo a1 = new SyncAccountDemo();

        Thread t1 = new Thread( a1 ) ;
        Thread t2 = new Thread( a1 ) ;

        System.out.println( "Starting thread 1 ");
        t1.start();
        System.out.println( "Starting thread 2 ");
        t2.start();
```

```
    }


    synchronized public void run() {
        int beginBalance = myAccount.getBalance();
        for ( long i=0 ; i < 500000 ; i++ ) {
            myAccount.deposit( 200 );
            myAccount.withdraw( 200 );
            if ( myAccount.getBalance() != beginBalance )
                System.out.println( "Iteration # " + i +
                                    " Begin balance = " + beginBalance
                                + " End balance = " +
myAccount.getBalance());
        }
    }
}
```

It is important to understand that synchronization is tied to an object, not to
the code. Multiple threads can all simultaneously execute the same synchronized
method as long as each is operating on a different object. However, multiple
threads cannot simultaneously execute even different synchronized methods if all
are operating on the same object.

This one modifier does the trick. When you run the program, you will notice
no output being produced that indicates balance mismatch. This means there
were no thread collisions. Here is what you will see:

```
Starting thread 1
Starting thread 2
```

Although we got the program to work, synchronizing the run() method
ruins the concurrency of the program, since no other thread can enter the method
until the current thread executes all the code. The second way to create synchronized code is more typically used and, as demonstrated next, achieves a finer gran-
ularity of object locking.

Imagine that you want to synchronize access to objects of a class that was not
designed for multithreaded access. That is, the class does not use synchronized
methods. Further, this class was not created by you, but by a third-party software
shop, and you do not have access to the source code. Thus, it is not possible for you
to add the synchronized qualifier to any of the methods within the class. In such
situations, you can use a synchronized(object) statement. Here, (object) is
a reference to the object being synchronized. All the code that needs to be thread

protected follow this statement enclosed in curly braces. This form of synchronization gives fine-grain control over exactly what you want to synchronize. In our example, since we are only interested in protecting the calls to the `withdraw()` and `deposit()` methods, we can synchronize the `Account` object only for these two statements. The revised code looks like this:

```java
public class Sync2AccountDemo  implements Runnable {
    private Account myAccount = new Account();

    public static void main ( String s[] ) {
        Sync2AccountDemo a1 = new Sync2AccountDemo();

        Thread t1 = new Thread( a1 ) ;
        Thread t2 = new Thread( a1 ) ;

        System.out.println( "Starting thread 1 ");
        t1.start();
        System.out.println( "Starting thread 2 ");
        t2.start();
    }
    public void run() {
        int beginBalance = myAccount.getBalance();
        for ( long i=0 ; i < 500000 ; i++ )
        {
            synchronized( myAccount )
            {
                myAccount.deposit( 200 );
                Thread.yield();
                myAccount.withdraw( 200 );
                if ( myAccount.getBalance() != beginBalance )
                    System.out.println( "Iteration # " + i +
                        " Begin balance = " + beginBalance +
" End balance = " + myAccount.getBalance());
            }
        }
    }
}
```

Note that this version produces a similar output as the `SyncAccountDemo` class. Like that class, it does not report any balance mismatch events, thereby confirming that there were no thread collisions. However, this way of synchronization is far more efficient and desirable since the duration for which the lock on the `myAccount` object is held has been made minimal. This means threads contending to acquire the lock on the same object will now wait for a shorter duration.

Communicating Between Threads to Avoid Race Conditions

That `java.lang.Object` class defines `wait()` and `notify()` methods that extend the functionality of threads. These methods serve as a channel of communication between the threads and can be extremely helpful when used in a scenario involving multiple cooperating threads. Interthread communication using `wait()` and `notify()` allows two threads to talk to each other about either an occurrence of or a lack of an event. In this way, the thread that is interested in processing the event need not spend its time constantly polling for the event.

The Classic Producer–Consumer Problem

A producer object produces data to be consumed by a consumer. A queue object is used to temporarily hold and transmit the data produced by the producer, and could be any Java container, such as an `ArrayList` or a `Vector`. The producer generates data (objects) and places them in the queue. The consumer gets the data from the queue and processes it in some way. In a multithreaded application that has multiple producers and consumers, the queue represents a shared, thread-safe container that is concurrently accessed by both producers and consumers. The whole idea is that the consumers (threads) are always consuming, but they can't consume if the queue becomes empty. The producer creates objects and puts them in the queue at anytime. This means the consumer has no idea when the producer will create objects and put them in the queue.

A mail queue inside an e-mail server is a typical example of a producer-consumer system. The client program (the consumer) will not know when an e-mail arrives from the e-mail server (the producer). However, as soon as it is sent, the client will have to be notified and has to start processing it. The mail server has to synchronize access between new, incoming messages and the client, which may just be downloading messages.

Another example could be an application that performs numerous asynchronous write operations on a stream. Asynchronous here means the application (the producer) invokes a large number of write operations on the stream, such as sending data packets across the network, without waiting for each operation to complete. Using a shared container such as a queue, the producer can simply put the data that needs to be processed into the right queue object and let the consumer thread, a process that sends data across a physical network, take care of performing the processing the data.

For this strategy to work, it is imperative that when the queue is full, the producer has to wait until the consumer is finished processing before generating more data. Similarly, the consumer has to wait for the producer to generate more data once it has finished processing all the available data. If we designed the producer and the consumer using a polling system, the consumer would waste many CPU cycles while it waited for the producer to produce. Similarly, the producer would poll if it wanted to post something to the queue, and if the queue were full, it would waste even more CPU cycles waiting for the consumer to empty the queue, and so on. Clearly, the polling strategy demands more resources and might not perform well in a real-life scenario. As a remedy, Java includes an elegant inter-process communication mechanism via the `wait()`, `notify()`, and `notifyAll()` methods. These methods are defined as final on the `java.lang.Object` class and are inherited by all the other classes. All three methods can only be called within a `synchronized()` method context.

When a thread enters a synchronized block, all other threads trying to get into the same block are automatically made to wait. The thread that successfully enters the synchronized block acquires the lock on the object. The lock is released only when the thread exits the synchronized block. Let's say you don't want this first thread to complete its run through the synchronized section, but you want it to relinquish the ownership of the lock. Using the `wait()` method on the object on which the lock is held, you can "freeze" the running thread and force it to give up the lock. The thread joins a waiting queue and stays there until it is awakened. The rest of this section refers to the pool of running threads that executed the `wait()` method as the "wait set." At this point, the second or third thread that was contending to acquire the lock on the same object gets its chance to do so and happily enters the synchronized section.

It is important to remember the `wait()` method is defined by the `java.lang.Object` class. We don't execute the `wait()` method on a thread. Instead, a thread executes the `wait()` method on an object within a synchronized block. In order for a thread to even execute the `wait()` method, it has to first acquire the lock on the object. So if the thread is waiting to acquire this lock, there is no way it will get to execute the `wait()` method or be put in the waiting queue. Here's the general form of using a `wait()` method:

```
synchronized public void SomeMethod() {
```

```
    try {
        wait();
    }
    catch ( InterruptedException e ){
            // optional exception handler code.
    }
}
```

Travel Advisory

The `wait()` method is declared to be throwing an `InterruptedException`. This means it must to be enclosed within a `try-catch` block to make the compiler happy. If the call to `wait()` is not enclosed within a synchronized section, an `IllegalMonitorState Exception` will be thrown at runtime.

Typically, a thread evaluates a condition to determine if it should execute `wait()`. This evaluation is normally done in a `while()` loop, not an `if-else` structure. Once a thread moves to the wait-set, it stops running and, at some point, has to be woken up. Otherwise, it dies. By using `notify()` or `notifyAll()` on a particular object, you can inform one or all of the waiting threads that their waiting period is over. Since more than one thread may be waiting in an object's wait-set, the plural version `notifyAll()` can be used to inform all the waiting threads that their waiting is over. This is particularly relevant either if all consumers can consume the very same object, or if there are different types of consumers and not all of them may be able to consume the object. The `notify()` method is appropriate if only one consumer can consume a given object from the queue and all consumers are interchangeable.

The following sample program illustrates an application of the producer-consumer scenario to a practical problem. Imagine a word processing application that checks the spelling of every word as the user types them. The spell checker process runs as a separate thread and consumes the list of words produced by the editor.

```
import java.util.Vector;

class WordList {
    static final int MAX_SIZE= 5;
```

```
    // Sample list of words for testing.
    static final String dictionary [] = {
                   "Monday", "Tuesday","Wednesday", "cat",
"rat","mat",
                   "boy","Java","World", "certification", "wonder-
ful",
                    "broom", "brick", "house", "mouse", "Thursday",
                    "August", "December", "Fall", "winter", "morn-
ing"
                };

    // Shared data buffer.
    private Vector NewWords = new Vector();

    private boolean listFull() { return ( NewWords.size() == MAX_SIZE
- 1) ; }

    private boolean listEmpty() { return NewWords.isEmpty(); }



    synchronized public void produce() {
          while ( listFull() ) {
             try {
                wait();
                System.out.println("List full. Producer waiting for
consumers to consume....");
                }
             catch (InterruptedException  e ) {}
          }

          // Generate a random number and pick a word from the dic-
tionary.
          int randomIndex = (int) (Math.random() *
dictionary.length);
            System.out.println( "Produced : " +
dictionary[randomIndex]);

       //add the new word to the list ...
```

```
        NewWords.addElement( new String(dictionary[randomIndex]) );

        //.. and notify the conumser
        notify();
    }


    // Called by Consumer
    synchronized public void consume() {
        while ( listEmpty() ) {
            try {
                System.out.println("List empty. Consumer waiting for
producer for more data....");
                wait();
            }
            catch (InterruptedException  e ) {}
        }

        // Get the last word from the word list.
        String message = (String)NewWords.lastElement();
        NewWords.removeElement( message );
          System.out.println( "Consumed : " + message);

        //.. and notify the producer
        notify();
    }
}


final class Producer extends Thread {
    private WordList wordList ;

    public Producer( WordList w ) {
        this.wordList = w ;
        this.start();
    }

    public void run() {
        try {
            while ( true ) {
```

```
            wordList.produce();
            // sleep for a random interval of time.
            sleep( (int) (Math.random() * 500 ));
        }
    }
    catch( InterruptedException e ) { }
  }
}


final class Consumer extends Thread {
    private WordList wordList ;

    public Consumer( WordList w ) {
        this.wordList = w ;
        this.setDaemon(true);
        this.start();
    }

    public void run() {
        try {
            while ( true ) {
                wordList.consume();
                // sleep for a random interval of time.
                sleep( (int) (Math.random() * 500 ));
            }
        }
        catch( InterruptedException e ) { }
    }
}


public class ProducerConsumerDemo {
    public static void main(String args[]) {
        WordList w = new WordList();
        Producer producer = new Producer( w );
        Consumer consumer = new Consumer( w );
    }
}
```

Consider the way the `WordList` class can be used. A consumer thread can consume objects from the list and do some work on it. Concurrently, a producer thread can put objects into the list for the consumer to work on. Therefore, `WordList` acts as a shared object or a data channel between the producer and the consumer.

The producer thread inserts new words into the `WordList` at any time, asynchronously with the consumer. The consumer thread can't consume anything if the list is empty. In order to avoid polling the `WordList` to see if it is not empty, the `wait()` method is used to suspend the consumer thread when the list becomes empty. Upon invoking the `wait()` method, the consumer thread gives up the lock it owns on the `WordList` object and moves into the waiting state.

Once the producer thread produces a word and adds it to the list, it notifies the waiting consumer thread that it should reevaluate its waiting condition. One (or all, if `notifyAll()` is used) consumer thread that is waiting for the list to become nonempty gets revived and immediately starts reevaluating whether it should wait again or can continue running. If `notifyAll()` is used, all the threads that are waiting are notified. Although all the waiting threads now get a chance to run, not all of them will start running simultaneously because of the synchronized code. Eventually, only one thread will get a chance to obtain the lock on the object, reevaluate the waiting condition, and start running.

The same `wait()`/`notify()` cycle repeats for the producer thread. Since the producer cannot simply keep producing but has to allow the consumer threads to process the words, the producer thread waits upon detecting a full buffer. When the list is full, it indicates that the consumer threads haven't had a chance yet to process the data, and hence, the producer thread executes the `wait()` method on the object, gives up its lock, and moves to the waiting pool. Once all the data has been processed, it gets notified by the consumer thread and starts running again, producing more words.

Due to the effective interthread communication achieved by these two cooperating threads, race conditions are eliminated. Here is some output from this program that shows the clean synchronous behavior:

```
Produced  : winter
Consumed : winter
Produced  : December
Consumed : December
List empty. Consumer waiting for producer for more data....
Produced  : August
Consumed : August
```

```
Produced  : World
Consumed : World
Produced  : Tuesday
Consumed : Tuesday
Produced  : certification
Consumed : certification
Produced  : brick
Consumed : brick
List full. Producer waiting for consumers to consume....
Produced : certification
Consumed : certification
```

User and Daemon Threads

Java supports two kinds of threads: user threads and daemon threads. Every thread is a user thread by default. Threads created by an application such as all the examples covered in this chapter are user threads.

Daemon threads are special background threads, often called server threads. Daemon threads are treated differently from regular threads. Any thread can be flagged as a daemon by calling the method setDaemon(true) on the thread. This method must be called before the thread is started. Notice how the word processing consumer thread is made daemon in our previous example Producer ConsumerDemo.

Normally, a Java process will run until all threads have completed execution. If daemon threads are the only threads running in a process, the Java runtime environment will end the process. That's because daemon threads are background threads that provide various services, and if only background threads are running, no services are being requested.

The method isDaemon() can be used to determine whether a running thread is a daemon thread. A thread created by a user thread is, in turn, a user thread. Similarly, a thread created by a daemon thread becomes another daemon thread.

The following program illustrates how daemon threads are handled by the JVM. The main() function starts two threads, one user and one daemon. The run() method is intentionally written to do more processing in the daemon thread and half as much processing in the user thread. This strategy will guarantee the user thread always completing before the daemon thread. Since the main() method itself is a user thread, thread t1 also becomes a user thread. Thread t2 is made daemon by calling setDaemon(true) on the thread object before starting the thread. The main() method terminates soon after starting the two threads.

Immediately after user thread t1 completes, the JVM detects that no more user threads are running and terminates all the daemon threads, in this case, the thread t2. Therefore, the daemon thread never completes, which is obvious in the output generated by the program.

```
public class UserDaemonDemo extends Thread {
    private String myName;

    public UserDaemonDemo( String sName ) {  myName = sName ; }
    public void run() {
        if ( isDaemon()) {
            System.out.println( "Daemon thread " + myName + " run-
ning...");
            for ( int i = 0 ; i < Integer.MAX_VALUE ; i++ ){
                if ( i%50 == 0 )
                    Thread.yield();
            }
        }
        else {
            System.out.println( "User thread " + myName + " run-
ning...");
            // Do some processing
            for ( int i = 0 ; i < Integer.MAX_VALUE/2 ; i++ ) {
                if ( i%50 == 0 )
                    Thread.yield();
            }
        }
        System.out.println(myName + " finished running");
    }
    public static void main( String s[] ) {
        Thread t1 = new UserDaemonDemo("Thread #1");
        Thread t2 = new UserDaemonDemo("Thread #2");
        t1.start();
        t2.setDaemon(true);
        t2.start();
        System.out.println("Exit from main method");
    }
}
```

The program generates the following output:

```
Exit from main method
User thread Thread #1 running...
Daemon thread Thread #2 running...
Thread #1 finished running
```

Travel Assistance

For more information, check out these sources: The Sun Java Threads tutorial at **http://java.sun.com/docs/books/tutorial/essential/threads/index.html**; the *Java Language Specification* at **http://java.sun.com/docs/books/jls/second_edition/html/j.title.doc.html**; the *Java Virtual Machine Specification, 2nd Edition* at **http://java.sun.com/docs/books/vmspec/2nd-edition/html/VMSpecTOC.doc.html**; *Thinking in Java* by Bruce Eckel at http://www.bruceeckel.com *Java in a Nutshell* by David Flanagan (O'Reilly Associates); *Taming Java Threads* by Allen Holub (Apress Books) and the excellent articles about threading on his web page, **http://www.holub.com/aiharticles.html.**

CHECKPOINT

✔ **Objective 8.01** Write code to define, instantiate, and start new threads using both **java.lang.Thread** and **java.lang.Runnable**

- Each Java Virtual Machine can support many threads of execution at once. These threads independently execute code that operates on values and objects residing in a shared main memory.
- Java threads are instances of the `java.lang.Thread` class. The `Thread` class implements the `java.lang.Runnable` interface that defines only one method: `public void run()`.
- Threads can be created by extending the `java.lang.Thread` class and overriding the `run()` method or by implementing the `java.lang.Runnable` interface by providing a nonabstract version of the `public void run()` method.

- Simply instantiating a thread object will not cause the thread to start running. The `start()` method must be invoked on the instance to make the thread run. The `run()` method will be eventually called on the object by the thread scheduler.
- The `start()` method may not be called more than once on the same object. An `IllegalThreadStateException` results if the thread was already started.
- Every thread has a priority. Threads with higher priority are executed in preference to threads with lower priority. Priorities can be set using the `setPriority()` method before starting the thread. If the priority is not in the range `Thread.MIN_PRIORITY` to `Thread.MAX_PRIORITY`, an `IllegalArgumentException` will be thrown.
- Every thread may or may not be marked as a daemon. When code running in some thread creates a new `Thread` object, the new thread has its priority initially set equal to the priority of the creating thread. The new thread becomes a daemon thread if, and only if, the creating thread is a daemon.
- All threads belong to one of the two categories: daemon and user. `Thread.setDaemon()` sets the thread as a daemon thread. Daemon threads are similar to background processes.
- When a Java Virtual Machine starts up, there is usually a single nondaemon thread (which typically calls the method named `main()` of some designated class). JVM exits when all user threads are dead. JVM will not exit after the execution of the `main()` method if some user threads are still running.
- `wait()`, `notify()`, and `notifyAll()` are instance methods on the `java.lang.Object` class because they operate on the object's monitor lock.
- `start()` and `interrupt()` are instance methods of the `Thread` class because they are used to control a specific thread.
- `sleep()` and `yield()` are static methods defined by the `Thread` class and always operate on the current thread.

✔ **Objective 8.02 Recognize conditions that might prevent a thread from executing.**

- `Thread.sleep()` and `Object.wait()` throw an `InterruptedException`, but this doesn't always stop a running thread. The thread could `catch` the exception and continue processing.
- A thread moving to the sleep state does not release the object's lock if it has any.

- When a task's `interrupt()` method is executed while it is waiting or sleeping, the task enters the ready state. The next time the task enters the running state, an `InterruptedException` is thrown.
- `Thread.yield()` simply lets the JVM thread scheduling mechanism call another thread if one is waiting for execution. In fact, the calling thread may immediately continue if there is no other thread waiting to run.
- `Thread.sleep()` always blocks the thread. The sleeping thread is awakened once the time specified elapses, or when it is interrupted by another thread, whichever occurs first.
- The `Thread.isAlive()` method returns false for new threads as well as dead threads.

✔ **Objective 8.03** Write code using `synchronized, wait, notify,` or `notifyAll` to protect against concurrent access problems and to communicate between threads. Define the interaction between threads and between threads and object locks when executing `synchronized, wait, notify,` or `notifyAll`.

- If two or more concurrent threads act on a shared variable, there is a possibility that the actions on the variable will produce timing-dependent results. If two threads are started instantaneously, which one runs first depends on the thread scheduler. It is even possible that the threads will not see each others' actions at all unless they synchronize.
- A synchronized code is guaranteed to be executed only by one thread at any given point of time. The thread entering the synchronized code obtains the ownership of the lock on the object being synchronized. The lock is released when the thread completes the execution of the method, either normally or abruptly. As a convenience, a method may be declared `synchronized`; such a method behaves as if its entire body was contained in a synchronized statement.
- The methods `wait()`, `notify()`, and `notifyAll()` of class `java.lang.Object` support an efficient transfer of control from one thread to another. Rather than simply "spinning" (repeatedly locking and unlocking an object to see whether some internal state has changed), which consumes computational effort, a thread can suspend itself using the `wait()` method until such time as another thread awakens it using notify.
- When a thread calls the `wait()` method, it releases the lock for the object on which `wait()` is called and goes to the waiting state. An object can have more than one thread in its waiting pool (or wait-set). A thread continues in the waiting state until it is interrupted or another thread

issues a call to `notify()` or `notifyAll()` on the same object.
- Calls to `wait()`, `notify()`, and `notifyAll()` must be enclosed in a synchronized block, otherwise `IllegalMonitorException` will be thrown. This means that at the time a thread invokes these methods on an object, it should own the lock on that object. Since these methods throw `InterrupredException`, the call should follow all the rules of compile-time exception handling.
- If more than one thread executes the `wait()` method on the same object and is therefore waiting in an object's waiting pool, a subsequent call to `notify()`/`notifyAll()` will make an arbitrarily selected thread run. There is no way to tell which thread will run first.

REVIEW QUESTIONS

1. Given that the class `MyThread` extends `java.lang.Thread`, which of the following statements correctly instantiates a `Thread` object and starts the thread?

A. `new MyThread().run();`
B. `new MyThread().start();`
C. `new Runnable(new MyThread()).start();`
D. `new Thread(MyThread).start();`

2. Which of the following statements are true? Select two.

A. All Java threads are instances of `java.lang.Runnable`.
B. Calling the `start()` method has the same effect as calling the `run()` method on a thread object.
C. The `run()` method is a `private` method belonging to the `Thread` class.
D. `java.lang.Thread` extends the abstract class `java.lang.Runnable`.
E. All `java.lang.Thread` is a subclass of `java.lang.Object`.

3. What output is produced by the following program?

```
public class CoolThread extends Thread {
    public static void main ( String s[] ) {
        Thread t = new Thread();
        t.start();
    }
    public void run(){ System.out.println( "Wonderful World");}
}
```

A. Wonderful World
B. Compiler error: Threads cannot be created in static contexts
C. Runtime error
D. None of the above

4. Which of these events will always cause a running thread to temporarily stop?

A. Calling a `sleep()` method on the thread
B. Calling a `yield()` method on the thread
C. The `run()` method calling `system.exit(0)`
D. Starting another thread with a higher priority
E. None of the above

5. The following program attempts to imitate a dice being thrown six times by generating six random numbers ranging from 1 to 6. Which of the following statements could be inserted in the commented line so the program will work as expected?

```
public class SixThrows extends Thread {
    private int Throws [] = new int[6];
    public static void main (String s[]) throws InterruptedException
{
        SixThrows myDice = new SixThrows();
        myDice.start();
        // missing line
        for ( int i=0 ; i< 6; i++ )
                   System.out.println(myDice.Throws[i]);
    }
    public void run() {
        // Fill the array with six random numbers.
        for ( int i=0 ; i< 6; i++ )
                   Throws[i] = (int)(Math.random() * 6);
    }
}
```

A. `myDice.sleep(100);`
B. `myDice.yield();`
C. `Thread.sleep(100);`
D. Nothing; the program will work fine without any changes

6. In a multithreaded application, use of synchronized code is necessary in order to:

A. Allow all the threads to run normally.

B. Protect shared resources from concurrent access.

C. Control the order of execution of threads based on their priority.

D. Make the code run faster.

E. Convert the application to an applet.

7. If thread x is waiting on a lock on object A, which of the following events will cause the thread to stop waiting and move to "ready to run" state?

A. Thread x executes `notify()` on object A.

B. Another thread executes `notifyAll()` on object A.

C. Another thread releases the lock on object A soon after completing a synchronized method.

D. JVM creates a second lock on object A for thread x.

E. The last daemon thread completes normally.

8. When code running in some thread creates a new `Thread` object, the new thread has its priority initially set equal to

A. `Thread.MIN_PRIORITY`

B. `Thread.MAX_PRIORITY`

C. Priority of the creating thread

D. `Thread.NORM_PRIORITY`

9. What happens when a thread executes a wait method on an object without owning its lock ?

A. Nothing happens.

B. An `InterruptedException` will be thrown.

C. The thread gets the ownership of the lock automatically.

D. An `IllegalMonitorStateException` will be thrown.

10. The `wait()` method

A. is a final method defined by `java.lang.Object`.

B. is an abstract method defined by `java.lang.Runnable`.

C. is a void method defined by `java.lang.Thread`.

D. is a native method defined by `java.lang.System`.

REVIEW ANSWERS

1. **B** To start a thread, you should use the `start()` method on either an instance of subclass of `Thread`, or on a `Thread` object constructed using an instance of an object that implements the `Runnable` interface.

2. **A** **E** `java.lang.Thread` implements the `run()` method defined in the `java.lang.Runnable` interface. Like all other Java classes, the Thread class is a subclass of the primordial `java.lang.Object` class.

3. **D** Note that 't' refers to an object of type `Thread`, not of type `CoolThread`. Therefore, `t.start()` eventually causes the `run()` method on `java.lang.Thread` class to be executed. The default implementation of the `run()` method does nothing. Hence, no output is produced.

4. **A** Note that a call to the `yield()` method may not always cause the thread to stop running. If no other threads are waiting to run, the current thread will simply continue running. Calling `system.exit(0)` will terminate the JVM and immediately kill all the running threads. Answer D is true only if the JVM implements a priority-based scheduling algorithm.

5. **C** Since the `start()` method returns immediately, the `main()` method may try to print the values too soon, before the `run()` method gets a chance to fill in the values. If for some reason the `run()` method starts executing after a small delay, the `main()` method will print zero values from the empty array. A small `sleep()` method helps the `main()` method wait for the `run()` method to complete execution. The `sleep()` is defined as a static method on the Thread class and makes the current thread sleep, which is the one executing the `main()` method.

6. **B** Synchronization is necessary to ensure critical sections are thread safe and shared resources are accessed by only one thread at a time. Use of synchronized code introduces additional overheads of locking and unlocking making the application run slower.

7. **B** A waiting thread can only be awakened by another thread, not by itself, and only `notify()` and `notifyAll()` can enliven a waiting thread. Answer D is obviously wrong since every object has only one lock. The type of the thread, user or daemon, will not affect the way `wait()`/`notify()` works.

8. **C** Not only the priority, but the new thread also inherits the "daemonness" of the parent thread.

9. **D** The call to `wait()`, `notify()`, and `notifyAll()` must be enclosed in a synchronized block. Failure to do so results in the exception being thrown at runtime.

10. **A** The `wait()` method is is a final method defined by `java.lang.Object`. So are the `notify()` and `notifyAll()` methods.

P A R T

III

Using the
Java API

AWT 1: The User Interface

	NEWBIE	SOME EXPERIENCE	EXPERT
ETA	30+ hours	15 hours	4 hours

Now comes the *fun* part. After going through all of the technical background of the Java language, finally getting to the point where you can actually put together a screen that *looks* good and does things is much more entertaining. In this chapter, we are going to talk about the visible aspects of a screen and how to control the layout. In the next chapter, we will discuss how to put functionality into the screen.

> **Exam Tip**
>
> The newer releases of Java include the Swing package, which has many improvements over the original AWT (Abstract Windowing Toolkit) components. Since much of Swing builds on the AWT, it is to your benefit to be sure that you have a good grounding in the AWT basics. However, since Swing is not covered on the exam, we will not be discussing it in this book.

Understanding the GUI

Interacting with the user is an immensely important part of any application. Making that interaction pleasant and functional is critical to the success of many projects.

The basis of the visible part of all Java GUIs is the `Component` class. Basically anything that you can see or use or interact with is a subclass of `Component`. This includes the more obvious components such as `Buttons` and `Lists` and `Scrollbars` as well as the background classes like the `Frame` or `Applet` that the screen might sit in.

> **Local Lingo**
>
> *GUI (graphical user interface)* is the term for a screen that the application uses to present and get information to and from the user.

Program Flow

Java code can be implemented using several possible approaches. An *application* works outside a browser at the operating system level (for instance, at the DOS prompt). An *applet* sits on an HTML page that is displayed by a browser, which creates the JVM (Java Virtual Machine) for the applet to run on. A *servlet* is rendered in an HTML page but uses the resources of a server to do its processing.

> **Exam Tip**
>
> Servlets are not covered on the Sun Certified Java 2 Programmer exam, so we won't be covering them here.

> **Local Lingo**
>
> *JVM (Java Virtual Machine)* is the name of the interpreter that takes your compiled code and executes it. Sun publishes the specifications that all vendors must use when they create their JVM for their browser.

> **Local Lingo**
>
> *HTML (HyperText Markup Language)* is used by web pages to tell the browser how to display the information in the web page. It is also used to place an applet on a web page.

Applications

The basic structure of an application was covered earlier in this book; we will address the initiating of a GUI in this chapter. When a stand-alone application is created, there must be some code in the main() method to kick off the GUI if there is to be one. Whatever visual class you decide to use must be created in the main() method of your driver class.

The most common component that is used for an application's GUI is a Frame. That Frame may then hold many other components, such as Panels and Panels within Panels, and so on, to provide the complexity that is needed.

Applets

Applets are inherently different from stand-alone applications in that they are a contract with the browser. The program running is actually the browser itself, which was probably written in some other language than Java, and there is an agreed upon set of method calls that the browser performs.

When an applet has been loaded, usually by a browser from a web page but sometimes from an applet viewer, the init() method is always called just once, and that is immediately before the `start()` method is called. The `stop()` method is called every time the web page with the applet is replaced and just before the applet is about to be destroyed.

So that is it—there are just these four methods:

- `init()`   Include code to create the applet for the first time here, for instance, to define the visual components of the GUI: all the buttons, input fields, drop-down lists, scrollbars, menus, and so on.
- `start()`   Include code that needs to be executed each time the page that the applet is on is redisplayed, for instance, to get any animation going that should only run while the page is being displayed. If you run animations or audio clips and such when a page is not being displayed, you will use up the user's resources needlessly.
- `stop()`   Include code that needs to be executed when the web page has just been replaced by another page, for instance, calls to stop any animations.
- `destroy()`   Include any resources that need to be explicitly released.

It is the responsibility of the applet programmer to make sure that these methods contain the correct code. If you don't have these methods, you will inherit the empty ones from Applet.

We are going to concentrate on the `init()` method during this chapter, and we will be using both applications and applets to demonstrate the use of the AWT classes.

Objective 9.01   Write Code Using Components

All of the objects that can be put together like tinker toys to create a user interface are part of the AWT (Abstract Windowing Toolkit). The AWT has classes for all sorts of windows and containers and widget-type elements like `Buttons`, `Menus`, `Fonts`, and `Scrollbars` that you might need on a screen. In addition, the AWT has the responsibility for managing all user events like mouse clicks and window manipulation. Therefore, if you are going to have a GUI in your program, you know you *must* make use of the classes in `java.awt.*;`. There are 10 or 11 additional subdirectories of the AWT that you might also need, but you can worry about those as you need them.

Travel Advisory

There is actually a class in the AWT that is called Toolkit. This class contains some very low-level utility-like methods. Do not confuse the Abstract Windowing Toolkit as a whole with this one class.

The general inheritance structure of the AWT, shown in Figure 9-1, descends from Object like everything else. Then it splits into Components, which are the pieces that make up the GUI, and the "helper" classes that participate in making the GUI work but are not directly visible to the end user. This includes things like Events, LayoutManagers, Graphics, Fonts, and so on.

The Components are further split up into specific widgit-like classes (Buttons, TextComponents, Labels, Scrollbars, and so on) and Containers that serve to hold all the pieces together and define *where* the widget-like things should be on the screen.

Local Lingo

Widget is a generic term for anything on a screen that the user can interact with.

Components

Let's start by talking about the widget-like components for your screen. The look of the components will be affected by the operating system (OS) that the JVM is running on. This is because for each component, the operating system has a

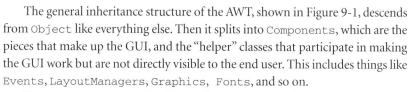

FIGURE 9-1   AWT class hierarchy

"heavy-weight peer" component behind it that is actually doing the work. The AWT components are influenced by this peer and pick up the "normal" look and feel for that OS. It is the AWT component's responsibility to provide the interface to the Java application and notify the peer of all happenings, and it is the peer's responsibility to render the component using native code.

Some of this OS influence has been reduced in the Swing components, but for now you only need to know that your GUI may look slightly different on different machines.

The `Component` class is the base class for all classes in the AWT with graphical representations, and it comes with a whole *bunch* of methods. So, of course, all the things on your GUI are going to inherit all of these methods. Many of these methods are about dealing with listeners (the topic of Chapter 10) and processing events, but some of them are useful for understanding your GUI, so we should mention them here.

The point of origin for a component is the upper-lefthand corner of the component. The location of your component can always be found using the `getX()` and `getY()` methods. This returns an integer, which represents the screen coordinates (in pixels) of the point of origin. Then the integer size in pixels of the component can be found using the `getHeight()` and `getWidth()` methods.

Component Appearance: Color, Size, and Font

The color of the component can be manipulated using the `setBackground` `(Color c)` method and feeding it a `Color` instance. Using the `setForeground` `(Color c)` method with the `Color` as a parameter can change the text or foreground. If you do *not* set the foreground or background color, the component will inherit them from the container that holds it.

All components have a preferred, minimum, and maximum size. The corresponding methods to get them are `getPreferredSize()`, `getMinimumSize()`, `getMaximumSize()`. The methods to set them are `setPreferredSize()`, `setMinimumSize()`, and `setMaximumSize()`. The preferred size of a component is generally "just big enough" to display whatever it needs to display. In general, it is best to allow a component to be its preferred size. However, the methods `setSize()` and `setBounds()` offer ways of controlling the component size. It should be noticed that in most cases there is a layout manager in effect and that *it* will be in control of the size of your components, so using `setSize()` and `setBounds()` on components in a container with a layout manager can be fruitless. Some of the layout managers will try to respect the component's preferred size if possible, but some don't pay attention at all. However, you *can* use these methods on the outer containers themselves with no interference.

Components use the methods `hide()` and `show()` to control visibility, but these have been deprecated in favor of `setVisible(false)` and `setVisible (true)`. In addition, it is possible to "gray out" a component and make it not functional by using the `setEnabled()` method and feeding it a false. Then you can return it to normal by using `setEnabled(true)`.

By default, the component will get the same font that the container holding it has. Of course, the container inherits its font from the container holding *it*, and so on. Luckily, components have a `setFont()` method available that takes a parameter of type `java.awt.Font` so that you can get the effect that you want.

The three pieces that make up a specific `Font` are the name of the glyph of the font, the style of the font (bold, italic, normal), and its size (for example, I am typing in 12 point). The Java Runtime Environment (JRE) comes with three built-in font glyphs: "Serif", "SansSerif", and "Monospaced". The `Font` class provides static fields for the styles `Font.PLAIN`, `Font.BOLD` and `Font.ITALIC`, and the special `Font.BOLD+Font.ITALIC`. The size is an integer.

The following is an example of creating your own personal font for your component:

```
Font myFont = new Font("SansSerif", Font.BOLD, 28);
myComponent.setFont(myFont);
```

Button

Let's start with a `Button`. Luckily, there are only two ways to construct a `Button`: with a `String` that will appear on the `Button`, or with no `String`. Then, as with all components, you have to add the `Button` to whatever container you are going to use. Let's start with a small sample.

First, this is the basic HTML to use:

```
<HTML><HEAD><BODY>
<APPLET code=MyApplet.class width=150 height=160>
</APPLET></BODY></HTML>
```

Next, perhaps the world's simplest applet:

```
import java.awt.*;
import java.applet.Applet;
class MyApplet extends Applet{
   public void init(){
```

```
    Button btn = new Button("My Button");
    add(btn);
  }
}
```

If you compile this and double-click your html file, your browser should display a small applet that looks like this:

My Button

Notice that the String that you used to construct the Button appears on the image of the button. Because you are adding the button to the Applet class that you are currently defining, there is an implied "this" for the add(btn). If you were adding the button to a container that was not the current class being defined, you would use the syntax myFrame.add(btn); to add it to the myFrame instance.

TextField and TextArea

One of the most commonly used components is the TextField to be used as an input field with only one line. There are two possible parameters when constructing a TextField: the default String that the TextField should display and the number of columns in the input area.

Travel Advisory

Later in this chapter, we will talk about LayoutManagers and how they impact the actual size of the components. If you have a LayoutManager in effect that uses its own logic for assigning component sizes, the input area of TextField and TextArea could be different than what you requested with your parameters.

Here are some examples of creating TextFields:

```
TextField tfield1 = new TextField();// a blank text field
TextField tfield2 = new TextField(20); // blank field of 20 columns
TextField tfield3 = new TextField("Yes"); // predefined text displayed
TextField tfield4 = new TextField("Both", 30); // predefined text in
                                               //30 columns
```

Notice that the user's input is not limited to the `TextField` viewing area. You can use your arrow keys to move back and forth in the input area to get to the hidden areas.

After the `TextField` has initially been created, you can change the value that the field contains by using the `setText(String s);` method. This is especially useful for clearing the screen or editing the user's input. In addition, the size of the viewing area can be reset using the `setColumn(int columns)` method.

`TextAreas` have multiple lines in them and allow you to set both the width and height of the viewing area of the text and to set the initial text and define which scrollbars are to be shown.

```
new TextArea(); //empty
new TextArea(60, 40); //rows and columns
new TextArea("Once upon a time . . .");
new TextArea("Once upon a time . . .", 4, 60);
new TextArea("Once upon a time . . .", 4, 60,
TextArea.SCROLLBARS_XXXX);
```

Because the user can enter text beyond the visible area of the `TextArea`, it is possible that scrollbars will be needed to access these lines. The `TextArea` class has four static fields that can be used as constants to set the scrollbars: `TextArea.SCROLLBARS_VERTICAL_ONLY`, `TextArea.SCROLLBARS_HORI-ZONTAL_ONLY`, `TextArea.SCROLLBARS_BOTH`, `TextArea.SCROLLBARS_NONE`. By default you get `SCROLLBARS_BOTH`. If you do not have scrollbars, the user can use the arrow keys to navigate the area.

Both `TextField` and `TextArea` are subclasses of `TextComponent` and as such inherit some common "text-editing" -like methods (most of the useful ones are up there). They also share some common text-related problems. The major problem with `TextComponent`s is fonts: not all fonts are equal. If you are using a proportional font, where the width of the letter varies as needed, the number of columns parameters becomes more of a problem. If you set up a TextField and initialize it to a string of "iiiiiiiiii", the `TextField` will be just wide enough to hold those ten *i*'s. The viewable field will *not* be wide enough to hold ten *W*'s and will not grow to accommodate the wider letter. If you initialize the field with a given number of columns, an average column width is used, whether you provide a string or not.

Label

A `Label` has no functionality. It is just there for information. You can change it using code, but the user cannot affect it at all. The basic syntax includes feeding in parameters for the `Label` text and an integer that indicates the positioning of the `String` in the `Label`. For example:

```
Label name = new Label("First Name");
Label filler = new Label(" ");
Label fillLater = new Label();
Label right = new Label("right side",Label.CENTER);
```

Here is a little code that you can use to test some `TextFields` and `Labels`.

```
import java.awt.*;
import java.applet.Applet;
class MyApplet extends Applet{
   public void init(){
      Label lbl = new Label("Enter Name:");
      add(lbl);
      TextField txt = new TextField("Joe Blow");
      add(txt);
      TextArea txtArea = new Area(5,20);
      add(txtArea);
   }
}
```

As you can see in Figure 9-2, it looks quite nice, doesn't it?

Canvas

Much like `Label`, `Canvas` has no functionality. It is just an area with no title, no border, no built-in behavior. It is just *there*. Well, that is, if you specifically give it

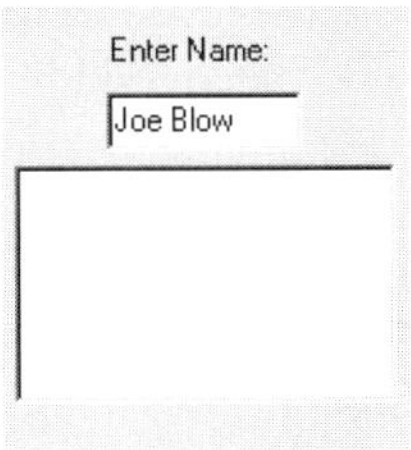

FIGURE 9-2   Label, TextField, and TextArea

some useful size. The constructor takes no parameters, just `Canvas can = new Canvas();`.

What it *can* do is send Mouse and Key events (which will be covered in Chapter 10), so it can be used to define an area of the screen the user can click in to do something. It can also be useful for drawing on, thus the name.

Checkbox

A `Checkbox` is a true/false component: it is either On or Off. It can be made with a `String` label as a parameter, and you can set whether you want it to start out as on or off.

```
Checkbox mar = new Checkbox("Married?", null, true);
Checkbox emp = new Checkbox("Employed?", false, null);
Checkbox o21 = new Checkbox("Over 21?" , true);
Checkbox male = new Checkbox("Male?");
```

Here is what the `Checkbox` looks like:

☑ Married?   ☐ Employed?   ☑ Over 21?   ☐ Male?

The default state for the `Checkbox` is false or Off. Notice that if you do not provide a `String` label, or at least the value "null" as the first parameter, you cannot provide either of the other parameters so you'll have a no-argument constructor. However, if you *do* provide the first parameter, you can feed in just the true/false state or both of the other two parameters in either order.

CheckboxGroup

Some programmers call the grouping of `Checkboxes` that work together a radio group, but in the AWT it is called a `CheckboxGroup`. The most common misconception about a `CheckboxGroup` is that because it is so involved with the GUI components, it must be a `Component` itself. Not so: it is just a grouping of related `Checkbox` components. In a `CheckboxGroup`, only *one* of the `Checkboxes` can be true at any given time.

```
CheckboxGroup age = new CheckboxGroup();
add(new Checkbox("0-18", age, true));
add(new Checkbox("19-40", false, age));
add(new Checkbox("41-100", age, false));
```

Here's what the CheckboxGroup looks like:

List

A `List` is a scrollable sequence of items. There are two things you can control about selection `Lists`. No matter how long the list of items is, you can name the number of items that will display at any one time without scrolling. You can also allow the user to select more than one item by turning `multipleSelection` on.

If you do not provide any parameters when you make your list, by default you will get four items showing, and `multipleSelection` will be turned off. However, *if* you name the number of items to display at once, you can turn on `multipleSelection` by adding true to the parameters.

```
List lst = new List(3);
lst.add("Detroit");
lst.add("Toronto");
lst.add("New York");
lst.add("Dallas");
lst.add("Denver");
add(lst);
List another = new List(5, true); //read an input file in a loop and
add each record to this list or something.
```

Here is the `List`:

```
Detroit
Toronto
New York
```

Choice

A `Choice` is very similar to a `List`. It allows you to add items and the user can select an item. However, it is displayed as a drop-down that displays all the items instead of a scrollable list in a window area. `Choice` does not give you the option of how many items to display. It initializes showing only the first item, and when the arrow is pushed it shows all the items. There is no `multipleSelection` option for `Choice`.

```
Choice lst = new Choice();
lst.add("Detroit");
lst.add("Toronto");
lst.add("New York");
```

```
lst.add("Dallas");
lst.add("Denver");
add(lst);
```

A Choice is shown here:

ScrollBar and ScrollPane

So what do you do if the screen that you want to show is bigger than the window the user has squeezed you into? There are two options. You can either explicitly add Scrollbars to your outermost container, or you can use a ScrollPane, which has built in Scrollbars.

You can create your own Scrollbar(s), such as:

```
Scrollbar upDown = new
Scrollbar(Scrollbar.VERTICAL);//there is also
           //Scrollbar.HORIZONTAL
myFrame.add(upDown, BorderLayout.EAST);
```

This allows you to name the orientation as shown. In its most complicated constructor, you can control the size and position of the slider using the following:

```
Scrollbar(int orientation, int startPosVal, int sliderSize, int
minVal, int maxVal);
```

Watch out: the parameters in this are not talking about pixels; it is a relative value. Scrollbar(Scrollbar.HORIZONTAL, 350, 25, 300, 500); will make a Scrollbar that can scroll the entire screen, where the screen runs from 300 to 500 units (200 units total). The initial slider position will start at 350, which is a fourth of the way from 300 to 500. The slider will be 25 units, which is an eighth of the total distance, so an eighth of the entire screen will be visible at one time.

The default values for Scrollbar are Scrollbar(VERTICAL, 0, 10, 0, 100);. This divides the screen into 100 units, starts the slider at the top, and makes the slider 10 percent of the entire length.

Alternatively, you can use ScrollPane, which does a great job of handling the scrollbars for you. ScrollPane will take in just *one* component, so you might want to consider making it a `Panel` or something that you can put other stuff in. Since you don't have to worry about the details of how big to make the slider and where to start it, all you have to do is tell the `ScrollPane` your personal preference on how the scrollbars are to be handled, also known as the scrollbarPolicy. The options are `ScrollPane.SCORRBARS_AS_NEEDED`, `ScrollPane.SCROLLBARS_ALWAYS`, and `ScrollPane.SCROLLBARS_NEVER`.

```java
import java.awt.*;
class Test extends Frame{
   Test(){
      ScrollPane myPane = new
ScrollPane(ScrollPane.SCROLLBARS_AS_NEEDED);
      Label myLabel = new Label("This is a very long sentence and
will need to be scrolled");
      myPane.add(myLabel);
      this.add(myPane);
      this.setSize(200,100);
      this.setVisible(true);
   }
   static void main(String args[]){
       Test t = new Test();
   }
}
```

In this example, we are creating the `ScrollPane` in the constructor for our outermost `Frame`. Then we are putting one really long label in the `ScrollPane` and putting the `ScrollPane` in the `Frame`. Now try stretching and shrinking the frame and watch the scrollbars disappear and reappear as needed (see Figure 9-3).

Notice that the `Scrollbar` appears by itself when the `Frame` is started because the entire component cannot be seen in the size that was set. When you stretch it out to show the whole thing, the `Scrollbar` disappears automatically.

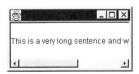
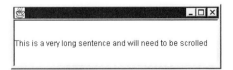

FIGURE 9-3 ScrollPane (a) with and (b) without Scrollbar

MenuBars, Menus, and MenuItems

MenuBars go in Frames, which are top-level windows. Notice that since Applet is *not* a Frame (it is a Panel), they do *not* take MenuBars. When MenuBars are added, they go in an area below the title and before the area controlled by the layout manager. You simply create the new MenuBar and use the setMenuBar() method of Frame to attach it to the Frame. Notice that you do not add() it to the Frame because that would put it in the layout area where it does not belong. You should also note that Menu's MenuItems and MenuBars are *not* subclasses of Components like the widgets that we have been describing up to now. They subclass the MenuComponent class and as such are part of the helper classes like Fonts and LayoutManagers. The add() method of Frame takes only Components, so remember to "set" your MenuBar.

```java
import java.awt.*;
class Test {
   public static void main(String args[]){
       Frame myFrame = new Frame("Menus and such");
       MenuBar mb = new MenuBar();
       myFrame.setMenuBar(mb);
```

Once you have a MenuBar you need something to go in it—a Menu or two, obviously.

```java
       Menu fileMenu = new Menu("File");
```

A Menu is much like a Choice in that it contains items or, in this case, MenuItems. A MenuItem can be just a selection, or it can be another Menu or a CheckboxMenuItem. Other than that, they are straightforward. They take in a String that is the display label.

Once you have defined your Menu, you can add MenuItems to it using the following:

```java
       MenuItem newFile = new MenuItem("New");
       MenuItem openFile = new MenuItem("Open");
       MenuItem closeFile = new MenuItem("Close");
       MenuItem saveFile = new MenuItem("Save");
       fileMenu.add(newFile);
       fileMenu.add(openFile);
```

```
fileMenu.add(closeFile);
fileMenu.addSeparator();   //Notice the divider;
fileMenu.add(saveFile);
```

When you have the MenuItems on a Menu, you can get rid of them later by
using the remove() method of Menu.

Now you can make submenus by adding Menus as MenuItems. Notice that
menu is a subclass of MenuItem, so this is possible. A CheckboxMenuItem is a
little different creature in that it has an On or Off state that is represented by showing a little check in front of it. When you are constructing it, you have the option
of including the beginning state of the item by including a boolean where "true"
is equal to On. By default, the state is Off. Later on you will be able to determine
what the state is by using the getState() method of CheckboxMenuItem.
They are added just like the other MenuItems.

```
Menu toolBars = new Menu("ToolBars");
toolBars.add(new CheckboxMenuItem ("Standard",true)); //will
start checked
toolBars.add(new CheckboxMenuItem ("Formatting"));//will
start unchecked
toolBars.add(new CheckboxMenuItem ("Drawing"));
fileMenu.add(toolBars);                 //add the submenu to the menu
```

Now you add the Menus to the MenuBar:

```
mb.add(fileMenu);
Menu viewMenu = new Menu("View");
mb.add(viewMenu);
```

There is also a special method for setting which Menu is to be the help Menu
for this Frame. Then depending on the operating system, the JVM can decide if
it has a special location that help menus should be in. You create it and its
MenuItems just like any other Menu, but you use the setHelpMenu() method:

```
Menu helpMenu = new Menu("Help");
mb.setHelpMenu(helpMenu);
myFrame.setSize(200,200);
myFrame.setVisible(true);
}
}
```

Figure 9-4 shows the `MenuBar, Menu,` and submenu.

 **FIGURE 9-4** Menus on a MenuBar

Objective 9.02 Write Code Using Containers

All of the things that make up a user screen need to be held in a manageable space. A portion of the subclasses of `Component` have been dedicated to the functionality of holding other components and are therefore called `Containers`. The AWT defines several containers to hold all of the pieces of the GUI, including `Windows, Frames, Panels, Applets`, and so on. Notice that a `Container` is first of all a `Component`. So what is different about it that makes it a container? The internal `Component` list that it has. In order to make this work, each `Container` manages a list of what it is holding and knows the order that these components were added to the list. This is important because the order that the components are added to the container drives the manner in which they are displayed on the screen.

When you add something to a container, you can either use the default `add(Component c)` method, or you can specify where you want to put it in the order of things by specifying the index to add it at `add(Component c, int index)`. This is going to be important when we start talking about `Layout Managers`.

First, let's go through some of the more common `Containers`. There are quite a few types of containers that belong to Swing, but we are not going to discuss the Swing classes because they are not on the exam. The remaining containers are `Panel, ScrollPane,` and `Window`.

`Windows` are the parents of `Frames` and `Dialogs`, and `Panels` are the parents of `Applets` (see Figure 9-5). However, `Panels` are also widely used in their own right to help with nesting containers to get a specific look to the screen, so it's common to see a `Panel` nested *in* an `Applet` or a `Frame`.

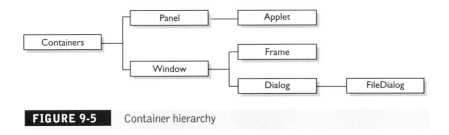

FIGURE 9-5   Container hierarchy

Windows and Frames and Dialogs

A `Window` is a top-level container. It has no titlebar, it has no borders. It does have a lot of methods that it can pass down to any subclasses like `Frames` and `Dialogs`.

It is possible to hide a `Window`, using `myWin.hide()`, and forget that it is there. Unfortunately, the operating system window peer hangs onto all the memory resources, waiting for the window to become visible again. In order to get rid of a `Window` completely, you can use `dispose()`, which tidies up on its way out. Luckily if you call `show()`, the system will rebuild the `Window` and get those resources back for you.

`Frames` and `Dialogs` are subclasses of `Window`, which means that they both have all of the "Window-like" behaviors of any `Window`. They also have a title, an icon, and the three buttons to minimize, maximize, and multiwindow. Notice that while the minimize and multiwindow buttons work by default, the X does not actually function without your code. This is to allow you to do stuff on the way out if you need to.

You just can't make a `Window` by itself. It *must* be owned by something that tacks it to the operating system, which means that you need a `Frame`. Luckily, it is very easy to make a `Frame`. All you really need to remember is that by default `Frames` have (0,0) size in pixels. This is very difficult to see (smile), so you should always call `setSize(int width, int height)` or `setBounds(int x, int y, int width, int height)` on your Frame. Even better, you can use `pack()` and let the layout manager decide what size is just right to honor the preferred sizes of all of the components and still show them all. If you choose to use the `setBounds()` method, the x and y parameters allow you to place the `Frame` at a specific location (in pixels) on the screen. The other thing is that you need to make sure to call `setVisible(true)` to insure that your `Frame` can be seen. Wait—are you wondering what happened to that `show()` method we just mentioned? Well, the `show()` method in `Component` (Window and Frame are Components) has been deprecated, which means that they are out of favor with Sun, and the new method `setVisible(boolean b)` is the preferred method to use.

```
import java.
import java.awt.*;
public class Test {
    public static void main(String[] a) {
        Frame f = new Frame ("World Most Simple Frame");
         //make lots of stuff for your screen here and add them to the
Frame
        f.setSize(200, 200);
        f.setVisible(true);
    }
}
```

This simple `Frame` is shown here:

This application has only a `main()` method and that creates just one component. The frame that we made is visible. It would have been nice if we had added
some buttons or other widgets before making it visible. Notice that when you set
the container visible, all of the components in it become visible also.

Another approach is that you can create a `MyGUI` class that has all the gizmos
and widgets in its constructor, and then create an instance of `MyGUI` in a `main()`
method somewhere:

```
import java.awt.*;
public class MyGUI extends Frame {
    //probably need to deal with the other super constructors also
    public MyGUI() {
        super("My Little Frame");//
         //make lots of stuff for your screen here
        f.setSize(300, 400);
        f.setVisible(true);
    }
    public static void main(String[] a) {
        MyGUI f = new MyGUI();
    }
}
```

In this case, we did all of the composition of the screen in the constructor of our Frame class. All that is left for the main() to do is create an instance of this class.

Because a Frame is a Window, you can use the dispose() method to get rid of the memory resources that tie the Frame to the underlying operating system.

> **Travel Advisory**
>
> Sooner or later you *will* forget to give your Frame a size and to do a setVisible(true) on your Frame. Then you will wonder why nothing is happening. Then you will kick yourself while saying, "I *knew* I was supposed to set those!" Be prepared. We all do it.

Dialogs

Dialogs are used to get immediate input from the user. A Dialog is just a pop-up window that can be made modal, which forces the user to deal with the pop-up before switching focus to some other window:

```java
import java.awt.*;
class Test {
    public static void main(String args[]){
        Frame myFrame = new Frame("Frame with Dialog");
        Dialog dia = new Dialog(myFrame,"Enter Name:");
        TextField name = new TextField(10);
        dia.add(name);
        myFrame.setSize(300,200);
        myFrame.setVisible(true);
        dia.setSize(120,60);
        dia.setVisible(true);
    }
}
```

Figure 9-6 shows the Dialog box.

Notice that the Dialog has to pass the name of the Frame that it belongs to as a parameter. A Dialog is a Window and therefore has a dispose() method to use.

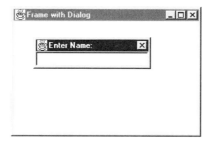

FIGURE 9-6   A Dialog with a TextField over a Frame

Panels

A `Panel` is basically a blank piece of paper. It has no title, no menubar area, no little X's in the corner. It has no methods of interest for you to use. It is a blank container for you to use to put other components in, or you can put it *inside* other containers as needed to create the look that you want.

Remember that `Applet` is a `Panel` with special powers built in by the browser.

Objective 9.03

Write Code Using the LayoutManager Classes of the `java.awt` Package

It is all well and good to be able to create a bunch of components that come up on a screen the way that you want them. It is quite another thing to be able to maintain that look while the user changes everything around as fast as possible. Without layout managers, the job of a screen designer would be a nightmare. If programmers had to worry about how screens look after users play with the size and shape, or how it looks on a different operating system, they would never get their jobs done. However, there are a variety of helper classes whose only job is to attempt to make the screen look as good as it can and as close to how you want it on whatever operating system is running it, without your having to tell it what to do. Containers use `LayoutManagers` to size components and organize the screen properly.

Controlling the Look

There are two general categories of `LayoutManagers`: those that require specific constraints from each component to tell the `LayoutManager` where to put them, and those that require no information from the components. The ones that need constraint information implement both `LayoutManager` and `LayoutManager2`; the simpler ones only implement `LayoutManager`. Let's start with the easy ones.

FlowLayout

`FlowLayout` and `GridLayout` don't take any constraint information from components when they are added to the container. They just look at the components that have been added to the list that the container keeps and load them up first-come, first-serve, starting from left to right.

    `FlowLayout` is the most basic layout manager, and as a result, it's the one that you have the least control over. `FlowLayout` really *tries* to honor the preferred size of a component. If you put several components on a screen that is wide enough to hold them, they will just line up from left to right. As you reduce the width of the screen, `FlowLayout` will shift the components down, much as words wrap in a text editor. `FlowLayout` is the default layout manager for `Panel`, and therefore also for `Applet` (as a subclass of `Panel`).

    When you create a `FlowLayout`, you do not need to pass it any parameters. This one is *easy*.

```
import java.awt.*;
class Test extends Frame {
    Test(){
    // An applet or Panel would not need this set but this is a Frame
    setLayout(new FlowLayout()); //force this Layout.
    add(new Button("one"));
    add(new Button("two"));
    add(new Button("three"));
    setSize(300,200);
    setVisible(true);
    }
    public static void main(String args[]){
       Test t = new Test();
    }
}
```

    The `FlowLayout` with three buttons is shown here:

Notice in the add statement we named the component to add, but we did not provide any other information about where to place it. The placement of the components shifts around as the window is resized to try and provide the best display.

There are two constructors for `FlowLayout` that allow you to indicate how you prefer the components to be justified or aligned in the rows on the screen. The class provides the fields CENTER, LEFT, RIGHT, LEADING, and TRAILING to use for this purpose. When specified, the LayoutManager tries to honor this request. The LEADING and TRAILING alignments follow the component's orientation, which helps when dealing with languages that read vertically or right to left. In English and Western European orientation, LEADING is the same as LEFT.

You can optionally also specify a vertical and horizontal gap to be left between components using the constructor `FlowLayout(int align, int hgap, int vgap)`.

GridLayout

Although components do not need to give `GridLayout` any information about their placement when they are added, `GridLayout` still requires that you tell it how you want the grid formatted when you set up the layout. It is going to use this grid to determine the size of each component that gets added, so forget about it paying any attention to the component's preferred size. The layout uses the dimensions of the grid, in rows and columns, that you want any components put into, and if you really want to get picky, you can tell it how much horizontal and vertical space to put between the components. If you *really* want to be lazy you can call it with no parameters, and it will create a one-row grid with as many cells as you add components. There is no minimum size for a grid so you *could* make it 1 × 1, but a typical way to set `GridLayout` up would be to do the following:

```
myPanel.setLayout(new GridLayout(3,4));
```

This would create a `GridLayout` with three rows and four columns to be set up in the Panel:

```
import java.awt.*;
class Test extends Frame {
    Test(){
```

```
    setLayout(new GridLayout(2,3));
    add(new Button("one"));
    add(new Button("two"));
    add(new Button("three"));
    add(new Button("four"));
    add(new Button("five"));
    add(new Button("six"));
    setSize(100,100);
    setVisible(true);
  }
  public static void main(String args[]){
    Test t = new Test();
  }
}
```

The Frame with a six-button GridLayout is shown here:

This code will create a screen with six buttons set up as two rows of three. The components are added from left to right, wrapping to the next row when the columns are all filled. If you don't add enough components to fill up the grid you have defined, the remaining sections are left blank.

Actually, if the number of rows is specified, either in the GridLayout constructor or using the setRows() method of GridLayout, the number of columns is ignored, but it is still a nice practice to put it in. It helps the next guy understand your code better. OK, so now you are asking, "How can I *not* specify the number of rows?" Well, you can set the value to 0 and set the columns parameter to a value when you create the GridLayout. Or, if you created the GridLayout using the no parameters constructor, you could use the setColumns(int cols) method to name the number of columns. Either way creates a situation where there are columns specified but no nonzero row value, and your columns will be honored.

With the previous code, if you comment out the last three buttons, the screen will have two rows of two columns with the last section empty.

If you add seven buttons, even though the grid is two by three, you will end up with two rows of four buttons, with the last section empty.

If you try to fit a component in an area of the grid that is not big enough to hold it (for instance, if the label on your button is too big for the space), the layout displays as much as it can.

While GridLayout is widely used when layering several containers on a single page, it does not come by default with any of the containers in the AWT, probably because there is no default grid setting that could be reasonably set up.

BorderLayout

BorderLayout is the other LayoutManager that comes by default with some containers. It is the default for both Windows and Frames. BorderLayout is interesting because it provides four side areas (NORTH, SOUTH, EAST, and WEST) to put things in, as well as a center square area. Of course, having these areas provided for you means that each component has to *tell* BorderLayout where it needs to go as it is added; otherwise, they will just get piled up in the center by default.

```java
import java.awt.*;
class Test extends Frame {
    Test(){
        add(new Button("b1"),BorderLayout.NORTH);
        add(new Button("b2"),BorderLayout.EAST);
        add(new Button("b3"),BorderLayout.SOUTH);
        add(new Button("b4"),BorderLayout.WEST);
        add(new Button("b5"),BorderLayout.CENTER);//default if no
placement is given
        this.setSize(200,200);
        this.setVisible(true);
    }
    public static void main(String args[]){
        Test t = new Test();
    }
}
```

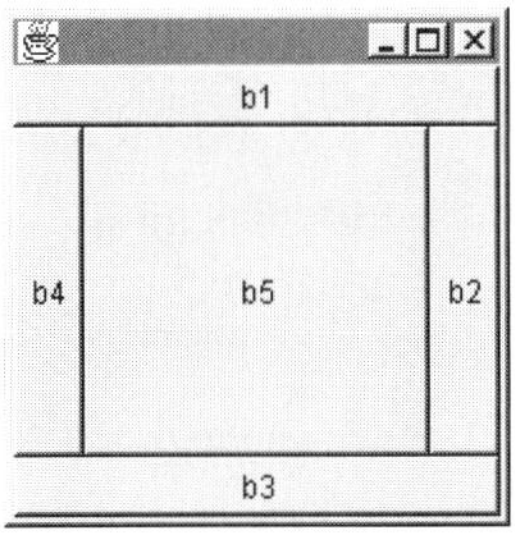

FIGURE 9-7   BorderLayout

Figure 9-7 shows `BorderLayout` in a `Frame`. You can see that this would be a great way to place scrollbars along the bottom or sides. Or SOUTH would be good for having a status bar and clock. If we left out the placement parameter when we did the add, all five buttons would be piled up in CENTER with only the last one showing.

This layout manager is kind of picky about the sizing of those five areas, so once again it is going to ignore some of your efforts to `setSize()` and the `preferredSize()` of the components that it holds. The NORTH and SOUTH areas go end to end of the container, so the width of components going in these areas is ignored, but it will try to honor the height. The EAST and WEST areas span the space between them, so their height is determined by what is leftover after NORTH and SOUTH get done, but their widths will try to be honored. Poor CENTER just gets the leftovers, not a chance of any component going in this area having any dimension honored. Notice that if you make the window wider, the `BorderLayout` area will be wider, so NORTH and SOUTH will get wider to insure that they still run edge to edge, and CENTER will get wider to fill the extra area, but the width of EAST and WEST will remain unchanged.

In the same way, when the window gets taller, EAST and WEST get taller to accommodate this, CENTER gets taller to fill the gap, but the NORTH and SOUTH remain unchanged.

Because `BorderLayout` takes constraints (the area parameters) when setting its components, it is not interchangeable with `FlowLayout` and `GridLayout`. Those layout managers do not know anything about keeping track of constraints, so they will get lost if they are in effect at the time you are placing the components, even if you pass in the placement parameter. When you add a component to a container, it first adds it to its internal list of components and then passes the component and its parameters to whatever layout manager is in effect *at that time*. This is the one and only time that you get to slide those parameters into the `BorderLayout` internal area tracking fields. If `BorderLayout` is not the one in control at add time, it never finds out about the placement parameters that were used when you added the component to the container.

```
import java.awt.*;
class Test extends Frame {
    Test(){
      setLayout(new FlowLayout()); //OOPs FlowLayout cannot track
constraints
      add(new Label("Top of Form"),BorderLayout.NORTH);// placement
ignored
      add(new Button("b2"),BorderLayout.EAST);//Frame has this
method signature
      add(new Button("b3"),BorderLayout.SOUTH);
      add(new Button("b4"),BorderLayout.WEST);
      add(new Button("b5"));
      setLayout(new BorderLayout());//BorderLayout can't find the
constraints
      this.setSize(400,200);
      this.setVisible(true);
    }
    public static void main(String args[]){
      Test t = new Test();
    }
}
```

Since BorderLayout was not in place at the time the buttons were added, the buttons didn't even have a chance to pick up the default placement (FlowLayout sure didn't set it for them when they were added).

Travel Advisory

When you add a MenuBar to a Frame it is added to the top of the window, *not* in the NORTH area of BorderLayout.

Combining LayoutManagers

Of course, using all that center space for one big button is a waste. It is much more common to stack another container inside the areas of BorderLayout (or any other layout) to get a more customized look to the screen:

```java
import java.awt.*;
class Test extends Frame {
    Test(){
        add(new Button("b1"),BorderLayout.NORTH);
        add(new Scrollbar(),BorderLayout.EAST);
        Panel status = new Panel(); //a little panel to put in SOUTH
later
        status.setLayout(new BorderLayout());
        Label message = new Label("status bar");
        status.add(message,BorderLayout.WEST);//we could put a clock in
EAST
        add(status,BorderLayout.SOUTH);
        add(new Button("b2"),BorderLayout.WEST);
        Panel pan1 = new Panel();
        pan1.setLayout(new GridLayout(3,1));
        List lst = new List(3, false);
        lst.add("Alabama");
        lst.add("Michigan");
        lst.add("Colorado");
        lst.add("Wyoming");

        pan1.add(lst);

        TextField txtf = new TextField(20);
        pan1.add(txtf);
        pan1.add(new Button("Do Stuff")); //a nameless Button
        add(pan1,BorderLayout.CENTER);
        this.setSize(200,200);
        this.setVisible(true);
    }
    public static void main(String args[]){
        Test t = new Test();
    }
}
```

You cannot add a `Window` to a container; therefore you cannot add a `Frame` to another `Frame`, but you *can* add `Panels` to `Frames`, and set their layout to whatever would work best. Figure 9-8 shows stacked containers and layout managers.

GridBagLayout

`GridBagLayout` is probably the reason that IDEs (Integrated Development Environments) are so popular. Nobody in their right mind would want to work with something as complicated as this layout without a tool to help out. It is covered on the exam, and you will probably get at least one question on it, however a complete discussion of all of the details of `GridBagLayout` is beyond the scope of this book. We will just discuss what you need for the exam, and there is a file on the website for this book that discusses the topic in detail.

You set the Layout the same as any other Layout:

```
myContainer.setLayout(new GridBagLayout());
```

`GridBagLayout` splits the screen up into a grid (surprise). The unique thing about it is that the rows and columns of this grid do not have to be the same width or height. The size of the components in the grid determines the size of the rows and columns. In addition, a component on the grid can span more than one section of the grid. To control the placement of a component, all of the information is gathered in a `GridBagConstraints` object and used when adding the component to the container with `GridBagLayout`. This part is not much different from setting a component into a particular area of `BorderLayout`. We are not going to discuss all of the parameters required to create a `GridBagConstraint`, but you need to know that the constructor can be either with no parameters:

```
GridBagConstraints();
```

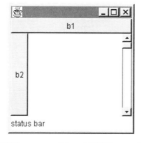

FIGURE 9-8   Stacking containers and LayoutManagers

or as complicated as:

```
GridBagConstraints(int gridx, int gridy, int gridwidth, int grid-
height, double weightx, double weighty, int anchor, int fill, Insets
insets, int ipadx, int ipady);
```

To add a component to a container using a `GridBagLayout` you can either:

- Add the component to the container and and use the
  `setConstraints()` method of `GridBagLayout` to tell the layout
  what the constraint values are for each component:
  ```
  add(myComponent);
  myComponent.setConstraints(myGridBagConstraints);
  ```

You can also set the constraints and then add the component.

- Name the `GridBagConstraints` instance as you are adding the component:
  ```
  add(myComponent, myGridBagConstraints);
  ```

Travel Assistance

http://java.sun.com/docs/books/tutorial/uiswing/layout/
custom.html

CardLayout

`CardLayout` is seldom used and has been replaced in Swing with a `JTabbedPane`.
However, it is fair game for the exam, so just for completeness we will gloss over it.
`CardLayout` offers the programmer a set of cards, each being exactly one component with a name that the layout tracks. It has the ability to display the cards, one at
a time, using the methods of the layout to flip through them, or by using the `String`
name of the card that was used when it was added to the layout manager to directly
access them. Of course, the intent is that the *one* component of the card is probably
going to be a `Panel` or something in turn to hold other components. Therefore, the
effect of a set of screens that can be accessed at will can be created. It is not a far
stretch to imagine a row of buttons across the top of each card looking a lot like
index card tabs, each calling the appropriate card to the top.

There are two methods that can be used to add a component to the layout:

```
addLayoutComponent(String name, Component c);
```

or

```
addLayoutComponent(Component c, Object name);
```

where the `Object` is a `String`.

By default, the first card added is the first displayed. The `CardLayout` relies on the `Container` that holds it to determine the ordering of the cards.

Travel Advisory

It is possible to set the LayoutManager to null using `setLayout`
`(null);` and do everything yourself. *Avoid the urge.* You will
be buying into *way* more problems than you can think of
right now.

LayoutManagers vs. Containers

Containers need to know what they contain. They need to know in what *order* those things were added. Then they pass off the constraints that were defined when each component was added to whatever layout manager is in effect at the time.

Layout managers get the information on what to display and the order from the container. Once they have that information, it is their job to do their best to display all of those components in a manner consistent with their rules and the constraints used to place them.

The problem with a window is that users can change it and move it about and what not. There is also that minimizing and resizing problem. Of course all of this is also the strength of using windows, so as programmers we have to deal with the problems related to keeping the appearance corrected to the new view.

Objective 9.04

Present a GUI with Specified Appearance and Resize Behavior

There are times when *you*, as the programmer, want to change the size or look of something that is already displayed on the screen. To handle these situations, you need to understand the graphics methods in addition to components that are available to you.

Everything that has a graphical representation in the AWT descends from the class Component . This representation is tracked through a graphics context. A graphics context holds the state information about how to render the component correctly onto the screen, so this includes things like the current color, font, clipping coordinates, and such things. The graphics context is something that the JVM keeps track of for you, so you would never create an instance of it yourself using the new operator. Instead, you ask the component to give you a copy of its graphics context by using the getGraphics() method, which then returns a Graphics object for use in housekeeping:

```
Graphics g = myComponent.getGraphics();
```

Once you have this object, you can use it to invoke the methods that the Component class has that are dedicated to maintaining its visual integrity. These methods are paint(), update(), and repaint().

There are about two dozen drawing methods in the Graphics class in the API that you need to be familiar with. They are summarized in the following table.

void	draw3DRect(int x, int y, int width, int height, boolean raised)
abstract void	drawArc(int x, int y, int width, int height, int startAngle, int arcAngle)
void	drawBytes(byte[] data, int offset, int length, int x, int y)
void	drawChars(char[] data, int offset, int length, int x, int y)
abstract boolean	drawImage(Image img, int x, int y, Color bgcolor, ImageObserver observer)
abstract boolean	drawImage(Image img, int x, int y, ImageObserver observer)
abstract boolean	drawImage(Image img, int x, int y, int width, int height, Color bgcolor, ImageObserver observer)

(Continued)

CONTINUED

abstract boolean	drawImage(Image img, int x, int y, int width, int height, ImageObserver observer)
abstract boolean	drawImage(Image img, int dx1, int dy1, int dx2, int dy2, int sx1, int sy1, int sx2, int sy2, Color bgcolor, ImageObserver observer)
abstract boolean	drawImage(Image img, int dx1, int dy1, int dx2, int dy2, int sx1, int sy1, int sx2, int sy2, ImageObserver observer)
abstract void	drawLine(int x1, int y1, int x2, int y2)
abstract void	drawOval(int x, int y, int width, int height)
abstract void	drawPolygon(int[] xPoints, int[] yPoints, int nPoints)
void	drawPolygon(Polygon p)
abstract void	drawPolyline(int[] xPoints, int[] yPoints, int nPoints)
void	drawRect(int x, int y, int width, int height)
abstract void	drawRoundRect(int x, int y, int width, int height, int arcWidth, int arcHeight)
abstract void	drawString(AttributedCharacterIterator iterator, int x, int y)
void	fill3DRect(int x, int y, int width, int height, boolean raised)
abstract void	fillArc(int x, int y, int width, int height, int startAngle, int arcAngle

(Continued)

abstract void	fillOval(int x, int y, int width, int height)
abstract void	fillPolygon(Polygon p)
abstract void	fillRect(int x, int y, int width, int height)
abstract void	fillRoundRect(int x, int y, int width, int height, int arcWidth, int arcHeight)

Keeping the Screen Clean

If you don't do anything with the housekeeping methods of component and the user changes something that affects the image of the component, such as moving a window over your stuff and then moving it away again, the system will send a message to the JVM. The system keeps track of where everything is displayed on the physical screen, so it knows what components are affected when any particular area of the screen needs tending to. The JVM will call the update() method of the component(s) affected, which then calls its paint() method. By default, the update() method clears the area and re-renders the components based on how they should look. This happens when the component is first constructed, shortly after the call to init() if it is an Applet, each time the component is clipped or minimized in any fashion, and again when it is restored or enlarged.

However, there are times when the programmer *wants* to change what the screen looks like. You may want to change a GIF file that is being displayed, or you may want to draw directly onto a component, like a Frame, or change the background color or whatever. Then you need to know how to modify the correct method to get the job done.

Paint

So how do you draw something on the screen? The area that you are going to draw on will be a component of some sort. There are four components that come with no special look to them by default. These are Applet, Canvas, Frame and Panel. Applet, Frame and Panel are truly intended to be containers although they can be drawn on, but Canvas has no other purpose than to be a drawing area. The Graphics class has a whole set of methods that can do all sorts of fun

> **Exam Tip**
>
> Any drawing method in the Graphics class is fair game in the exam.

drawing-like things. You should be familiar with these methods for the exam; we will use a few of them here so that you can get the hang of it.

That is where the `paint()` method comes in handy. Since we know that the system is going to make a call to `update()` and then `paint()` whenever it is needed, we can override `paint()` to include code that draws things.

Let's say that we have a component; this time we'll use a `Frame`. If we want to render an image of a `String` on the `Frame` we can use the `drawString()` method of `Graphics`. The common version of this method takes a `String` and the x and y coordinate of where to put the image. Notice that since you are not specifying anything else, the current default font and color from the container will be used for this drawing:

```
import java.awt.*;
class Test extends Frame{
    public void paint(Graphics g){
        g.drawString( "My Painting", 50, 100 );  //This is our artwork
    }
    public static void main(String args[]){
        Test t = new Test();
        t.setSize(300,400);
        t.setVisible(true);
    }
}
```

The frame is shown here:

Now we have a simple frame that includes a drawing of a `String`. When drawing in `Graphics`, the "pen" always starts at the upper-lefthand corner, so the `String` was drawn using the coordinates (50,100) as the upper-left corner of the drawing area. Every time that you cover up and uncover this Frame, a new call to `update()` happens and the `paint()` method is called. This is good.

But what if you *change* what you want to paint? You could call the `paint()` method directly. Let's try and draw a colored oval. To do that, you need to change the `Color` of the graphics context for the component and pass it a `Color` instance that represents the color that you want.

You could, of course, create your own color combination using the available constructors for the `Color` class. To do this, you need to pass parameters that are integers for the numerical representation of the correct combination of red, green, and blue (in that order) to create your `Color`:

```
Color c = new Color(100, 40,170); // a very nice purple thank you.
```

However, the `Color` class has a whole set of static fields that are intended to make this easier. For instance, `Color.orange` holds an instance of `Color` that has the numerical representation of the correct combination of red, green, and blue to create a very nice orange background. The `Color` fields that are available to you in the Color class are `Color.black`, `Color.blue`, `Color.cyan`, `Color.darkgrey`, `Color.grey`, `Color.green`, `Color.`, `Color.light-grey`, `Color.magenta`, `Color.orange`, `Color.pink`, `Color.red`, `Color.white`, and `Color.yellow`.

Now we can change the color using `Graphics g = getGraphics();` and then change the color by using `g.setColor(Color.blue);`.

In the following example, we are going to draw an oval using the `drawOval(int x, int y, int width, int height);` method of `Graphics`. The `mouseClicked()` method is going to slide the oval over and down and call the `paint()` method each time the mouse is clicked.

```
import java.awt.*;
import java.awt.event.*;
class Test extends Frame implements MouseListener{
    int xCoord=0, yCoord=0;
     Test(){
       addMouseListener(this);
       setSize(300,400);
       setVisible(true);
    }
    public void mousePressed(MouseEvent e){
      Graphics g = getGraphics();
       g.setColor(Color.blue);
```

```
    paint(g);
  }
  public void mouseClicked(MouseEvent e){};
  public void mouseReleased(MouseEvent e){};
  public void mouseEntered(MouseEvent e){};
  public void mouseExited(MouseEvent e){};

  public void paint(Graphics g){
      xCoord += 10;
      yCoord += 15;
      g.drawOval(xCoord,yCoord, 50,100);
  }
  public static void main(String args[]){
    Test t = new Test();
  }
}
```

The following `Frame` shows the moving oval:

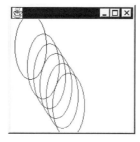

If you play with this you will notice a problem right away. It does paint the new oval on the screen, but it leaves the old stuff still there. However, when you minimize or cover up the Frame, or when you bring it back, the system calls update, which clears the screen and leaves you with just the one oval from this paint call.

This makes it clear that if *you* want to get rid of the previous oval when drawing a new one, you should be calling `update()` instead of `paint()`. Try replacing the `paint(g);` in the `mouseClicked()` method above with `update(g);` and see the difference.

When a container paints itself, it in turn calls the `paint()` method of every component that it owns, insuring that everything is recovered correctly.

Update

So when would you do anything *other* than calling update() instead of paint()? Up to now, we have been working on the assumption that you want a clean screen each time you paint, and calling update() provides that. However, there are times that you might want to make sure that the things that you draw *stay* drawn, even if the operating system makes a call to update() and skips any direct calls that you might have to paint—oops, all your previous stuff is gone.

By default, update() clears and then calls paint(). However, if you override update() to *only* call paint(), that clearing is bypassed, and your stuff stays put.

```
public void update(Graphics g){
    paint(g);
}
```

That's it. That should be the only tweaking that you ever have to do to update. Either leave it alone, or override it as above.

Repaint

All that explanation about how fun it is to play with paint(), and now I am going to tell you not to use it. "What?!" you say. The problem with a direct call to paint() is that it causes the paint() method to happen each and every time the call happens. Makes sense. But sometimes those calls get fed *very quickly* to the system and end up bogging it down. Since this has caused problems quite often, Sun invented the repaint() method to buffer those calls and insure that only a reasonable number of them happen per second. The limit is set at about 100 calls per second (depending on the operating system), which is *way* faster than the human eye can see.

When you call repaint() in your code, a call is made to update(), which in turn calls paint(). This means the screen has been cleared and recreated from scratch in a controlled manner. It has the added advantage that you do not have to pass it a Graphics object. The flip side of this is that since you are *not* passing it a Graphics context, you need to make sure that any messing around that you do to the Graphics context always happens in paint(). Of course, you should be doing that anyway (*always*), so that any times that the system calls update() without your involvement, all your stuff will get painted. If you tuck your drawings into some other method and the system calls paint() as a response to the user messing with the window, your stuff will *disappear*. Remember: *always* draw in paint(), and *always* call repaint().

The following example shows a `Frame` that has a rectangle and an oval drawn on it. Just for fun, we are switching the colors each time the user clicks on the `Frame`. To make it even more entertaining, this sample uses `MouseListener`, which we will cover in Chapter 10 (so just believe me for now). It also looks for the window closing, so that you can X out of the `Frame` without using CTRL-C (I get so tired of doing that). Again, this will be covered in the next chapter.

```java
import java.awt.*;
import java.awt.event.*;
class Test extends Frame implements MouseListener{
    int index = 0;
    Color []colors = {Color.red,Color.green,Color.blue};
     Test(){
        enableEvents(AWTEvent.WINDOW_EVENT_MASK);
        addMouseListener(this);
        setSize(300,400);
        setVisible(true);
    }
    public void processWindowEvent(WindowEvent e){
        if (e.getID() == WindowEvent.WINDOW_CLOSING) {
            super.processWindowEvent(e);
            //do closing stuff
            System.exit(0);
        }
    }
    public void mousePressed(MouseEvent e){
        setBackground(colors[index]); //just for the fun of it
        repaint();                         // Notice we are calling repaint
    }
    public void mouseClicked(MouseEvent e){};
    public void mouseReleased(MouseEvent e){};
    public void mouseEntered(MouseEvent e){};
    public void mouseExited(MouseEvent e){};

    public void paint(Graphics g){    // Notice that the drawing hap-
pens IN paint
        index += 1;
```

```
      index = index % 3;
      g.setColor(colors[index]);
      g.fillRect(80,80, 100,50);
      g.fillOval(80,200, 100,50);
   }
   public static void main(String args[]){
      Test t = new Test();
   }
}
```

The following `Frame` shows the fillOval and fillRect methods being called with changing colors:

You should never need to directly call `update()` because you are calling `repaint()` instead.

In this example, we used the `fillOval()` and `fillRect()` methods of `Graphics`, both of which take in the x and y coordinates of where to start, and the width and height that you want them drawn. For fun, we set up an array of colors so that clicking the mouse causes the drawings to change colors. Since we are now using `repaint()` like cautious programmers, the setColor activity must happen in `paint()` and not in the `mouseClicked()` method.

Fonts in Graphics

If you need to change the `Font` of the `String` that you are drawing on a `Component`, you can do so by the `Graphics` context, much as we changed the `Color` previously. An example of creating your own personal `Font` could be the following:

```
Font myFont = new Font("Serif", Font.ITALIC, 18);
```

Once you have the `Font` that you want, you can set the `Graphics` context by using `g.setFont(myFont);`

drawImage

Java uses `Images` to render graphical representations of its components. An empty `Image` instance can be created using the `createImage(int width, int height)` method of `Component`. `Toolkit` has several `createImage()` methods that can be used,

```
Image cool = Toolkit.getDefaultToolkit().createImage("myPic.jpg");
```

or

```
Toolkit.getDefaultToolkit().createImage(new URL("http://www.h.com/
imgs/7.jpg");
```

`Images` can also be created from GIF or JPEG files using the `getImage(URL)` method or the `getImage(Url URLDirectory, String path)` method of Applet. Toolkit has methods `getImage(URL)` and a `getImage(String filename)` that can be used in a Frame. Notice that if you use the `getImage()` methods of `Toolkit`, you get a fresh copy of the `Image` each time you use it. If it is called in `paint()`, that can be quite often. If you use the `createImage()` method, you are creating a copy of the image that can be accessed over and over, sort of like caching the object, except it does *not* go out and see if the JPEG file has been modified since the last time; it is more efficient but less "real time".

What you need to know is how to manipulate an `Image` using the `drawImage()` method of `Graphics` that lets you put the `Image` on your `Applet` or `Frame`.

```
import java.awt.*;
import java.applet.Applet;
class MyApplet extends Applet{
    Image myImage;
    public void init(){
        try{
          //to use getDocumentBase() the .gif must actually BE in the
          //same directory as the html
           myImage = getImage(getDocumentBase(),"Jungle.gif");
        }
        catch(Exception e){}
```

```
    }
    public void paint(Graphics g){
        boolean b = g.drawImage(myImage, 20, 20, this);
    }
}
```

In this case, the `Jungle.gif` file is sitting in the same directory with the html, so we could use the `getDocumentBase()` method to return a URL. If that is not the case, you'll need to replace that call with `new URL("file:c://whateverDirectory")` or `new URL("http://whatever Server")`, for example:

```
myImage = getImage("c://data/images","Jungle.gif");
```

The `Image` object has a graphics context of its own separate from the graphics for the applet, so it is possible to modify the Image after you have captured it or created it.

```
import java.awt.*;
import java.applet.Applet;
class MyApplet extends Applet{
    Image myImage;
    public void init(){
        myImage = createImage(200,200);
        Graphics myG = myImage.getGraphics();//get the graphics for
the new Image
        myG.fillOval(10,10,50,80); //draw on the Graphics
        myG.drawString("This is fun", 10,100);
    }
    public void paint(Graphics g){
        boolean b = g.drawImage(myImage, 20, 20, this);
    }
}
```

The following image shows the oval and string:

Here we created a new `Image` and got its `Graphics` context; then we started using the methods of `Graphics` to modify what is to be displayed.

Resizing and Clipping

So what if the `Graphics` object we have is too big? There is a `setClip()` method that lets us trim the viewing area. One version of this method takes in a `Shape` object, but the most common version is the following:

```
public void setClip(int x, int y, int width, int height)
```

If we modify the code above, we can cut the oval in half:

```
import java.awt.*;
import java.applet.Applet;
class MyApplet extends Applet{
    Image myImage;
    public void init(){
        myImage = createImage(200,200);
        Graphics myG = myImage.getGraphics();//get the graphics for
the new Image
        myG.fillOval(10,10,50,80); //draw on the Graphics
        myG.drawString("This is fun", 10,100);
    }
    public void paint(Graphics g){
        g.setClip(20,20,40,120);  // added this line
        boolean b = g.drawImage(myImage, 20, 20, this);
    }
}
```

The following `Image` is clipped in half:

CHECKPOINT

✔ **Objective 9.01** Write code using Components.

- Components that you need to be familiar with include Buttons, Labels, TextFields, TextAreas, Labels, CheckBoxes, CheckBoxGroups, and so on. You should be able to add them, customize them, and use their special methods.
- Menus, MenuItems and MenuBars are not Components but subclass MenuComponent instead. MenuBars are set on Frames outside of the layout area.

✔ **Objective 9.02** Write code using Containers.

- Frame, Applet, Panel, and Dialog are Containers. Frame and Dialog are subclasses of Window; Applet is a subclass of Panel.

✔ **Objective 9.03** Write code using the LayoutManager classes of the **java.awt** package. Distinguish the responsibilities of layout managers from those of containers.

- LayoutManagers worry about location and size constraints; Containers worry about the order that components were added.
- FlowLayout is the default for Panel and Applet, BorderLayout is the default for Frame and Dialog. By default, all components are added to the CENTER of BorderLayout.
- GridLayout relies only on the row's value that is set. If it is not available, it will honor the column's value. No container has GridLayout for a default layout. GridBagLayout takes a bunch of constraint information in a GridBagConstraint object to figure it out.

✔ **Objective 9.04** Present a GUI with specified appearance and resize behavior.

- For graphics drawing, always remember to put your drawing code in the paint() method, but make the call to repaint().
- Leave update() alone if you want the screen cleared before each call to paint(), but override it to contain *only* a call to paint() if you want to avoid having it cleared each time.

REVIEW QUESTIONS

1. Given the following code, which statement is true?

```
import java.awt.*;
class Test extends Frame {
    Button b1, b2, b3;
    Test(){
      b1 = new Button("b1");
      b2 = new Button("b2");
      b3 = new Button("b3");
      add(b1);
      add(b2);
      add(b3);
      this.setSize(400,200);
      this.setVisible(true);
    }
    public static void main(String args[]){
      Test t = new Test();
    }
}
```

    A. No buttons will display because there is no `init()` method.

    B. Three buttons will display in a row, each just wide enough for the label. The look of the button will depend on the underlying operating system.

    C. No buttons will display because there is no LayoutManager set.

    D. Three buttons will display in a row, and the look is platform independent.

    E. One button will display in the center. It will occupy all the available space. The look of the button will depend on the underlying operating system.

2. Given the following code, which statement is true?

```
import java.awt.*;
import java.applet.*;

class Test extends Applet {
    Button b1, b2, b3;
```

```
    Panel p = new Panel();
   public void init(){
     b1 = new Button("Push Me");
     this.setLayout(new BorderLayout());
     p.setLayout(new BorderLayout());
     p.add(b1, BorderLayout.WEST);
     add(p,BorderLayout.SOUTH);
   }
}
```

A. The code will get a compiling error because you cannot put BorderLayout on a panel.

B. The code will compile but will not display because there are no `setSize()` and `setVisible()` methods.

C. The code will compile and display. Panel p will occupy a strip at the bottom of the applet. The button will be on the left side of the strip.

D. The code will compile. The button will be in a strip running down the entire left side of the screen.

E. The code will compile. The button will display and will occupy the entire strip at the bottom of the screen.

3. Given the following code, which statement is true?

```
import java.awt.*;
class Test extends Frame {
    Scrollbar sb = new Scrollbar(Scrollbar.VERTICAL, 0, 60, 0, 300);
   public Test(){
     this.add(sb, BorderLayout.SOUTH);
     this.setSize(400,400);
     this.setVisible(true);
   }
   public static void main(String args[]){
       Test t = new Test();
   }
}
```

A. The Scrollbar will be added to the bottom strip. The control arrows will be on the left and right of the Scrollbar.

B. The Scrollbar will be added to the bottom strip. The control arrows will be on the top and bottom of the scrollbar and will run the entire width of the screen.

C. The Scrollbar will be added to the right strip. The control arrows will be on the top and bottom of the scrollbar and will be the width of the scrollbar.

D. The code will get a compile error because you cannot put a vertical scrollbar on the bottom strip of the screen.

E. The Scrollbar will be added, but the south parameter will be ignored because the default LayoutManager for Frame is FlowLayout.

4. If a panel has a GridLayout set to (4,3), what will be the effect of adding 13 components to the panel?

A. The number of columns will be honored, and the system will add an additional row to be able to accommodate all of the components.

B. Only the first 12 components will be displayed.

C. The twelfth and thirteenth components will be fit together in the last grid space.

D. The number of rows will be honored, and the system will add an additional column to be able to accommodate all of the components.

E. You will get a compile error stating that you have a null pointer exception.

5. Which syntax will add a Checkbox named Maple to a CheckBoxGroup named Trees and set it to default to checked? Select two.

A. `add(new Checkbox("Maple", true, Trees));`

B. `Checkbox Maple = new Checkbox(true, Trees);`

C. `add(new Checkbox("Trees", "Maple", true));`

D. `add(new Checkbox("Maple", true, new CheckboxGroup("Trees")));`

E. `add(new Checkbox("Maple", Trees, true));`

6. A Label has a foreground color of blue and a 12-point plain sans-serif font. The Label is added to a Panel that has a foreground color of red and a background color of green, with an 18-point font. The default foreground color for Components is set to black. The default background color for Components is set to gray. Which is true about the Label?

A. The letters on the Label will be black on a field of gray and the letter size will be 12 point.

B. The letters on the Label will be blue, and the background will be green with a 12-point plain sans-serif font.

C. The letters on the Label will be red, and the background will be green with an 18-point plain sans-serif font.

D. The letters on the Label will be blue, and the background will be gray with a 12-point plain sans-serif font.

E. The letters on the Label will be black, and the background will be green with an 18-point plain sans-serif font.

7. CheckboxGroup is a Container. True or False?

8. If you create a TextField on a Panel using `new TextField("Enter val-ues");` and then the user enters a long String value, which of the following statements are true?

   A. The TextField stays the same size and the text inside it wraps.
   B. The contents of the TextField are truncated.
   C. The TextField becomes wider to accommodate the new Font.
   D. The TextField stays the same size and the user must use the arrow keys to navigate the text.
   E. The TextField stays the same size, but a ScrollBar appears for the user to navigate the text.

9. To draw the screen with something new and replace what was there before, you need to do which of the following:

   A. Override the `repaint()` method and call `paint()`.
   B. Override the `paint()` method and call `repaint()`.
   C. Override the `update()` method to have a call to `clear()` and call `repaint()`.
   D. Add a `graphics()` method to your code and call `repaint();`
   E. Call `super.paint();`

10. What does the following `paint()` method draw?

```
public void paint(Graphics g){
    g.drawLine(30, 40, 50,60);
}
```

   A. A line starting at 30 pixels over on the x axis and 40 pixels up on the y axis and going to a point 50 pixels over on the x axis and 60 pixels up on the y axis.

B. A line starting at 30 pixels to the right of the upper-lefthand corner and 40 pixels down from the upper-lefthand corner and going to a point 50 pixels over from the left and 60 pixels down from the top.

REVIEW ANSWERS

1. **E** A is incorrect because only Applets require an `init()` method. B would be the answer if the LayoutManager were FlowLayout, but the default for Frame is BorderLayout. C is incorrect because Frame has a default LayoutManager. D is incorrect both because it describes a FlowLayout and because the look of components is platform dependent. E is correct.

2. **C** You can put any layout manager on a Panel, and Applets do not need `setSize()` and `SetVisible()` called. D would be true only if p had not been put in the SOUTH of the applet. E would be true only if the button had been put in NORTH, SOUTH or CENTER.

3. **B** Vertical scrollbars have their controls on the top and bottom, so A is incorrect. The scrollbar was placed in the south, not the right as stated in C, and that placement will be honored. You *can* put a vertical scrollbar in the south strip, so D in incorrect. E is incorrect because the default LayoutManager for Frame is BorderLayout.

4. **D** If both the rows and columns are set for GridLayout, the system uses the row number and calculates how many columns are required to be able to position all of the components in the grid, so D is true.

5. **A** **E** When creating a Checkbox you can order the parameters either `name/CheckboxGroup/Boolean Checked` or `name/Boolean Checked/CheckboxGroup`. All the constructors for Checkboxes that have a title must have the title first in the list, so B and C are incorrect. There is no constructor for `CheckboxGroup` that takes any parameters, so D is incorrect.

6. **B** The label specifically set the foreground to blue 12 point, so the letters on the label will be blue 12 point. Components inherit background colors that are not explicitly set from their immediately enclosing container, so the label will have the green background of the panel.

7. **False** CheckboxGroup is not a subclass of Container; its only superclass is Object. It is a logical grouping, not a special holder.

8. **D** The visual components do not change shape after they are constructed on a screen, so C is incorrect. The contents of the TextField cannot be damaged, so B is not true. There is no functionality in TextField to navigate up and down, so wrapping is not a possibility. ScrollBars do not appear unless there is code to make them appear. D is true.

9. **B** Both B and C will get something to appear on the screen, but only B will completely replace what was there before.

10. **B** The Graphics methods determine their location starting from the upper-lefthand corner of the container.

AWT 2:
Making the
Screen Work

	NEWBIE	SOME EXPERIENCE	EXPERT
ETA	12+ hours	6 hours	2 hours

So far, we have talked a lot about how to make the GUI (graphical user interface) look pretty, but nothing we've talked about so far actually *does* anything. We have made buttons, but when you push them, nothing happens.

Travel Assistance

You can get assistance in understanding these concepts from Sun's tutorial at **http://java.sun.com/docs/books/tutorial/uiswing/events/index.html,** but be aware that it uses Swing in its examples and Swing is not covered on the exam.

Objective 10.01

State the Event Classname for Any Specified Event Listener Interface in the `java.awt.event` Package

A user does all sorts of stuff while sitting at a screen—pushes buttons, maximizes and minimizes windows, enters text, selects things from lists, pushes radio buttons, and so on. Sooner or later, the programmer has to deal with how to handle this input.

Events: What Are They?

When interfacing with a user at a keyboard, there must be some method for the operating system to detect what the user is doing and get that information to the application. This is done is by creating events. When the user interacts with the hardware, it is detected by the operating system and the JVM wraps the information about the source of the event in an appropriate type of Java object called an AWTEvent. Luckily, we don't need to know how this is done; we just need to deal with it. The AWTEvent holds the information about what **kind** of an event it is considered to be in Java, and an instance of the actual Event class gets placed in the EventQueue for the component. Figure 10-1 shows the AWT Event hierarchy.

If the interaction was performed with a mouse, a MouseEvent is created. If the interaction was performed on a keyboard, a KeyEvent is created. If the interaction

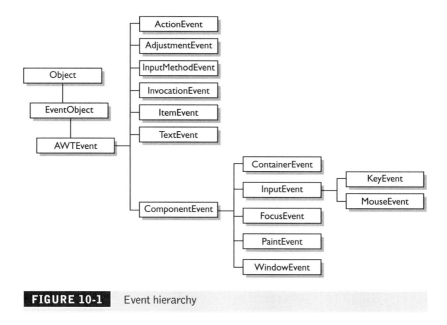

FIGURE 10-1   Event hierarchy

was performed on a window, a `WindowEvent` is created. All of the events that are handled by the visible components and have event masks are listed in Table 10.1. While we will be using many of the `Event` classes in the examples, some are not designed to be used with the Event Listener model or are beyond the scope of the exam. In particular, `PaintEvent` and `InvocationEvent` are not discussed in this chapter.

TABLE 10.1   **AWTEvents for the Visible Components, with Event Masks**

Event	Mask
java.awt.event.ActionEvent	ACTION_EVENT_MASK
java.awt.event.AdjustmentEvent	ADJUSTMENT_EVENT_MASK
java.awt.event.ComponentEvent	COMPONENT_EVENT_MASK
java.awt.event.ContainerEvent	CONTAINER_EVENT_MASK

(Continued)

TABLE 10.1 *Continued*

Event	Mask
java.awt.event.FocusEvent	FOCUS_EVENT_MASK
java.awt.event.InputMethodEvent	INPUT_METHOD_EVENT_MASK
java.awt.event.ItemEvent	ITEM_EVENT_MASK
java.awt.event.KeyEvent	KEY_EVENT_MASK
java.awt.event.MouseEvent	MOUSE_EVENT_MASK
java.awt.event.MouseMotionEvent	MOUSE_MOTION_EVENT_MASK
java.awt.event.TextEvent	TEXT_EVENT_MASK
java.awt.event.WindowEvent	WINDOW_EVENT_MASK

Event Enabling

There are several ways of dealing with events. The most basic involves having the component process the event itself. This is done using explicit event enabling.

The components, as provided by Sun, do not handle events automatically. Therefore, you need to subclass the component that you want to try this with and "turn on" the functionality. You do this by invoking the method enableEvents() in your component subclass and passing in an indicator that tells it *what* kind of events you are going to handle. The indicators are called masks and are defined in the AWTEvent class as fields. There is a mask for each kind of event that can be handled. The enableEvents() method is inherited from Component, so *all* of the visible GUI things can do this. Of course, for the enableEvents() functions to work, you need to make the call somewhere in the constructor or initiating code for your component.

A sample of the call would be as follows

```
enableEvents (AWTEvent.TEXT_EVENT_MASK,
              AWTEvent.FOCUS_EVENT_MASK);
```

There are a few other Event classes in JDK1.2 that relate to events that are not on the exam, so we will not be covering them here.

Now that you have turned on explicit event handling, you have to handle the events. The event is going to look for a method in your class called process XXXEvent(XXXEvent e) for instructions on what to do. The Component class, which is the parent for all of the visible components, has a whole set of these processXXXEvent() methods, one for each of the kinds of events that can be handled by any component. There are a few classes that have additional process XXXEvent() methods that only relate to a subset of the visible components. In your component subclass, you need to override the processXXXEvent() method that you are interested in and put in code to make it do what you want it to do.

For instance, you can call enableEvents(AWTEvent.ACTION_EVENT_MASK); and know that any action event that happens against your component will cause your class's processActionEvent() method to be called, which will allow you to be able to control any ActionEvent() that happens on your component.

> ### Travel Advisory
>
> BE CAREFUL! During this processXXXEvent() method, you not only need to do whatever *you* want to happen when the event happens, you also need to call the *super.processXXXEvent(e)* method if the superclass has stuff in *its* method that needs to get done. This is to insure that any listeners on the superclass are still dealt with. You don't want to be breaking what is already there when you add your functionality!

Sample of Event Enabling

```java
import java.awt.*;
import java.awt.event.*;
class Test extends Button {
   Test(String s){ //constructor
      super(s); //call Button constructor
      enableEvents(AWTEvent.ACTION_EVENT_MASK);//turn on handling
   }
   public void processActionEvent(ActionEvent e){ //use it
      System.out.println("ActionEvent"); //do cool stuff
      super.processActionEvent(e); //get the super stuff done
   }
```

```
public static void main(String args[]){
    Test t = new Test("Button"); //make a Button
    Frame f = new Frame("test"); //make a Frame
    f.add(t); // put the Button on the Frame
    f.setSize(400,300);
    f.setVisible(true);
}
}
```

Travel Advisory

If you use enableEvents, the `processXXXEvent()` notification happens *before* any listener notification that might also need to happen, and *then* it notifies the listeners. So even though you cannot know which listener is going to get notified first, you *do* know that the `processXXXEvent()` method will be first.

Once you have called `enableEvents`, just override the `processXXXEvent()` method, and life is good.

Objective 10.02

Write Code to Implement Listener Classes and Methods

Most of the time, the functionality that is the reaction to an event is handed off to another class, called a listener, whose only job is to sit around waiting for that particular kind of event to happen and then deal with it. This is called the Event Delegation Model and allows the programmer to keep the code that creates the cosmetics of the GUI separate from the code that actually *functions*. When a listener is added to a component, the appropriate `enableEvents()` is automatically called for you. Event Delegation is the cleanest and most common way of event handling in use today. Even Swing uses the Event Model to handle all of its events, so it is important that you understand it well.

> **Local Lingo**
>
> A *listener* is a class whose job is to wait around until it is notified that an event has happened, deal with it and then, if needed, it make a call back to the component that requested it to listen.

> **Travel Advisory**
>
> You *cannot* combine event delegation with event enabling.

Delegating to Listeners

The concept of delegating is very simple:

1. You create an object that is an instance of a GUI component of some sort (you should be pretty good at that by now).
2. You create an object that is an instance of a listener that knows what to do if the component delegates an event to it.
3. You link them together (also known as registering the listener with the component) using the addXXXListener() method of the component and passing in the listener.

That's it. Not so bad. Of course, first you have to have a class that is a listener and *knows* what to do. Therefore you may also have to create that functional listener class. The listeners provided by Sun are all just interfaces waiting for an implementation, so unless you have some generic listeners that have been created locally and that actually *do* what you want them to do, you will need to create a usable listener class.

Actually, the most complicated part of the whole topic is that there are lots of combinations of ways that you can accomplish those three or four steps, so recognizing the setups that are valid is important. We will go through most of them one at a time. But first, make sure that you are familiar with all of the listener interfaces that are available and what methods that you must implement for each one. Understand that they are all subinterfaces of java.util.EventListener. Table 10.2 shows all of the interfaces that are covered on the Certification Exam.

TABLE 10.2 Listeners and Methods

Interface	Methods That Must Be Implemented
java.awt.ActionListener	`actionPerformed(ActionEvent e)`
java.awt.AdjustmentListener	`adjustmentValueChanged` `(AdjustmentEvent e)`
java.awt.ComponentListener	`componentHidden(ComponentEvent e)` `componentMoved(ComponentEvent e)` `componentResized(ComponentEvent e)` `componentShown(ComponentEvent e)`
java.awt.ContainerListener	`componentAdded(ContainerEvent e)` `componentRemoved(ContainerEvent e)`
java.awt.FocusListener	`focusGained(FocusEvent e)` `focusLost(FocusEvent e)`
java.awt.InputMethodListener	`caretPositionChanged` `(InputMethodEvent e)` `inputMethodTextChanged` `(InputMethodEvent e)`
java.awt.ItemListener	`itemStateChanged(ItemEvent e)`
java.awt.KeyListener	`keyPressed(KeyEvent e)` `keyReleased(KeyEvent e)` `keyTyped(KeyEvent e)`
java.awt.MouseListener	`mouseClicked(MouseEvent e)` `mouseEntered(MouseEvent e)` `mouseExited(MouseEvent e)` `mousePressed(MouseEvent e)` `mouseReleased(MouseEvent e)`
java.awt.MouseMotionListener	`mouseDragged(MouseMotionEvent e)` `mouseMoved(MouseMotionEvent e)`

(Continued)

TABLE 10.2 *CONTINUED*	
Interface	**Methords That Must Be Implemented**
java.awt.TextListener	textValueChanged(TextEvent e)
java.awt.WindowListener	windowActivated(WindowEvent e)
	windowClosed(WindowEvent e)
	windowClosing(WindowEvent e)
	windowDeactivated(WindowEvent e)
	windowDeiconified(WindowEvent e)
	windowIconified(WindowEvent e)
	windowOpened(WindowEvent e)

Exam Tip

Yes, you *do* need to be familiar with *all* of these.

The Standard Setup and KeyEvents

The easiest setup to discuss is the one in which everything is in its own class: one class for the GUI component (we can use one that Sun provides), a separate class for your new listener, and a third class to be the "driver" application that uses them. This is the class with the `main()` method.

The Basic Setup

Pick a GUI thing, any GUI thing that's visible, and make an instance of it. Let's pick a TextField. OK, now make one. That's easy: `TextField tf = new TextField("This is my TextField")`, as shown in Figure 10-2.

Now, make a listener class by implementing one of the listener interfaces. Make sure it's one that will *work* on the particular component that you picked. For instance, `TextField` has a whole laundry list of `addXXXListeners` that it has inherited from its various superclasses, but nowhere in there does it have an `addWindowListener()` method, so don't make that kind of listener for it. In this

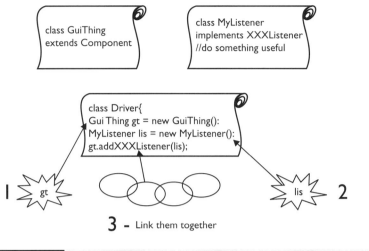

case, let's add a `KeyListener` so we can mess with the user's input. I LOVE
`KeyEvents`, they make me feel SO powerful <smile>! In our new class, we will
find fun stuff to do with the three methods that `KeyListeners` need to implement: the `KeyPressed()`, `KeyReleased()`, and `KeyTyped()` methods. First,
let's try to print something out to the console to see if it works:

```
import java.awt.event.*;
class MyListener implements KeyListener{
   public void keyPressed(KeyEvent e){
       System.out.println("A key was Pressed");
   }
   public void keyReleased(KeyEvent e){
       System.out.println("A key was Released");
   }
   public void keyTyped(KeyEvent e){
       System.out.println("A key was Typed");
   }
}
```

Notice that we have implemented all three of the methods of the `KeyListener`
interface. They don't **do** much, but we included them.

Now we have to make our `TextField` and a `MyListener` and link them
together:

```
import java.awt.*;
import java.awt.event.*;
class Test {
   public static void main(String args[]){
       Frame f = new Frame("test");
       TextField t = new TextField("This is the default"); //make a
       //GUI thing
       MyListener lis = new MyListener(); //make a listener
       t.addKeyListener(lis); //link the GUI thing and the Listener
       f.add(t);
       f.setSize(400,300);
       f.setVisible(true);
   }
}
```

Compile the listener. `TextField` comes already compiled by Sun. Compile the Test driver. Execute the Test driver. Put the cursor on the `TextArea` and type away.

Notice what is happening here. Something happens to the `TextField`, and the `TextField` sends (delegates) the Event to the listener.

Use CTRL+C on the DOS screen to break out of the application when you are done playing, or you will be stuck forever. A listener that knows when to exit would be a good idea, but we won't do that yet.

If all went well, you'll be able to watch the printout to the console as you pressed and released keys. Note that pressing some keys does not actually *type* anything, which is why they cause keyPressed Events. Also, note that a combination of a `keyPressed` of SHIFT and a `keyPressed` of "a" causes a `keyTyped` of "*A*".

Travel Assistance

Adding a listener automatically "turns on" enableEvents.

Messing with the Input

Now comes the fun part. When a key is used, the `KeyEvent` that is created contains the information on *what* is pressed or typed. The data is stored in the `KeyEvent`, and there are methods provided to query for it. The `getKeyChar()`

method lets you work with the logical characters as you would see them on the keyboard; the `getKeyCode()` method lets you work with the integer value that each character is assigned. You can tinker with these values in your `KeyEvent` methods using the `setKeyChar()` method. <evil grin>. Let's set it up so that whatever the user presses, the `TextField` displays the next biggest character.

If we modify the `keyTyped()` method of our listener slightly, we can use the `getKeyChar()` method to capture what happened and the `setKeyChar()` method to change the value of what happened.

```
public void keyTyped(KeyEvent e){
    char whatKey = e.getKeyChar(); //get the information from the
    //event
    System.out.println(whatKey + " was pressed"); //do stuff
    e.setKeyChar(++whatKey); // mess with the event by incrementing
    //it <grin>
}
```

KeyEvent Constants

The next useful thing to know about `KeyEvents` is that they come with a whole set of constants built-in that relate to the `KeyCode` for all the possible inputs on a keyboard. For example, there is a VK_A constant that relates to the `KeyCode` for "a", and there is a VK_3, and a VK_ASTERISK, and so on. Notice that these are integer values, not character representations. They are very useful for making readable code to manipulate `keyPresses`. There are also `KeyCodes` for keys that do not actually *type* anything but have other functions, such as VK_ENTER, VK_BACK_SPACE, and so on.

To do the next "trick" you need to be clear on the difference between a `keyPress` and a `keyTyped`. You can press the SHIFT key all you want and nothing is going to get typed. However, to get a `KeyTyped` of a capital *A*, you need a `keyPressed` of SHIFT and a `keyPressed` of "*a*" with no `keyReleased` in between.

Using the `KeyCode` masks, we are going to hide all of the user's entry. If we add one line of code to the `keyPressed()` method, all of the users input will be crossed out. Notice that this happens even if we leave the `KeyChar` untouched.

```
public void keyPressed(KeyEvent e){
    System.out.println("A key was Pressed");
    e.setKeyCode(KeyEvent.VK_X);
}
```

These examples are perhaps not the most useful thing to do; however, in real life if you need to prevent your user from entering numbers or special characters, you can look at what the character is and, based on your logic, switch what the value is, cover it up, or even get rid of it.

The Embedded Driver Setup

The test driver that we used in the previous example is just a `main()` method floating in an otherwise useless class. Many folks choose to embed the main method that uses the component and the listener *inside* either one of those classes. For instance, we could put the `main()` method in the new MyListener class that we just wrote and then execute MyListener (watch out for the import statements when moving the code over):

```
import java.awt.*;
import java.awt.event.*;
class MyListener implements KeyListener{ // Notice that this class
is a listener
   public void keyPressed(KeyEvent e){
       System.out.println("A key was Pressed");
   }
   public void keyReleased(KeyEvent e){
       System.out.println("A key was Released");
       e.setKeyCode(KeyEvent.VK_X);
 }
   public void keyTyped(KeyEvent e){
       char whatKey = e.getKeyChar();
       System.out.println(whatKey + " was pressed");
       e.setKeyChar(++whatKey);
   }
   public static void main(String args[]){ //the driver code is in
the listener
       Frame f = new Frame("test");
       TextField t = new TextField("This is the default"); ..//make a
GUI thing
       MyListener lis = new MyListener(); //make a listener
       t.addKeyListener(lis); //link the GUI thing and the listener
       f.add(t);
       f.setSize(400,300); //don't forget
```

```
        f.setVisible(true);
    }
}
```

Having the `main()` method in one of the other two classes sometimes makes life easier, especially for testing purposes. However, it could be considered bad style because it blurs class responsibilities.

Inner Listeners

Another possibility is to include your listener class entirely *inside* the class that is going to use it. This is a good way to organize the classes so that they are easily maintainable—but you should only do this if the listener class is so specialized that only this class will ever use it, or its function is extremely simple. Notice that in the following example there is only *one* top level class. The top level class has an inner class that is a listener, and the driver code in the `main()` is in the outer class. This is getting much more streamlined.

The TextListener class is useful if you want to listen for *any* kind of a change to the Text without paying too much attention to what keystrokes the user keyed in.

```java
import java.awt.*;
import java.awt.event.*;
class MyTextArea extends TextArea{
    MyTextArea(int rows, int cols){ //the constructor
        super(rows, cols); //call the super constructor
        MyTextArea.MyListener lis = this.new MyListener(); // make a
listener
        this.addTextListener(lis); //link the GUI thing and the
Listener
    }
    //This is the inner class
    private class MyListener implements TextListener{
        public void textValueChanged(TextEvent e){
            System.out.println("Something Changed"); //respond to
TextEvent
        }
    }
```

```
    public static void main(String args[]){ //the driver code
        Frame f = new Frame("test");
        MyTextArea t = new MyTextArea(10,30); //make a GUI thing
        f.add(t);
        f.setSize(400,300);
        f.setVisible(true);
    }
}
```

All this code does is create a simple frame with one TextArea, and every time something text-like happens in the TextArea, a message is displayed.

Anonymous Classes

There is one more way to **really** streamline the code, and that would be to make your inner class anonymous. In the previous example, we created a listener and gave it a name just so we could use that name to feed the `addTextListener()` method. If you use an anonymous class, you can put the whole definition of the listener *in* the parameter for the `addTextListener()`.

The concept of anonymous classes was presented earlier as a way to define and use a class exactly one time — all at once. These classes are never given a name because they never need to be referenced any place but the spot where they are defined. The most common use of these anonymous classes is listener classes:

```
guiThing.addActionListener(new ActionListener(){//implement the
methods here});
```

Of course, when you stuff a bunch of methods in the brackets that are basically just the input parameter for the method `addXXXListener()`, it gets to looking a bit like a maze, but if you can get the syntax correct, it *does* allow for a rather elegant implementation. However, you really do *not* want to be doing this if you are going to have a lot of statements in the anonymous class. It gets much too complicated very quickly.

In this example, the only thing that the button does is close the frame, which is a very useful thing to do.

```
import java.awt.*;
```

```
import java.awt.event.*;
class Test extends Frame {
   Button b = new Button("Push Me to Close this application");
   public Test(){ //this is the constructor for the frame
       this.add(b);
       b.addActionListener(new ActionListener(){
           public void actionPerformed(ActionEvent e){
               System.exit(0);
           }
       } );
       this.setSize(300,50);
       this.setVisible(true);
   }
   public static void main(String args[]){
       Test t = new Test();
   }
}
```

In the following example, a `WindowListener` listens for the user clicking the X to close the window.

```
import java.awt.*;
import java.awt.event.*;
class Test extends Frame {
   Button b = new Button("Close using the X");
   public Test(){ //this is the constructor for the frame
       this.add(b);
       this.addWindowListener(new WindowListener(){
           public void windowClosing(WindowEvent e){System.exit(0);}
           public void windowActivated(WindowEvent e){};//zillions of
empty methods
           public void windowClosed(WindowEvent e){};
           public void windowDeactivated(WindowEvent e){};
           public void windowDeiconified(WindowEvent e){};
           public void windowIconified(WindowEvent e){};
           public void windowOpened(WindowEvent e){};
       });
```

```
        this.setSize(300,100);
        this.setVisible(true);
    }
    public static void main(String args[]){
        Test t = new Test();
    }
}
```

Notice that even though we didn't put any actions in the other methods, this is still a complicated bit of code to stuff in an anonymous class, and we would *not* suggest doing it this way. Instead, you should use the adapter for the `WindowListener` so that you do not *need* to implement all those unnecessary methods in the anonymous class. Adapters are a simple way to use listeners that have lots of methods; they are covered in more depth in the next section.

Event Adapters

If you are working with `ActionListeners`, `ItemListeners`, `TextListeners`, and so on, implementing an interface is no problem. These listeners have only one method in them, and you have to override that method to get anything done. However, some listeners have lots of methods. For instance, `WindowListener` has seven and `MouseListener` has five, for example. The rule is if you implement a listener, you have to provide implementations for *all* of the methods. That means that even if you are just using *one* method, you have to type empty methods for the rest of them. What a pain. I always forget to do it, and end up getting a compiler error and have to go back and add them in. Even more pain.

Turns out that the folks at Sun thought it was a bit of a pain too, so they provided a set of adapters for the listeners in the API. Adapters are just classes that implement the listeners for you and provide the empty methods. This allows you to extend them, override the one or two that you want, and inherit the rest. This is a nice convenience factor. Of course, Sun only provided adapters for those listeners that have more than one method to override (it would be sort of silly to have an adapter that didn't save you any effort).

The only problem with adapters is that if you are already extending something else, you can't use adapters. If you can use adapters, however, it is a piece of cake. You just add the adapter method that does the work right in with all of the other methods in your component or driver class. This is the same anonymous class as in the previous example but using an adapter instead of an interface:

```
import java.awt.*;
import java.awt.event.*;
class Test extends Frame {
   Button b = new Button("Close using the X");
   public Test(){ //this is the constructor for the frame
       this.add(b);
       this.addWindowListener(new WindowAdapter(){ //this is an
anonymous adapter
          public void windowClosing(WindowEvent e) //only override
what you want
          {System.exit(0);}
       } );
       this.setSize(300,100);
       this.setVisible(true);
   }
   public static void main(String args[]){
       Test t = new Test(); //make the Frame
   }
}
```

Now we have a *very* streamlined way to close a window without bothering with all of the other methods that WindowListeners can use. Elegant.

The one caution that should be mentioned is that most applications are constantly changing. It is possible that in the future the class that you have extending an adapter may need to extend something else. If you already had it set up as implementing a listener, it's no problem. However, if you used an adapter, it will require more work to update.

Travel Advisory

Be sure to check your spelling. If you make a typographical error spelling the method name when implementing a listener, you will get a compile error that tells you so. However, if you make a typographical error spelling a method name when you extend an adapter, it becomes a different method that never gets called, and you may end up wondering why nothing *works*.

Determine the Affected Component, Mouse Position, Nature, and Time of Event

Events know a lot about themselves, and it is possible to query this information so that the application can make decisions on how to handle each event.

Event Information

Most GUIs have more than one component on the screen. It is possible to make a separate listener that knows exactly what to do for each and every component, but this could involve a lot a lot of separate classes. It is also possible (although not necessarily recommended as a matter of style) to have one listener and add that listener to lots of components and then let that listener figure out which component it is dealing with. To do that, the listener needs some information from the event that was fired: it needs to know which component fired the event. The listener can use the `getSource()` method that all components inherit from `EventObject` to do this:

```
import java.awt.*;
import java.awt.event.*;
class Test extends Frame implements ActionListener{
    Button b1 = new Button("Close");
    Button b2 = new Button("Write to console");
    public Test(){ //this is the constructor for the frame
        this.setLayout(new FlowLayout());
        b1.addActionListener(this);
        b2.addActionListener(this);
        this.add(b1);
        this.add(b2);
        this.setSize(300,100);
        this.setVisible(true);
    }
    public void actionPerformed(ActionEvent e){
```

```
    if (e.getSource() == b1)
        System.exit(0);
    if (e.getSource() == b2)
        System.out.println("Button b2 was pushed");
}
public static void main(String args[]){
    Test t = new Test();
}
}
```

Here we have a `Frame` with two buttons that are using the *same* listener. In this case, the Test class *is* the listener. When an action occurs, the method has to check the event to find out the source so that it knows what to do. All events know their source, and you can use the `getSource()` method to identify it.

Finding Screen Position and Time

One of the more fun things to do is to play with `MouseEvents`. Mouse clicks are just a `MousePressed` with a `MouseReleased`. When a `MouseEvent` happens on a `component`, you can use the `getX()` and `getY()` methods to find the location of the click. Alternately, you can choose to get the same information back as an instance of `Point` (which has an X and a Y). Either way, you get information to play with. You can even get the number of clicks on the component at a particular coordinate using `getClickCount()`.

`MouseEvents` are also a subclass of an `InputEvent` like `KeyEvent`. That means that they inherit a `getWhen()` method that gives you the time-stamp (in milliseconds) of when the event happened.

Just for fun, this example also shows an implementation of `MouseMotion Listener`. The two methods that it includes, `mouseMoved()` and `mouseDragged()`, differ only in that the dragged event happens if a button was pushed. If no button was pushed when the mouse changed location, the `mouseMoved()` method is called.

```
import java.awt.*;
import java.awt.event.*;
class Test extends Frame {
    Test(){ //construct the Frame
        MyInnerMouseListener lis = new MyInnerMouseListener();
        MyInnerMouseMotionListener lis2 = new
```

```
MyInnerMouseMotionListener();
      this.addMouseListener(lis); //add the inner Mouse listener to
this Frame
      this.addMouseMotionListener(lis2); //add the inner
MouseMotion listener
      this.setSize(400,400);
      this.setVisible(true);
   }
   class MyInnerMouseListener extends MouseAdapter{
      int intX, intY, cnt;
      long myTime, lastTime;
      public void mouseClicked(MouseEvent e){
         cnt = e.getClickCount();
         intX = e.getX(); // get the mouse position
         intY = e.getY();
         lastTime = myTime; //store the time of the last
         myTime = e.getWhen(); //get the time of this click
         //print out all the information that you found
         System.out.println("Click #" + cnt + " at " + intX + " , "
+ intY + " at " + yTime + " it's been " + (myTime-lastTime) +
" milliseconds");
      }
   }
   class MyInnerMouseMotionListener implements MouseMotionListener{
      public void mouseDragged(MouseEvent c){
         System.out.println("Mouse dragged after clicking a but-
ton");
      }
      public void mouseMoved(MouseEvent e){
         System.out.println("Mouse moved without clicking any but-
ton");
      }
   }
   public static void main(String args[]){
      Test t = new Test();
   }
}
```

In this code, we chose to use the `MouseClicked()` method to get our information. All we are doing is finding the *x*, the *y*, and the *when* and storing them. Then in the println, we are calculating how long it has been in milliseconds since the last click.

Putting More than One Listener on a Component

Often you need to do different things depending on what event happens to a component. For instance, if a `Button` gets focus, you may want to put an outline around the label so that the user is aware of that fact. However, if the `Button` has an action against it, like being pushed, then you would want to process whatever the `Button` does:

```java
import java.awt.*;
import java.awt.event.*;
class Test extends Frame implements ActionListener, FocusListener{
    Button b1 = new Button("Close");
    Button b2 = new Button("Write to console");
    public Test(){ //this is the constructor for our frame
        this.setLayout(new FlowLayout());
        b1.addActionListener(this);
        b1.addFocusListener(this);
        b2.addActionListener(this);
        b2.addFocusListener(this);
        this.add(b1);
        this.add(b2);
        this.setSize(300,100);
        this.setVisible(true);
    }
    public void focusGained(FocusEvent e){
        if (e.getSource() == b1)
            b1.setBackground(Color.red);
        if (e.getSource() == b2)
            b2.setBackground(Color.green);
    }
    public void focusLost(FocusEvent e){
        if (e.getSource() == b1)
```

```
            b1.setBackground(Color.gray);
        if (e.getSource() == b2)
            b2.setBackground(Color.gray);
    }
    public void actionPerformed(ActionEvent e){
        int i = e.getID();
        if (i == ActionEvent.ACTION_FIRST){
            System.out.println("Action First");
    }

        String par = e.paramString();
        System.out.println("id = " + i + " param = " + par);
        if (e.getSource() == b1)
            System.exit(0);
        if (e.getSource() == b2)
            System.out.println("Button b2 was pressed");
    }
    public static void main(String args[]){
        Test t = new Test();
    }
}
```

This frame has two `Buttons` and implements both a `FocusListener` and an `ActionListener`. Because you can ask the event where it came from, it becomes easy to use one listener and link it to many components.

Here we are using the source of the `FocusEvent` to know which button has focus and decide what colors to use. We are also using the source of the `ActionEvent` to know which button was pushed so that we know what to do.

Now that we've shown you that approach, we'll regress and say that it might be better (as a matter of style) to have separate FocusListeners for each of the buttons. It's your choice, but it is cleaner to give each button an anonymous class, as in the following example:

```
b1.add(new FocusListener() {
  public void focusGained(FocusEvent ev) {
b1.setBackground(Color.red);}
  public void focusLost(FocusEvent ev) {
b1.setBackground(Color.gray);}
});
```

Notice that each event also has an integer value, which is an ID that identifies what type of event it is, as well as defined field constants that can be used to reference that ID. The value of this ID can be found by using the `getID()` method of `AWTEvent`. `FocusGained` can be referenced by `FocusEvent.FOCUS_GAINED` and so on. This is available so that if you choose to use `enableEvents()` and provide code in `processXXXEvent()`, you have a way of asking the event what kind of XXXEvent it is.

For instance, in our code, if we have an `Event` e (in this example it would need to be a `WindowEvent`) we can say the following:

```
import java.awt.*;
import java.awt.event.*;
class Test extends Frame{
  Test(){
    enableEvents(AWTEvent.WINDOW_EVENT_MASK);
  }
  public void processWindowEvent(WindowEvent e){
    if (e.getID() == WindowEvent.WINDOW_CLOSING) {
      super.processWindowEvent(e);
      //do closing stuff
      System.exit(0);
    }
  }
  public static void main(String args[]){
    Test t = new Test();
    t.setSize(300,400);
    t.setVisible(true);
  }
}
```

In this code, you can't extend `WindowAdapter` because you are already extending `Frame`. There is a whole slew of methods in `WindowListener` to implement. Being able to identify the ID of the `WindowEvent` in the above code allows you to "get away with" just `enablingEvent()`, and not having to implement `WindowListener`.

CHECKPOINT

✔ **Objective 10.01** State the event classname for any specified event listener interface in the **java.awt.event** package.

- You need to be able to state the event classname for any specified event listener interface in the java.awt.event package, including the methods that they provide. Make sure that you have a handle on all of the listener topics we have gone over.
- You should be able to enableEvents using the Mask for the Event class.
- Remember that enableEvents(XXX_EVENT_MASK) turns on event processing and you use the processXXXEvent(XXXEvent e) methods to react to the event. You should be familiar with all of the listener interfaces and the methods that they declare. You have seen code that uses these listeners to process events in a variety of arrangements. We have gone over anonymous classes to do simple handling of events.
- Event adapters are available as an alternative to listeners that have more than one method in them.

✔ **Objective 10.02** Write code to implement listener classes and methods.

- The Event Delegation Model uses listener classes to handle events. You should be able to use any listener interface. You should be able to provide code in listener methods to make the components function properly.
- We have talked about extracting information from events to identify the source of the event and using that information to decide what to do. We have covered putting multiple listeners on a component. Finally, we have determined the mouse position and time of the event from information requested from the event.

✔ **Objective 10.03** In listener methods, extract information from the event to determine the affected component, mouse position, nature, and time of the event.

- In listener methods, you can extract information from the event to determine the affected component, mouse position, nature, and time of the event. You should be able to use this information to control your GUI.
- By now, you should be ready to handle almost any question on events and listeners that might be on the Exam.

REVIEW QUESTIONS

1. Given the following code, which statement is true?

```
import java.awt.*;
import java.awt.event.*;
class Test extends Frame {
   public Test(){
       this.setSize(400,400);
       this.setVisible(true);
   }
   public static void main(String args[]){
       Test t = new Test();
       t.addWindowListener(new WindowAdapter(){
           public void windowClosing(WindowEvent e)
               {System.exit(0);}
           }
       );
   }
}
```

A. The code will get an error compiling because class Test does not implement `WindowListener`.

B. The code will get an error compiling because it should be coded `t.addWindowListener(this);`

C. The code compiles and runs cleanly.

D. The code will get an error compiling because the anonymous class should create a new `WindowListener`.

E. The code will get an error compiling because the rest of the methods of `WindowListener` are missing.

2. Given the following code, which statement is true?

```
import java.awt.*;
import java.awt.event.*;
class Test extends Frame {
   MyListener lis = new MyListener();
   public Test(){
       this.addKeyListener(lis);
```

```
        this.setSize(400,400);
        this.setVisible(true);
    }
    public static void main(String args[]){
        Test t = new Test();
    }
}
//*******************
class MyListener extends KeyAdapter{
    public void KeyPressed(KeyEvent e){
        System.out.println("got " + e.getKeyChar());
    }
}
```

A. The code compiles and runs cleanly. The console displays a statement for each key pressed.

B. The code compiles and runs cleanly, but nothing displays on the console.

C. The code will get a compiler error because the `keyPressed()` method is misspelled.

D. The code will get a compiler error because class Test should implement `KeyListener`.

E. The code will get a compiler error because the rest of the methods of `KeyListener` were not implemented.

3. If you create several listeners and add all of them to the same component, which of the following statements is true?

A. The listeners will get notified of an event in the order that they were added.

B. The listeners will get notified of an event all at the same time.

C. There is no way to know in which order the listeners will get notified.

D. Only one of the listeners will get notified and it is not possible to know which one it will be.

E. Only the listener that should handle the event will get notified.

4. Given the following code, which statement is true?

```
import java.awt.*;
import java.awt.event.*;
class Test extends Frame {
```

```
    public Test(){
        MyListener lis = new MyListener();
        addMouseListener(lis);
        setSize(400,400);
        setVisible(true);
    }
    public static void main(String args[]){
        Test t = new Test();
    }
}
//******************
class MyListener implements MouseListener{
    int intX, intY;
    public void mousePressed(MouseEvent e){
        intX = e.getX();
        intY = e.getY();
        System.out.println("Mouse click at " + intX + " , " + intY);
    }
}
```

A. The code compiles and runs cleanly. Each mouse click causes the coordinate to display on the console.

B. The code compiles cleanly but displays nothing to the console because `mouseClicked` is not implemented.

C. The code will get a compiler error because the Test class does not implement `MouseListener`.

D. The code will get a compiler error because the rest of the methods of `MouseListener` have not been implemented.

E. The code will get a compiler error because `MyListener` should have extended `MouseAdapter`.

5. Given the following code, which of the following statements is true?

```
import java.awt.*;
import java.awt.event.*;
class Test extends Button implements ActionListener{
    String source;
    public Test(String s){
        super(s);
```

```
        addActionListener(this);
    }
    public void actionPerformed(ActionEvent e){
        source = e.getActionCommand();
        System.out.println("Event from " + source);
    }
    public static void main(String args[]){
        Test myBtn = new Test("My Button");
        Frame f = new Frame();
        f.add(myBtn);
        f.setSize(400,400);
        f.setVisible(true);
    }
}
```

   A. This compiles and runs cleanly. Each time the button is pressed a state-ment appears on the console saying "Event from My Button".
   B. The code will get a compile error because it is missing a `myBtn.addActionListener()` statement.
   C. The code compiles cleanly but does nothing because it is missing the `myBtn.addActionListener()` statement.
   D. The code will get a compiler error because Frame does not process `ActionEvents`.
   E. The code will get a compiler error because the rest of the methods of `ActionListener` have not been implemented.

6. What is the class of listener that you can extend to inherit their methods called?

   A. Enablers
   B. Events
   C. Delegators
   D. Adapters
   E. EventModels

7. The statement `enableEvent(AWTEvent.ACTION_EVENT_MASK);` enables the processing of action events. What method needs to be overridden to han-dle those events?

   A. `processActionEvent(ActionEvent e);`
   B. `actionPerformed(ActionEvent e);`

C. `handleActionEvent(ActionEvent e);`

D. `enableEvent(ActionEvent e);`

E. `actionEvent(ActionEvent e);`

8. When using explicit event enabling, the `processXXXEvent()` method is called before any listeners. True or False?

9. A class cannot both extend MouseAdapter and implement `MouseListener` with no compile errors or runtime errors. True or False?

10. An adapter can be used to create an anonymous class. True or False?

REVIEW ANSWERS

1. **C** This is a correct implementation of an anonymous listener class. In this case, we used an adapter instead of an interface, so D is incorrect. We did not need to also implement `WindowListener`, and we inherit the extra methods from `WindowAdapter`, so A and E are incorrect. B is incorrect because "this" is an object of class Test, which is not a listener.

2. **B** The method `KeyPressed()` is spelled differently from the `keyPressed()` method in `KeyAdapter`; therefore it will not override it, so A is incorrect. However, it will compile cleanly as a different method, so C is incorrect. The `keyPressed()` method inherited from `KeyAdapter` will be called when each key is pressed and will not print anything to the console as described in B. Extending `KeyAdapter` is a valid alternative to implementing `KeyListener`, so D is incorrect. When you extend a class you do not need to implement all of the methods in the subclass, so E is incorrect.

3. **C** There is no relationship between the order of adding listeners and the order that they are notified, so A is incorrect. The listeners will not get notified at the same time, so B is incorrect. They will all get notified, so D and E are incorrect. They will get notified one at a time, and you cannot be sure of that order, so C is correct.

4. **D** When you implement an interface, you must implement all of the methods of the interface so D is true, it cannot compile cleanly. The driver class does not need to be the class that implements the listener as stated in C. While extending `MouseAdapter` is a valid alternative to implementing `MouseListener`, not using that approach does not cause any compiler errors.

5. **A** This is a correct implementation of a class that is its own listener. The addActionListener(this) statement replaced the myBtn.addAction Listener() statement. Button processes ActionEvents, and there are no other methods in ActionListener to implement.

6. **D** Event adapters are actual implementations of Event listener interfaces.

7. **A** The method processActionEvent(ActionEvent e) is available in all classes that handle ActionEvents.

8. **True** This is the only case where it is known that one event handler will get called first. Any additional listeners will get notified after, and it is not possible to know in which order they will get notified.

9. **False** It is possible to do both with no problem; however, you can get rid of the "implement MouseListener" statement with no changes to the code required.

10. **True** Either a listener adapter or a listener interface can be used to create an anonymous class as a parameter into the addXXXListener() method.

java.io Package

	NEWBIE	SOME EXPERIENCE	EXPERT
ETA	12–14 hours	8–10 hours	4–6 hours

373

Like C, C++, and most other modern languages, the Java language itself has no built-in input or output capability. Instead, the Java Development Kit (JDK) includes a standard library known as the java.io package. It is a large collection, consisting of 10 interfaces and 66 classes. Fortunately, you don't need to master each one to pass the exam. The objectives identify four main sets of classes upon which you'll be tested:

- **File**   A class whose instances represent a file or directory.
- **Input and output byte streams**   Classes that provide access to files, sockets, and arrays as ordered sets of bytes.
- **Input and output character streams**   Classes that provide access to files, sockets, and strings as ordered sets of characters.
- **RandomAccessFile**   A class that enables access to a file as if it were a persistent array of bytes, with reading and writing allowed at any position in the file.

There are a number of other important classes (such as StreamTokenizer and IOException and its subclasses, ObjectInputStream and Object OutputStream), but they are not included in the objectives tested on the exam and so will not be covered here.

Navigate with the `File` Class

Exam questions for this objective test your ability to write code that uses objects of the File class to navigate a file system. This section provides a detailed description of the class and its methods, as well as examples of using it to test file attributes, create and delete files, work with filename components, and list the contents of a directory.

Overview

An instance of the java.io.File class is an object that represents a file or directory name in the file system. Ordinarily it corresponds to a particular physical file, but not always. To check for a file's existence, for example, you could create a File object that represents the path name and then call its exists() method to determine whether the underlying file is actually there.

This version turns out to be quite useful in listing directory contents, as you will see.

The remainder of this section discusses the methods in the File class in detail, grouping them according to their main function.

Checking File Attributes

Table 11.1 lists methods that can be used to test the attributes of the underlying file or directory.

TABLE 11.1   Methods for Testing File Attributes

Method Name	Description
boolean canRead()	Returns true if the application has read permission to the file.
boolean canWrite()	Returns true if the application has write permission to the file.
boolean isDirectory()	Returns true if the underlying file system object is a directory.
boolean isFile()	Returns true if the underlying file system object is an ordinary file (not a directory).
long lastModified()	Returns the time at which the underlying file was last modified. The time is stated in milliseconds, suitable for use in java.util.Date constructor.
long length()	Returns the number of bytes in the underlying file. Returns zero for directories.

Comparing Pathnames

The File class contains four methods for comparing path names and testing for equality, as listed in Table 11.2.

File implements the java.lang.Comparable interface by implementing the compareTo(Object obj) method. This means that the following is true:

- Arrays of File objects can be sorted with the static sort(Object[] a) method of the java.util.Arrays class.

TABLE 11.2 Methods for Comparing `File` Objects

Method Name	Description
`int compareTo` `(File pathname)`	Compares this filename to another, returning a negative number, zero, or a positive number, depending on whether this filename is less than, equal to, or greater than the other filename.
`int compareTo` `(Object obj)`	Another version of the same method, this time allowing (in principle) arbitrary objects to be compared. Only other `File` objects can actually be specified without causing a `ClassCastException`.
`boolean equals` `(Object obj)`	Returns true if the object parameter refers to the same path name as the `File` object.
`int hashCode()`	Computes a hash code value that enables the `File` object to be used as the key in a Hashtable.

- An iterator obtained from a `java.util.TreeSet` containing `File` objects will return them in sorted order.
- If `File` objects are used as keys in a `java.util.TreeMap`, the keys of the map can be retrieved in sorted order with `Map.keySet().iterator()`.

Operating on Underlying Files

Every `File` object is associated with an underlying file or directory in the file system, which may or may not exist. Using methods in `File`, you can perform programmatically the ordinary operations on the file that you could from a command line or shell: you can create and delete files, rename them, and set their attributes. Table 11.3 lists the methods provided for these purposes.

Extracting and Transforming Names

Every operating system has its particular syntax for naming files. Usually, this includes some notion of absolute and relative names (that is, if the file system is tree structured, as is the case with Unix and Win32 operating systems) with a root

TABLE 11.3	Methods That Perform Operations on Underlying Files
Method Name	**Description**
`boolean createNewFile()`	Creates a zero-length file corresponding to the path name of this `File`, if it does not already exist.
`static File createTempFile(String prefix, String suffix)` `static File createTempFile(String prefix, String suffix, File dir)`	Creates a new file in the default temporary directory whose name begins with *prefix* and ends with *suffix*. If *suffix* is null, `.tmp` is used as the suffix. The second form of the method allows a different directory to be specified.
`boolean delete()`	Deletes the file or directory.
`void deleteOnExit()`	Causes the file or directory to be deleted when the virtual machine is terminated.
`boolean exists()`	Returns true if the underlying file already exists.
`boolean mkdir()` `boolean mkdirs()`	Creates the underlying directory. Returns true if the creation was successful. `mkdirs()` creates any intermediate directories as needed.
`boolean renameTo (File dest)`	Renames the underlying file to the path name specified in *dest*. Returns true if the operation was successful.
`boolean setLastModified (long time)`	Changes the modification date of the underlying file to *time*.
`boolean setReadOnly()`	Sets the appropriate underlying file attribute to prevent write operations.

specifier and one or more names separated by a file separator character. The File class provides access to the individual components of the name and provides means for transforming filenames from relative to absolute form and to URLs. Table 11.4 describes the methods available for these purposes.

TABLE 11.4 Methods for Extracting and Transforming Name Components

Method Name	Description
File getAbsoluteFile() String getAbsolutePath()	Converts the path name to absolute form.
File getCanonicalFile() String getCanonicalPath()	Converts the path name to its canonical form.
String getName()	Returns the name portion of the filename (that is, does not return the directory).
String getParent() File getParentFile()	Returns the parent directory of the file.
String getPath()	Returns the path name that was specified in the constructor.
boolean isAbsolute()	Returns true if the path name is absolute.
String toString()	Returns the path name (equivalent to getPath()).
URL toURL()	Converts the path name to a file: URL.

The canonical form of a filename is similar to the absolute form but additionally takes care of resolving ".." and "." references in the name. In Java 2, the absolute path, canonical path, and parent directory can be returned in either String form or as File objects. The toURL() method is also new with Java 2 and can be very useful in working with XML parsers and other classes that deal with URLs.

The following program illustrates the values returned by these methods:

```
import java.io.*;
```

```
public class NameTester
{
   public static void main(String[] args)
      throws IOException
   {
      // Get a file name from the command line
      // and create a File object for it

      String fileName = args[0];
      File file = new File(fileName);

      // Display file attributes

      System.out.println("Names components of " + fileName + ":");
      System.out.println("absolute:   " + file.getAbsolutePath());
      System.out.println("canonical:  " + file.getCanonicalPath());
      System.out.println("name:       " + file.getName());
      System.out.println("parent:     " + file.getParent());
      System.out.println("path:       " + file.getPath());
      System.out.println("URL:        " + file.toURL());
   }
}
```

For simple names, it prints the following:

```
D:\book\chap11\examples\01>java NameTester myfile.txt
Names components of myfile.txt:
absolute:    D:\book\chap11\examples\01\myfile.txt
canonical:   D:\book\chap11\examples\01\myfile.txt
name:        myfile.txt
parent:      null
path:        myfile.txt
URL:         file:/D:/book/chap11/examples/01/myfile.txt
```

Note that the absolute form of the filename was extracted from the underlying file system. In addition, the parent component is null, because the filename is relative.

Listing Directory Contents

If a `File` object represents a directory, it can be used to get the names of the files in the directory. Calling these methods recursively allows you to explore the file system to any depth you wish. Table 11.5 summarizes the methods that support this technique.

TABLE 11.5   Methods for Listing Directory Contents

Method Name	Description
`String[] list()`	Returns the names of all files and subdirectories in this directory.
`String[] list (FilenameFilter filter)`	Returns the names of all files and subdirectories in this directory that are accepted by the specified filter.
`File[] listFiles()`	Returns the names of all files and subdirectories in this directory as `File` objects.
`File[] listFiles (FileFilter filter)` `File[] listFiles (FilenameFilter filter)`	Returns the names of all files and subdirectories in this directory accepted by the specified filter as `File` objects.
`static File[] listRoots()`	Returns an array of `File` objects representing the roots of the file system (for example, the drive letters for Win32).

The `list()` method returns an array of strings for every entry in the directory, not including "." or "..". The list will also include any hidden files. If there are no files in the directory, the method will return an empty array (length 0). If the `File` object does not refer to a directory, null is returned. A `FileFilter` or `FilenameFilter` can be used to restrict the set of returned files to just those that are accepted by the filter.

Exam Tip

Note that the values returned by String[] list() and String[] list(FilenameFilter filter) are simple filenames without any directory information. To convert them to File objects, you need to use the two-argument form of the File constructor, specifying the directory File object as the first parameter and the filename as the second.

The following program, FileLister, shows how to navigate a file system recursively with these methods. The purpose of the program is to list all files in a specified directory and its subdirectories that end in a specified character string (extension).

```java
import java.io.*;

public class FileLister
{
   private String suffix;

   public FileLister(String suffix)
   {
      this.suffix = suffix;
   }
   public void showMatches(File dir) throws IOException
   {
      String[] entries = dir.list();
      for (int i = 0; i < entries.length; i++) {
         File entry = new File(dir, entries[i]);
         if (entry.isFile() && entry.getName().endsWith(suffix))
            System.out.println(entry.getPath());
         else if (entry.isDirectory())
            showMatches(entry);
      }
   }
   public static void main(String[] args)
      throws IOException
   {
```

```
      File rootDir = new File(args[0]);
      String suffix = args[1];
      new FileLister(suffix).showMatches(rootDir);
   }
}
```

The `main()` method accepts a directory name and a suffix, then creates a `FileLister` object and invokes its `showMatches()` method, passing it a `File` object that represents the starting directory. The `showMatches()` method uses `File.list()` to get a list of the entries in the directory, then examines each entry to see if its name matches the specified suffix. It prints the names of those that match. If the entry is a subdirectory, `showMatches()` calls itself with the subdirectory `File` object. In just a few lines of code, then, it can explore the entire directory tree.

As an alternative to testing the filename for a match, you can use a `FileFilter` or `FilenameFilter`. To do so, you need to write a class that implements one of these interfaces. Implementing `FileFilter` requires that you supply the following method:

```
public boolean accept(File pathname)
```

The `accept()` method can perform any test you like on the path name. It should return true if the file should be included. The older `FilenameFilter` interface works similarly but uses an `accept()` method that takes a directory name and path name:

```
public boolean accept(File dir, String name)
```

In the example, you can use a `FileFilter` for testing whether a file has a particular extension. This filter class can be defined as follows:

```
public class ExtensionFilter implements FileFilter
{
   private String ext;
   public ExtensionFilter(String ext)
   {
      this.ext = ext;
   }
   public boolean accept(File path)
   {
      return
```

```
        path.isDirectory() ||
        path.getName().endsWith(ext);
    }
}
```

Note that the filter accepts either files whose names end with the specified extension, or any directory. It accepts directories because if it didn't it could not be used in recursive enumerations of directory contents.

Objective 11.02

Use Stream Readers and Writers

Questions for this objective test your ability to write code that uses the InputStreamReader and OutputStreamWriter classes to translate between characters and byte streams and to determine when to use conversion to the platform default encoding, as opposed to conversion to a specific encoding.

Overview

A little background information is in order. We are accustomed to thinking of bytes and characters as basically the same thing. Most people that have been programming for a long time have used ASCII or EBCDIC encoding to store characters in 8-bit bytes. This works well as long as all you intend to store is English language text and numbers.

As internationalized applications have become more widespread, it has become increasingly important to be able to represent other character sets. Early attempts to handle this requirement involved complicated systems of single- and double-byte character sets. A better solution has emerged in the Unicode standard, which uses 16 bits to represent each character. This allows for 65,536 possible characters, which makes it possible to allocate unique code points for a wide variety of languages and special needs.

Java uses Unicode as its basic internal representation of character data. When this data is written to byte output streams, the 16-bit characters must be converted to 8-bit equivalents. Obviously, not all possible characters can be mapped at once—only a selected subset for a particular language is included. The specific mapping used is known as a *character encoding*.

A character encoding is a set of rules that transform a set of characters to a corresponding set of bytes (usually one-to-one, but not necessarily). Most western languages can be represented by ASCII or an extended version known as ISO-8859-1. Other languages have their own standard encodings. The complete set of encodings supported by the Java 2 platform can be found at **http://java.sun.com/ j2se/1.3/docs/guide/intl/encoding.doc.html.** For any given Java 2 virtual machine, one of these encodings will be used as the *platform default encoding*.

Byte Stream and Character Classes

To accommodate all this, the `java.io` package provides two parallel systems of classes, one for byte streams and one for characters. This section provides a quick overview of these classes and their relationships.

Exam Tip

If a test question includes the words "character encoding," you can be sure it will test your understanding of the fact that characters and bytes are not synonymous.

The byte stream input classes (shown in Figure 11-1) all derive from the class InputStream. They include the following:

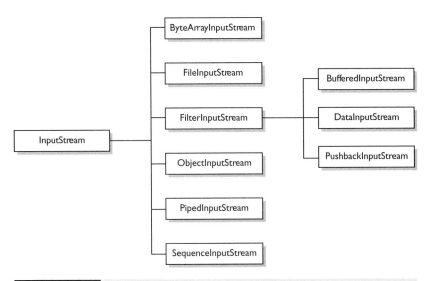

FIGURE 11-1 java.io.InputStream and its subclasses

- `InputStream` The abstract base class. Defines the basic read methods that all input streams implement.
- `ByteArrayInputStream` An input stream that allows an array of bytes to be read as if it were a file.
- `FileInputStream` An input stream for reading bytes from a file in a file system.
- `FilterInputStream` A stream that reads bytes from another input stream, usually performing some transformation on the bytes. This file and its subclasses are considered in more depth in Objective 11.03.
- `BufferedInputStream` A `FilterInputStream` that reads large chunks of bytes into an array and satisfies read requests from the array.
- `DataInputStream` A `FilterInputStream` that allows reading Java primitive types from a stream of bytes.
- `PushbackInputStream` A `FilterInputStream` that allows bytes to be "unread" by being pushed back to the stream where they can be read again.
- `ObjectInputStream` An input stream that allows serialized objects to be read from byte streams and reconstituted into objects.
- `PipedInputStream` An input stream that receives its input from a PipedOutputStream, usually one running in another thread. Supports communication between threads using input and output operations.
- `SequenceInputStream` An object that allows a set of input streams to be read back-to-back as if they were one big stream.

A corresponding set of classes for byte stream output (shown in Figure 11-2) is derived from the `OutputStream` class. These include the following:

- `OutputStream` The abstract base class from which all byte stream output classes are derived. Contains the basic write methods that send bytes to an output destination.
- `ByteArrayOutputStream` A class that stores its output in an array of bytes instead of writing it to a file. The internal buffer can be accessed with the `toByteArray()` method.
- `FileOutputStream` An output stream that writes bytes to a file in a file system.
- `FilterOutputStream` Analogous to `FilterInputStream`, this class writes bytes to another output stream, usually performing some transformation on the stream. This class will be discussed at greater length in Objective 11.03.
- `BufferedOutputStream` A `FilterOutputStream` that stores output in an intermediate buffer, then writes large chunks to minimize I/O time.

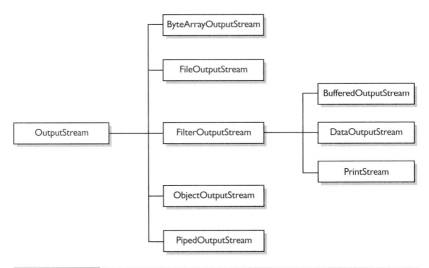

FIGURE 11-2   java.io.OutputStream and its subclasses

- **DataOutputStream**   A `FilterOutputStream` that allows primitive Java data types to be written to another output stream.
- **PrintStream**   A `FilterOutputStream` with convenience methods for writing primitive Java data types.
- **ObjectOutputStream**   A class that writes serialized objects as bytes stream.
- **PipedOutputStream**   A class that writes data to a `PipedInput Stream`, usually in another thread.

For reading character streams, `java.io` provides the `Reader` class and its subclasses, as seen in Figure 11-3:

- **Reader**   The abstract base class from which all other character reader classes are derived.
- **BufferedReader**   A reader that gets characters from a large internal buffer to minimize I/O time.
- **LineNumberReader**   A `BufferedReader` that keeps track of the line number.
- **CharArrayReader**   A reader similar to `ByteArrayInputStream` but one that reads from a character array rather than a byte array.
- **FilterReader**   Base class for classes that `read` from another Reader and perform transformation on the input.
- **PushbackReader**   A `FilterReader` that allows characters read from a stream to be "unread" by being pushed back on the input reader.

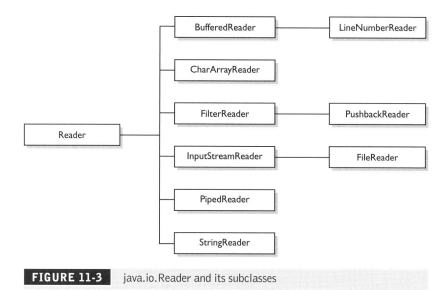

FIGURE 11-3   java.io.Reader and its subclasses

- **InputStreamReader**   A reader that converts an input byte stream to a stream of characters.
- **FileReader**   An InputStreamReader over a FileInputStream.
- **PipedReader**   A reader that gets characters from a PipedWriter, usually in another thread.
- **StringReader**   A reader that allows a String to be read using input operations, as if it were a file.

Completing the structure is the java.io.Writer class and its subclasses, shown in Figure 11-4. These classes allow characters to be written to an output destination, such as a file or a String:

- **Writer**   The abstract base class for all character stream writer classes. Contains the basic write methods that all these classes implement.
- **BufferedWriter**   A writer that uses an internal buffer to minimize write operations to the output destination.
- **CharArrayWriter**   A writer that stores output in an array of characters. The array can be accessed with the toCharArray() method.
- **FilterWriter**   A writer that sends output to another writer, usually transforming it in some way.
- **OutputStreamWriter**   A writer that converts character data to bytes according to some character encoding.
- **FileWriter**   An OutputStreamWriter over a FileOutputStream.
- **PipedWriter**   A writer that produces character data to be read by a PipedReader, usually in a different thread.

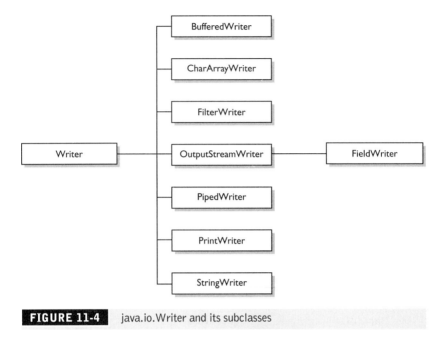

FIGURE 11-4   java.io.Writer and its subclasses

- **PrintWriter**   A writer that prints objects to a character stream using their `toString()` representation.
- **StringWriter**   A writer that sends output to a string. The data can be retrieved with the `toString()` method.

InputStreamReader

An `InputStreamReader` reads a stream of bytes in some character encoding and converts them to the corresponding Unicode characters. It provides the following constructors:

```
InputStreamReader(InputStream in, String enc)
```

which creates a character stream reader over the specified input stream using the specified encoding, and

```
InputStreamReader(InputStream in)
```

which creates a character stream reader over the specified input stream using the platform default encoding.

The combination of `InputStreamReader` with an underlying `FileInput Stream` is common enough that there is a convenience class named `FileReader` that combines the two operations into one class.

OutputStreamWriter

An `OutputStreamWriter` converts Unicode characters according to a designated character encoding and writes them to an output stream. It has the following constructors:

```
OutputStreamWriter(OutputStream out, String enc)
```

which creates a character stream writer over the specified output stream using the specified encoding , and

```
OutputStreamWriter(OutputStream out)
```

which creates a character stream writer over the specified output stream using the platform default encoding.

As was the case with `InputStreamReader`, there is a convenience class named `FileWriter` that combines the operations of `OutputStreamWriter` and `FileOutputStream`.

When to Specify the Encoding

Every Java Virtual Machine has a platform default encoding. This is set in native Virtual Machine startup code, usually according to the default locale. Its value can be determined from the system property `file.encoding`. In most cases, the default encoding is sufficient. But when files are destined to be read by systems using a different language or different character system (such as EBCDIC), a specific encoding should be employed.

An example will make this clearer. `GreekTextGenerator`, shown in the following listing, creates a file containing the Greek alphabet. This is easy enough to generate using Unicode character literals for the letters alpha through omega. (The astute reader will note that there are 24 letters in the Greek alphabet but 25 characters in the string. The reason for this is that sigma has two representations, one for when it appears at the end of a word and one for when it appears anywhere else. However, we can't write the string directly to the FileOutputStream—it has no methods that allow for this; they're only for writing bytes or arrays of bytes.

Instead, we use an OutputStreamWriter to convert the string to bytes and wrap it in a PrintWriter to give us convenient access to writing lines:

```
import java.io.*;

public class GreekTextGenerator
{
   public static void main(String[] args)
      throws IOException
   {
      String alphabet =
            "\u03b1\u03b2\u03b3\u03b4\u03b5"
         + "\u03b6\u03b7\u03b8\u03b9\u03ba"
         + "\u03bb\u03bc\u03bd\u03be\u03bf"
         + "\u03c0\u03c1\u03c2\u03c3\u03c4"
         + "\u03c5\u03c6\u03c7\u03c8\u03c9" ;

      FileOutputStream stream =
         new FileOutputStream("alphabet.txt");

      OutputStreamWriter writer =
         new OutputStreamWriter(stream);

      PrintWriter out = new PrintWriter(writer);

      out.println(alphabet);
      out.flush();
      out.close();
   }
}
```

But look at the results—it's nothing but question marks:

```
00000: 3f3f 3f3f 3f3f 3f3f 3f3f 3f3f 3f3f 3f3f ????????????????
00010: 3f3f 3f3f 3f3f 3f3f 3f0d 0a              ?????????..
```

This is because the platform default encoding on my Windows NT system (Cp1252 - Windows Latin-1) has no way to represent these characters. To correct this problem, you need to specify a particular encoding in the OutputStream Writer constructor:

```
    OutputStreamWriter writer =
        new OutputStreamWriter(stream, "ISO8859_7");
```

This time, the output contains distinct characters:

```
00000: e1e2 e3e4 e5e6 e7e8 e9ea ebec edee eff0 ................
00010: f1f2 f3f4 f5f6 f7f8 f90d 0a               ...........
```

To read from a byte stream that uses this encoding, you need to perform the analogous operations of using an InputStreamReader that specify the appropriate encoding, as shown in the following program:

```java
import java.awt.*;
import java.awt.event.*;
import java.io.*;
import javax.swing.*;
import javax.swing.event.*;

public class GreekTextDisplayer extends JPanel
{
   public GreekTextDisplayer() throws IOException
   {
      // Start with a stream of bytes

      FileInputStream stream =
         new FileInputStream("alphabet.txt");

      // Convert to characters with an InputStreamReader
      // using the appropriate encoding

      InputStreamReader reader =
         new InputStreamReader(stream, "ISO8859_7");

      // Use BufferedReader to read lines

      BufferedReader in = new BufferedReader(reader);

      // Read Greek text

      String text = in.readLine();
```

```
    in.close();

    // Create a label to display the text

    JLabel label = new JLabel("The text is " + text);
    label.setFont(new Font("Serif", Font.PLAIN, 20));
    label.setForeground(Color.black);

    add(label);
  }

  public static void main(String[] args)
    throws IOException
  {
    JFrame frame = new JFrame();
    frame.setTitle("Greek Text");
    frame.getContentPane().add
       (new GreekTextDisplayer(), BorderLayout.CENTER);
    frame.setSize(400, 80);
    frame.setVisible(true);
  }
}
```

The resulting output properly displays the Greek text:

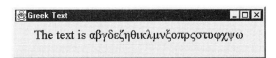

 ## **Filter Input and Output Streams**

Objective 11.03

Questions in this section of the exam will test your ability to create properly constructed instances of `FilterInputStream`, `FilterOutputStream`, and their subclasses.

Overview

Streams can be chained together to allow each one to reformat or otherwise build on the output of another. This allows highly functional composite input streams to be built up from simple reusable components, much like pipes in a Unix shell. The `java.io` package provides the `FilterInputStream` and `FilterOutput Stream` classes for this purpose, as well as several useful subclasses of each. As Figure 11-5 illustrates, filter streams can wrap any other kind of stream, including other filter streams.

To apply a filter stream over a given input or output stream, all you need to do is invoke the filter stream's constructor, passing it a reference to the stream to be filtered. For example, to read Java primitive data types from a socket connection, you would need code like the following:

```
Socket socket = new Socket(hostName, portNumber);
InputStream socketIn = socket.getInputStream();
DataInputStream in = new DataInputStream(socketIn);
```

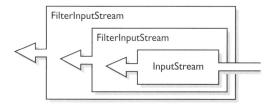

FIGURE 11-5   Nesting input streams with FilterInputStream

Creating your own subclass that extends `FilterInputStream` provides a natural way to handle reading more complex objects from an underlying byte stream. For example, in a hurricane-tracking application, you might have an `Observation` object that contains the latitude, longitude, and wind speed of a storm at a particular time. If you have a collection of these objects that can be read from a network connection, you could define an `ObservationInputStream` class that extends `FilterInputStream` and contains a `readObservation()` method which parses the observation data from the input stream. You could then read hurricane observation objects like this:

```
Socket socket = new Socket(hostName, portNumber);
InputStream socketIn = socket.getInputStream();
ObservationInputStream in =
```

```
      new ObservationInputStream(socketIn);
while (true) {
   Observation obs = in.readObservation();
   if (obs == null)
      break;
   // Do something with this observation
}
```

Why bother to extend `FilterInputStream` rather than just reading directly from the socket in the `ObservationInputStream`? Because it gives you greater flexibility in how you obtain the data. Suppose it sometimes comes from the network and sometimes from the local file system. For the latter case, all you need to change is to use a `FileInputStream` in place of the input stream returned by the socket.

The remainder of this section covers exam topics you'll need to know that relate to `FilterInputStream`, `FilterOutputStream`, and their respective subclasses.

FilterInputStream and Its Subclasses

The `FilterInputStream` class is the base class for all input streams that wrap and transform other input streams. While it is not an abstract class, there is little reason to use it directly. More often, you will use one of its subclasses, either those supplied by the `java.io` package or those you write yourself. The JDK contains `FilterInputStream` subclasses in the `java.util.zip` and `java.security` packages, but these are not included in the exam objectives and will not be considered here.

Exam Tip
Remember that only `InputStream` and its subclasses can be used in the constructor of a `FilterInputStream`. Not every input class in the `java.io` package satisfies this criteria (for example, `java.io.StreamTokenizer` and `java.io.RandomAccessFile` do not). In particular, any class with the word "`Reader`" in its name is a subclass of the character-oriented `java.io.Reader`, not of `java.io.InputStream`.

You create a `FilterInputStream` by invoking its constructor and passing it a reference to another `InputStream` object:

```
FilterInputStream(InputStream in)
```

The constructor does not throw any exceptions.

The `FilterInputStream` class takes care of two things on behalf of its subclasses:

- It stores a reference to the input stream in a protected instance variable named `in`. This allows subclasses to read from the underlying stream as necessary to transform it in constructing the higher-level objects that they return.
- It closes the underlying input stream when its own `close()` method is called.

Table 11.6 lists methods defined in `FilterInputStream`.

TABLE 11.6	Methods in the FilterInputStream Class
Method Name	**Description**
`int read()`	Invokes the single-byte `read()` method of the underlying input stream and returns the result.
`int read(byte[] b)`	Reads at most `b.length` bytes from the underlying input stream into the byte buffer specified. Returns the number of bytes read.
`int read(byte[] b,` `int start, int length)`	Invokes the corresponding method on the underlying input stream.
`long skip(long n)`	Ignores the next *n* bytes from the input stream.
`int available()`	Returns the number of bytes that can be read without blocking.
`void close()`	Closes the underlying input stream.
`void mark` `(int readlimit)`	Marks the current input stream position for later use with the `reset()` method. May be a no-op if the input stream does not support the `mark()` and `reset()` functionality.
`void reset()`	Repositions the input stream to the last position marked with the `mark()` method.
`boolean` `markSupported()`	Returns `true` if this input stream supports the `mark()` and `reset()` methods.

All these methods except `mark()` and `markSupported()` throw `java.io.IOException`.

The exam objective is to be able to select valid constructor arguments from a list of classes in the `java.io` package. Let's examine, then, the four subclasses of `FilterInputStream` that the package contains.

BufferedInputStream

As its name suggests, `BufferedInputStream` creates an internal save area for incoming data so that it can read a large block of bytes in a single operation and return them as necessary. The class has two constructors:

```
BufferedInputStream(InputStream in)
```

This creates a buffered input stream over the specified input stream using a buffer of the default size (2048 bytes, in case you're interested).

```
BufferedInputStream(InputStream in, int size)
```

This form of the constructor allows you to specify the buffer size.

For the input stream argument to the constructor, you can specify any object from a class that inherits directly or indirectly from `java.io.InputStream`. It is very common to see other `FilterInputStream` objects being used in this role.

Since it has an internal buffer, `BufferedInputStream` can implement the `mark()` and `reset()` methods. These methods allow you to save a reference to the current position within the input stream and to reposition the stream back to the marked positions.

The `java.io` package contains a filtering `BufferedReader` that performs the analogous function on character streams.

DataInputStream

Input streams consist of individual bytes. `DataInputStream` allows you to read an input stream and construct the higher-level Java primitive data types from these bytes: `boolean`, `byte`, `char`, `double`, `float`, `int`, `long`, and `short`. It also supports reading unsigned bytes and shorts, returning them as `int` values. This functionality is spelled out in the `DataInput` interface, which both `DataInputStream` and `RandomAccessFile` implement. `DataInputStream` is most commonly used to read values written by `DataOutputStream`.

In addition to primitive types, `DataInputStream` can read strings in a special format. Strings present a bit of a problem: how do you know the length? To deal with this issue, DataInputStream uses a modified version of UTF (UCS

Transformation Format) that represents strings linearly in two components: an unsigned short specifying the number of characters in the final string, followed by a series of 1-, 2-, or 3-byte groups, one for each character. The length of each byte group is indicated by a particular bit pattern in the first byte.

`DataInputStream` has one simple constructor:

```
DataInputStream(InputStream in)
```

FilterOutputStream and Its Subclasses

The `FilterOutputStream` class plays a similar role to that of `FilterInput Stream`, being the base class for all output streams that wrap and transform other output streams. It has a single constructor:

```
FilterOutputStream(OutputStream out)
```

The underlying output stream reference is stored in a protected variable so that subclasses can use it to write their output.

FilterOutputStream defines five methods, all of which simply delegate their operations to the corresponding methods in the underlying output stream. The methods are listed in Table 11.7.

TABLE 11.7   Methods in the FilterOutputStream Class

Method Name	Description
`void write` `(int b)`	Writes the specified byte to the underlying output stream.
`void write` `(byte[] b)`	Writes the contents of the byte array to the underlying output stream. Does so by calling the three-argument form of the method listed next.
`void write` `(byte[] b, int` *start*`, int` *length*`)`	Writes the subset of the byte array described by the specified start and length to the underlying output stream. Invokes the single-byte `write(int b)` method.
`void flush()`	Calls the `flush()` method of the underlying output stream.
`void close()`	Calls the `flush()` and `close()` methods of the underlying output stream.

All these methods throw `java.io.IOException`.

There are subclasses of `FilterOutputStream` in the `java.io`, `java.util.zip`, and `java.security` packages, but we will focus only on those mentioned in the exam objectives:

- `BufferedOutputStream`
- `DataOutputStream`
- `PrintStream`

BufferedOutputStream

Like its input counterpart, `FilterOutputStream` has a subclass that uses an internal buffer to store data so that it can be written efficiently in a single block. This means that writing to a stream does not usually require a physical write. `BufferedOutputStream` has two constructors:

`BufferedOutputStream(OutputStream out)`

which creates a buffered output stream over the specified output stream, using a buffer of the default size (512 bytes—you would think it would be the same as the default for `BufferedInputStream`, wouldn't you?), and

`BufferedOutputStream(OutputStream out, int size)`

which allows you to specify the output buffer size.

DataOutputStream

This is a companion to `DataInputStream` and implements the `DataOutput` interface. It has the constructor you are expecting:

`DataOutputStream(OutputStream out)`

Like `DataInputStream`, this class is a bridge between byte streams and Java primitive types: `boolean`, `byte`, `char`, `double`, `float`, `int`, `long`, and `short`. It also write strings in three different formats: as bytes, as characters, and using the modified UTF-8 format described earlier.

`DataOutputStream` is often used to write output that will subsequently be read with `DataInputStream`.

PrintStream

Like DataOutputStream, PrintStream provides methods for writing Java primitive data types but with two main differences:

- It can be set to flush the output buffer automatically after each operation.
- It never throws IOException.

There are two constructors:

PrintStream(OutputStream *out*)

which creates a print stream over the specified output stream, and

PrintStream(OutputStream *out*, boolean *autoFlush*)

which creates a print stream over the specified output stream which flushes the output buffer after each print operation.

PrintStream supports only the platform default encoding and for this reason is not widely used since JDK 1.1 introduced the PrintWriter class.

Objective 11.04   # Read and Update Files

Questions in this section of the exam test your knowledge of how to read, write, and update files using the FileInputStream, FileOutputStream, and RandomAccessFile classes. These classes deal with the operating system's file system (that is, the disk drives, diskette drive, and CD-ROM drive) using native method calls.

FileInputStream

FileInputStream is a commonly used class that reads bytes from a file in the file system. It is frequently used indirectly as the underlying input stream to a DataInputStream or InputStreamReader. It has three constructors:

FileInputStream(String *name*)

opens an input stream to the file with the specified name. If the file does not exist, the constructor throws a FileNotFoundException.

```
FileInputStream(File file)
```

calls the constructor listed above, passing it `file.getPath()` as its *name* parameter, and

```
FileInputStream(FileDescriptor fd)
```

creates a second input stream over an already open file.

FileOutputStream

As you might expect, `FileOutputStream` writes bytes to a file in the native file system. It is often wrapped in a `BufferedOutputStream` to increase its throughput or in a `PrintWriter` so that it can convert characters to bytes. `FileOutput Stream` has four constructors:

```
FileOutputStream(String name, boolean append)
```

opens an output stream that writes to the file having the specified *name*. If the *append* flag is true and the file already exists, data will be written starting at the end of the file rather than replacing the file contents.

```
FileOutputStream(String name)
```

opens an output stream that writes to the file having the specified *name*. Calls the previously described constructor with *append* = false.

```
FileOutputStream(File file)
```

opens an output stream to the file specified in the *file* argument. Calls the `FileOutputStream(String name)` constructor passing *file*.`getPath()` as its *name* argument.

```
FileOutputStream(FileDescriptor fd)
```

opens an output stream to an already open file, if the underlying operating system allows it. Note that this is the only constructor that does not automatically create a new file if one does not exist.

The `OutputExample` class in the following listing illustrates how to use `FileOutputStream` to create a file and write to it. It has an array of strings representing the first verse of a poem. After opening the output stream, the program reads each string in the array, converts it to an array of bytes using the platform default encoding, and then writes the byte array and a line separator to the output stream. After the array of strings is written, the program flushes and closes the output file.

```java
import java.io.*;

public class OutputExample
{
   private static final String CRLF =
      System.getProperty("line.separator");

   private static final String[] lines = {
      "     Simple Gifts",
      "",
      "'Tis a gift to be simple",
      "   'Tis a gift to be free",
      "'Tis a gift to come down ",
      "   where we ought to be ",
      "And when we find ourselves ",
      "   in the place just right",
      "'Twill be in the valley",
      "   of love and delight. ",
   };

   public static void main(String[] args)
      throws IOException
   {
      OutputStream out = new FileOutputStream("simplegifts.txt");

      for (int i = 0; i < lines.length; i++) {
         byte[] text = lines[i].getBytes();
         out.write(text);
         out.write(CRLF.getBytes());
      }
      out.flush();
```

```
        out.close();
    }
}
```

When invoked, this program creates a file with the following contents:

```
    Simple Gifts

'Tis a gift to be simple
    'Tis a gift to be free
'Tis a gift to come down
    where we ought to be
And when we find ourselves
    in the place just right
'Twill be in the valley
    of love and delight.
```

Exam Tip

Is the `flush()` method call strictly necessary? We can't say for sure in this case, because the `FileOutputStream` `close()` method is implemented in native code. It's a different story with `FilterOutputStream` and any of its subclasses; their `close()` method explicitly calls `flush()`.

Ordinarily, if we run this program again, we'll simply replace the output file with another copy. But by using the two-argument form of the `FileOutput Stream` constructor, we can specify that output should be appended, rather than replacing the file. `UpdateExample` in the following listing shows how we can write the second verse of the poem to the same file:

```
import java.io.*;

public class UpdateExample
{
    private static final String CRLF =
        System.getProperty("line.separator");
    private static final String[] lines = {
```

```
        "",
        "When true",
        "    simplicity is gained",
        "To bow and to bend",
        "    we shall not be ashamed",
        "To turn, turn will",
        "    be our delight",
        "'Till by turning, turning we",
        "    come 'round right.",
    };
    public static void main(String[] args)
        throws IOException
    {
        OutputStream out =
            new FileOutputStream("simplegifts.txt", true);
        for (int i = 0; i < lines.length; i++) {
            out.write(lines[i].getBytes());
            out.write(CRLF.getBytes());
        }
        out.flush();
        out.close();
    }
}
```

After we run `UpdateExample`, the file now contains the entire poem:

```
Simple Gifts

'Tis a gift to be simple
   'Tis a gift to be free
'Tis a gift to come down
   where we ought to be
And when we find ourselves
   in the place just right
'Twill be in the valley
   of love and delight.

When true
   simplicity is gained
```

```
To bow and to bend
   we shall not be ashamed
To turn, turn will
   be our delight
'Till by turning, turning we
   come 'round right.
```

RandomAccessFile

RandomAccessFile allows bytes or Java primitive data types to be read from or written to any position of a file. It has a seek() method that positions the file pointer to the desired byte number, and a getFilePointer() method that returns the current position.

RandomAccessFile implements both the DataInput and DataOutput interfaces, enabling it to behave like a DataInputStream or DataOutput Stream that can be positioned anywhere in the file. Note, however, that RandomAccessFile inherits from java.lang.Object directly, not InputStream or OutputStream, so you cannot use it as the underlying stream in a filter input or output class. (Well, sort of. You can get its file descriptor by calling getFD() and then create a FileOutputStream or FileInputStream using their file descriptor constructors. This is hardly necessary, however, since RandomAccessFile provides all their methods and more.)

RandomAccessFile has two constructors:

RandomAccessFile(String *name*, String *mode*)

opens the specified file for random access. The mode must be r –(read only) or rw –(read and write).

Local Lingo

If the mode is rw, then the underlying file is created if it does not already exist. There is no w mode.

Exam Tip

Pay careful attention to the file mode in any question about RandomAccessFile. If it is not rw, then write methods will fail.

RandomAccessFile(File *file*, String *mode*)

opens the specified file for random access and calls the other constructor using
file.getPath() for its name parameter.

RandomAccessFile is a versatile and useful class that is often used to read
binary file formats. The following example illustrates how to use RandomAccess
File to read metadata from a database in .dbf format. It features these methods:

- **void seek(long** *pos***)**   Positions the file pointer
- **byte readByte()**   Reads a single byte
- **void readFully(byte[]** *b***)**   Reads an array of bytes
- **int read()**   Reads an ASCII character

```
import java.io.*;

/**
 * An example of using a RandomAccessFile to read
 * metadadta from a file in dBase format.
 */
public class RandomAccessExample
{
   public RandomAccessExample(String fileName)
      throws IOException
   {
      // Open the dBase file for random access

      RandomAccessFile raf = new RandomAccessFile(fileName, "r");

      // Field descriptors are 32-byte structures,
      // beginning at offset 32 into the header.

      final int DESCRIPTOR_OFFSET = 32;
      final int DESCRIPTOR_LENGTH = 32;

      // Read and print each field descriptor

      for (int fieldNumber = 0;; fieldNumber++) {

         long pos = DESCRIPTOR_OFFSET
            + fieldNumber * DESCRIPTOR_LENGTH;
```

```
raf.seek(pos);

// A 0x0D byte signals the end of field
// descriptors

byte b = raf.readByte();
if (b == 0x0D)
   break;

// If not end of descriptors, this is the
// first byte of a field name.  Read the
// rest of the name.

byte[] buffer = new byte[11];
buffer[0] = b;
raf.readFully(buffer, 1, 10);

// The name is exactly 11 bytes, in
// ASCII with trailing zeros

int z = 0;
while (buffer[z] != 0)
   z++;
String name = new String(buffer, 0, z);

// The next byte is the field type:
// C, N, L, D, or M

char type = (char) raf.read();

// Skip 4 bytes of the field address

raf.skipBytes(4);

// Then read the one-byte field length

int length = raf.readByte();
```

```
        // Print results

        StringBuffer sb = new StringBuffer();
        sb.append("Field ");
        sb.append(fieldNumber + 1);
        sb.append(": name=");
        sb.append(name);
        sb.append(", type=");
        sb.append(type);
        sb.append(", length=");
        sb.append(length);
        System.out.println(sb);
      }
      raf.close();
   }


   /**
    * Mainline
    */
   public static void main(String[] args)
      throws IOException
   {
      String fileName = args[0];
      new RandomAccessExample(fileName);
   }
}
```

Using this program to read the NUTR_DEF.DBF file in the U. S. Department
of Agriculture Nutrient Database for Standard Reference (freely available for
downloading at **http://www.nal.usda.gov/fnic/foodcomp/Data/SR13/sr13.html**),
you get the following output:

```
D:\>java RandomAccessExample NUTR_DEF.DBF
Field 1: name=NUTR_NO, type=C, length=3
Field 2: name=UNITS, type=C, length=6
Field 3: name=TAGNAME, type=C, length=20
Field 4: name=NUTRDESC, type=C, length=60
Field 5: name=IFDA_NO, type=C, length=3
```

Describe Permanent Effects on the File System from Using FileInputStream, FileOutput Stream, and RandomAccess File

Objective 11.05

The final exam objective in this section tests your ability to describe the permanent effects on the file system of constructing and using `FileInputStream`, `FileOutputStream`, and `RandomAccessFile` objects.

Since `FileInputStream` only reads data, which is a nondestructive operation, using it has no effects on the file system (other than perhaps slowing things down if you open `FileInputStream`s by the hundreds). `FileOutputStream` can have three effects, depending on the constructor used and the state of the file before the operation, as listed in Table 11.8.

TABLE 11.8 Permanent Effects of FileOutputStream on the File System		
Constructor	**File Exists?**	**Effect**

`FileOutputStream(File file)`
`FileOutputStream(String name)`
`FileOutputStream(String name, false)`
`FileOutputStream(String name, true)`
	false	New file is created.

`FileOutputStream(File file)`
`FileOutputStream(String name)`
`FileOutputStream(String name, false)`
	true	File is cleared; output begins at the first byte.

`FileOutputStream(String name, true)`	true	Output is appended to end of existing data.

`RandomAccessFile` can affect the existence and length of files in the file system. If the file does not already exist, the results of opening a `RandomAccessFile` depend on the *mode* parameter in the constructor:

Local Lingo

An existing file can be cleared (set to zero length) with the single statement *new FileOutputStream(fileName).close()*.

- If mode = r, the constructor will throw FileNotFoundException.
- If mode = rw″, the constructor will attempt to create a new file

With RandomAccessFile, bytes can be written to any position in the file, even beyond the current end of file. If a write occurs beyond end of file, the file size will be extended, with the byte positions that were skipped filled with binary zeroes. When the file is closed, its length will reflect any change in the highest byte position written. Alternatively, you can set the file size explicitly with setLength().

CHECKPOINT

✔ **Objective 11.01** Write code that uses objects of the File class to navigate a file system. File is a class that represents a path name in the underlying file system. It contains methods for checking file attributes, comparing path names, operating on underlying files, extracting filename components, and listing directory contents.

✔ **Objective 11.02** Write code that uses objects of the classes InputStreamReader and OutputStreamWriter to translate between Unicode and either platform default or ISO 8859-1 character encoding and distinguish between conditions under which platform default encoding conversion should be used and conditions under which a specific conversion should be used. These classes provide the bridge between Unicode characters and their representations as byte output and input streams. They use the platform default encoding by default but can be used with any supported encoding.

✔ **Objective 11.03** Select valid constructor arguments for FilterInputStream and FilterOutputStream subclasses from a list of classes in the java.io package. These classes allow you to wrap other byte streams to transform the data (for example, from bytes to Java primitive types and back) and to provide additional functionality (for example, I/O buffering).

✔ **Objective 11.04** Write appropriate code to read, write, and update files using `FileInputStream`, `FileOutputStream`, and `RandomAccessFile` objects, classes that read and write byte streams from the underlying file system. FileInputStream and FileOutputStream are usually wrapped in filter streams that handle character conversion and line-based I/O. `RandomAccessFile` allows complete flexibility in reading binary files from any position within the file.

✔ **Objective 11.05** Describe the permanent effects on the file system of constructing and using `FileInputStream`, `FileOutputStream`, and `RandomAccessFile` objects. `FileOutputStream` can create new files, clear existing ones, or append data to them, depending on the constructor used and whether the file already exists. RandomAccessFile can also affect the existence and length of a file.

REVIEW QUESTIONS

1. The following code is run on a Windows NT platform. Which of the following statements correctly describe the output?

```
Map map = new HashMap();

File file1 = new File("MYFILE.TXT");
File file2 = new File("myfile.txt");

map.put(file1, file1);
map.put(file2, file2);

for (Iterator it = map.keySet().iterator(); it.hasNext();) {
   File file = (File) it.next();
   System.out.println(file);
}
```

    A. The single line "`MYFILE.TXT`".
    B. The single line "`myfile.txt`".
    C. Both "`MYFILE.TXT`" and "`myfile.txt`".
    D. The program will get a runtime exception when `map.put(file2, file2)` is executed.
    E. The absolute path names of both "MYFILE.TXT" and "myfile.txt".

2. Under what circumstances will the temporary file created by the following statement be deleted? (Select two.)

```
File tf = File.createTempFile("PLM", null, dir);
```

- **A.** The file will be deleted when the Virtual Machine is terminated.
- **B.** The file will not be deleted automatically.
- **C.** The file will be deleted when the `dir.close()` method is executed.
- **D.** The file will be deleted when the `tf.close()` method is executed.
- **E.** The file will be deleted when the `tf.delete()` method is executed.

3. Which of the following statements correctly describe the results of executing the following code? (Assume that the `c:\temp` directory contains just one file, named `xyz`).

```
File dir = new File("c:\\temp");
String[] entries = dir.list();
File file = new File(entries[0]);
FileInputStream in = new FileInputStream(file);
```

- **A.** The last line will throw an `IOException` because file will point to the ". " directory.
- **B.** The last line will throw an `IOException` because file will point to the ".." directory.
- **C.** The code will attempt to open a file named `xyz` in the current directory.
- **D.** The code will not compile because there is no `FileInputStream` constructor that takes a `File` argument.
- **E.** The last line will throw a `NullPointerException`.

4. Which of the following are methods in the `File` class that can be invoked to set the path name of the underlying file?

- **A.** `setPath(String pathName)`
- **B.** `setPathName(String pathName)`
- **C.** `setFile(String pathName)`
- **D.** `setFileName(String pathName)`
- **E.** None of the above.

5. After the following code has been executed, what methods can be invoked to reset the *read-only* attribute of the file so that it can be opened for output? (Assume that the file already exists before the code is executed.)

```
File file = new File("myfile.txt");
file.setReadOnly();
```

    A. `file.clearReadOnly();`
    B. `file.setReadOnly(false);`
    C. `file.setWriteOnly();`
    D. `file.chmod("+w");`
    E. None of the above.

6. The following code assigns the Unicode characters values for the first three letters of the Greek alphabet to the variables *alpha*, *beta*, and *gamma*, respectively. Assume the platform default encoding does not contain mappings for those characters. What will happen when the code is executed?

```
public static void main(String[] args)
   throws IOException
{
   OutputStream stream = new FileOutputStream("data.out");
   OutputStreamWriter out = new OutputStreamWriter(stream);

   char alpha = '\u03b1';
   char beta  = '\u03b2';
   char gamma = '\u03b3';

   out.write(alpha);
   out.write(beta);
   out.write(gamma);

   out.flush();
   out.close();
}
```

    A. The first `out.write()` statement will throw an `Unsupported EncodingException`.
    B. No data will be written to the file.
    C. The file will contain six bytes (three 16-bit characters).
    D. The file will contain three bytes of ASCII question marks (???).
    E. The first `out.write()` statement will throw a `NullPointerException`.

7. Which of the following are valid classes for use in a FilterOutputStream constructor? (Select two.)

A. DataOutput

B. DataOutputStream

C. RandomAccessFile

D. FilterOutputStream

E. StringWriter

8. The code in the following method gets a compilation error. What is the problem?

```
public void sayHello(OutputStream stream)
{
   try {
      PrintStream out = new PrintStream(stream);
      out.println("Hello, world");
   }
   catch (IOException e) {
      e.printStackTrace();
   }
}
```

A. The code in the try block does not throw IOException.

B. The print stream is never closed.

C. PrintStream does not accept an OutputStream parameter in its constructor.

D. PrintStream requires a boolean autoFlush parameter in its constructor.

E. PrintStream is deprecated.

9. Which of the following interfaces does RandomAccessFile implement?

A. Externalizable

B. Serializable

C. DataOutput

D. OutputStream

E. InputStream

10. What will be the contents of myfile.dat after the following code is executed?

```
public static void main(String[] args)
    throws IOException
{
    FileOutputStream out = new FileOutputStream("myfile.dat");
    out.write(1);
    out.write(2);
    out.write(3);
    out.flush();
    out.close();

    out = new FileOutputStream("myfile.dat", true);
    out.write(1);
    out.flush();
    out.close();
}
```

A. 0x010203

B. 0x01020301

C. 0x01

D. 0x00000001000000020000000300000001

E. 0x01000000020000000300000001000000

REVIEW ANSWERS

1. **A** This is a tricky one. Recall that the `File` class overrides the `equals()` method to take into account the underlying operating system's notion of equal path names. On DOS and Win32 systems, filenames are not case sensitive. On these platforms, then, `file1.equals(file2)` will be true. Therefore when the `map.put(file2, file2)` line is executed, the `HashMap` code finds that the entry already exists and does not replace the key (only the value).

2. **B E** Don't let the method name (`createTempFile`) fool you. The file is not automatically deleted—that is the job of the `deleteOnExit()` method. You can delete the file manually with its `delete()` method.

3. **C** The `list()` method returns just the filename, not the full path. Therefore, the `entries[0]` string contains just "xyz", not "c:/temp/xyz".

Consequently, the file variable points to a name relative to the current directory. The " . " and " . . " directory entries are not included in the list.

4. **E** File objects are immutable. You can only set the path name in the constructor.

5. **E** Strangely enough, the File class provides no method for resetting this attribute.

6. **D** OutputStreamWriter substitutes question marks for any character not found in its character encoding.

7. **B** **D** A is wrong because DataOutput is an interface, not a subclass of OutputStream, as required. C is wrong because RandomAccessFile is also not a subclass of OutputStream, although it implements the DataOutput interface. E is wrong because Writer classes are not byte output streams.

8. **A** Neither the constructor nor the println() method throws any exceptions, so the try/catch block is not valid. E is almost true, but PrintStream is not in fact marked as deprecated.

9. **C** RandomAccessFile is neither externalizable nor serializable. Output Stream and InputStream are classes, not interfaces. RandomAccessFile also implements DataInput, but that does not appear in the list of answers.

10. **B** The append=true flag in the second open means that write operations will take place at the end of the existing file, so A and C are wrong. D and E incorrectly assume that the write() method writes a 32-bit integer rather than just the low-order byte. E also incorrectly assumes that integers are written in little-endian format.

The **java.util** Package

	NEWBIE	SOME EXPERIENCE	EXPERT
ETA	8–10 hours	5–8 hours	3–8 hours

Virtually all programs use data structures that represent collections of objects: a set of playing cards in a game program, a list of choices in a combo box, a stack of tokens being parsed into expressions, or a mapping of state code abbreviations to state names. The Java language itself has only one means of representing collections: the array. While arrays will work as basic containers, they have several drawbacks:

- Arrays have a fixed length that cannot be changed. If you need to add elements to a full array, you need to create a new one and copy the old elements into it. Likewise, if you have fewer elements than the array can hold, you have no simple way to indicate that an array slot is empty (for primitive data types, that is).
- If you need to maintain elements in a particular order, you have to sort the array yourself. Arrays have no built-in sorting or searching functionality, nor any notion of an order other than the arrangement of elements according to array index.
- Arrays provide no means of mapping keys to values.

The standard pre-Java 2 class library had a fairly small set of classes that worked with collections, for example, the `Vector`, `Hashtable`, `Stack`, and `Properties` classes. Java 2 significantly revamped this capability with a comprehensive new collections framework. This framework, contained in the `java.util` package, consists of three components:

1. A set of *interfaces* that describe the behavior of different types of collections
2. Classes that are *implementations* of those interfaces
3. *Algorithms* that can be used on classes implementing the interfaces.

The remainder of this chapter explores the main interfaces and classes that support the functionality of the collections framework.

Exam Tip

There are other types of classes in the `java.util` package that deal with dates, resources, and events, but the exam objective focuses entirely on the collections framework. You should concentrate your study efforts on those classes and interfaces.

Make Appropriate Selection of Collection Classes/Interfaces

One of the benefits of using interfaces instead of classes is that you can define a specific set of methods that an object must handle, define a variable of that type, and then assign any object that implements that interface to the variable. The object may be an instance of a class that has other methods and implements other interfaces, but the compiler will ensure two things:

- Every method required by the interface is supported by the object.
- No methods other than those required by the interface are ever called on the object.

The practical value of this is that you can write code using just the interface types and have it operate on a variety of concrete classes. For example, if you are writing a sort routine, you might define an interface called Sortable with a compare() method that indicates which of two Sortable objects is greater. You can write the sort algorthim entirely in terms of Sortable objects. If you later come up with a RomanNumeral class, your sort routine can operate on arrays of that type, as long as RomanNumeral declares that it implements Sortable and provides a compare() method.

The collections framework is organized around interfaces. There are a few top-level interfaces that define general behavior: adding and removing members of a collection, testing whether it contains a particular member, and retrieving

---

Exam Tip

It is essential to understand the difference between the class of an object and the type of the variable to which it is assigned. When you see an instance variable of type Runnable, for example, you know it contains an object of a class that implements that interface—one that has a run() method, in this case. But that simply describes the role that object is playing in the code, not the class it actually belongs to.

members one by one. These interfaces are then extended by others that define other specific behaviors. There are also abstract and concrete classes that serve as basic implementations of these interfaces.

Overall, the framework classes are organized into the following four categories:

- Collections interfaces and classes
- Mapping interfaces and classes
- Iterators
- Utility classes

Let's consider each of these categories in greater detail, taking a look at the classes they contain, the behavior they support, the algorithms they use, and examples of their use.

Collections Interfaces and Classes

The most basic interface in the framework is the `Collection` interface. It represents a simple group of elements, and has two main characteristics:

- Elements are not assumed to be in any particular order. Note that this does *not* mean that the elements may not in fact be maintained in some order, only that there are no methods in the interface that depend on this fact.
- Duplicates and null elements are permitted.

`Collection` has two subinterfaces, `List` and `Set`, which modify these characteristics. Figure 12-1 shows the interface hierarchy that descends from `Collection`, as well as the concrete classes that implement these interfaces.

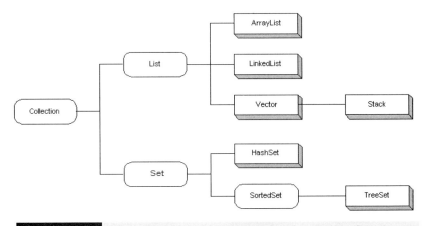

FIGURE 12-1   Collection interface hierarchy and implementation classes

The only assumption you can make about the members of a Collection object is that they are instances of java.lang.Object or one of its subclasses, not primitives like int or float. The methods in the Collection interface, as well as all the other interfaces in the framework, work with Object parameters and return values. For this reason, you must cast elements retrieved from a Collection to the desired data type. For example, if you have stored a Date object in a Map like this:

```
Map dm = new HashMap();
dm.put("TODAY", new Date());
```

then you retrieve it like this:

```
Date today = (Date) dm.get("TODAY");
```

Table 12.1 lists the methods that comprise the Collection interface. (The table does not include the hashcode() and equals() methods, even though the interface specifies them, because they are defined in java.lang.Object, and therefore automatically have at least default implementations in every class.)

TABLE 12.1 Methods Defined by the Collection Interface	
Method Name	**Description**
boolean add(Object *o*)	Loosely speaking, adds the specified object to the collection and returns true. If the implementing class does not allow duplicates and the object already exists in the collection, returns false.
boolean addAll (Collection *c*)	Adds all the elements of collection *c* to this collection.
void clear()	Removes all elements of the collection.
boolean contains(Object *o*)	Returns true if this collection contains the specified object.
	(Continued)

TABLE 12.1 *Continued*

Method Name	Description
`boolean containsAll (Collection c)`	Returns true if this collection contains every element of collection c.
`boolean isEmpty()`	Returns true if the collection contains no elements.
`Iterator iterator()`	Returns an object that can be used to retrieve every element of the collection, one at a time.
`boolean remove(Object o)`	Removes the specified object from the collection. Returns true if the collection changed as a result.
`boolean removeAll (Collection c)`	Removes every element of collection c from this collection.
`boolean retainAll (Collection c)`	Removes every element from this collection that is not an element of collection c. Equivalent to converting this collection to the intersection of the two collections.
`int size()`	Returns the number of members of the collection.
`Object[] toArray()`	Creates an array of the same size as this collection and copies all the members of the collection into it.
`Object[] toArray (Object[] o)`	Creates an array large enough to hold all elements of this collection and copies the elements into it. If the `Object[] o` parameter array is large enough, it will be used to hold the results. Otherwise, a new array will be allocated.

There are no concrete classes in the java.util package that implement Collection directly, since it is not particularly useful as is. However, Collection is frequently used as the data type of a variable or the return type of a method. Using it in this manner allows the compiler to verify that you aren't relying on any hidden assumptions about the behavior of the collection beyond what is spelled out in the interface.

In the examples that follow, we'll use that approach, defining our variables to be of type Collection, even though they contain instances of a concrete class DemoCollection (which extends LinkedList, just because we had to pick something.) The complete definition of DemoCollection is just this:

```
public class DemoCollection extends LinkedList {}
```

Using the Collection Methods

We'll demonstrate how the collection methods work by creating and modifying groups of musical instrument names.

add() and addAll()

The first example demonstrates the use of the add() method:

```
Collection stringTrio = new DemoCollection();
stringTrio.add("Violin");
stringTrio.add("Viola");
stringTrio.add("Cello");
System.out.println("String trio is " + stringTrio);
```

Nothing complicated here: just three calls to add(), passing it a String parameter each time. The results are what you'd expect:

```
String trio is [Violin, Viola, Cello]
```

Note that all we had to do to print the contents of the collection was to concatenate it to a string literal and pass the result to System.out.println(). Our code doesn't add the square brackets, list the individual elements, or put commas between them. This is all done by the collection's toString() method.

We can make a string quartet from the trio by adding a violin to an empty collection, then calling addAll() to add the elements of the string trio.

```
Collection stringQuartet = new DemoCollection();
stringQuartet.add("Violin");
stringQuartet.addAll(stringTrio);
System.out.println("String quartet is " + stringQuartet);
```

Note the duplicate elements in the result:

```
String quartet is [Violin, Violin, Viola, Cello]
```

remove() and removeAll()

Building on this collection by removing the extra violin and adding a piano, the following code uses the remove() and add() methods:

```
Collection pianoQuartet = new DemoCollection();
pianoQuartet.addAll(stringQuartet);
pianoQuartet.remove("Violin");
pianoQuartet.add("Piano");
System.out.println("Piano quartet is " + pianoQuartet);
```

with the following result:

```
Piano quartet is [Violin, Viola, Cello, Piano]
```

The removeAll() method works by invoking remove() repeatedly, once for each of the elements in the collection parameter object.

retainAll()

The retainAll() method corresponds to the notion of the intersection of two sets. The following code creates two collections with certain elements in common, then uses retainAll() to restrict the second collection to just those elements it shares with the first:

```
Collection hsTrio = new DemoCollection();
hsTrio.add("Violin");
hsTrio.add("Clarinet");
hsTrio.add("Piano");
System.out.println
    ("L'Histoire du Soldat trio is " + hsTrio);

Collection group = new DemoCollection();
```

```
group.add("Flute");
group.add("Oboe");
group.add("Violin");
group.add("Clarinet");
System.out.println("Original group: " + group);
group.retainAll(hsTrio);
System.out.println("After retainAll " + hsTrio + " : " + group);
```

The output shows the contents of each of the collections and the results of invoking retainAll():

```
L'Histoire du Soldat trio is [Violin, Clarinet, Piano]
Original group: [Flute, Oboe, Violin, Clarinet]
After retainAll [Violin, Clarinet, Piano] : [Violin, Clarinet]
```

"Violin" and "Clarinet" were the only elements common to both collections, and they are the only ones that remain after retainAll().

contains() and containsAll()

The Collection interface has methods to determine if a collection contains a particular element or set of elements. Using collections built in the preceding examples, this code illustrates use of the contains() and containsAll() methods, with both true and false results:

```
System.out.println
    (stringTrio + " contains Clarinet? "
    + stringTrio.contains("Clarinet"));

System.out.println
    (hsTrio + " contains Clarinet? "
    + hsTrio.contains("Clarinet"));

System.out.println
    (pianoQuartet + " contains " + stringTrio + "? "
    + pianoQuartet.containsAll(stringTrio));

System.out.println
    (stringTrio + " contains " + duo + "? "
    + stringTrio.containsAll(duo));
```

```
System.out.println
    (stringTrio + " contains " + stringQuartet + "? "
    + stringTrio.containsAll(stringQuartet));
```

The results are shown here:

```
[Violin, Viola, Cello] contains Clarinet? false
[Violin, Clarinet, Piano] contains Clarinet? true
[Violin, Viola, Cello, Piano] contains [Violin, Viola, Cello]? true
[Violin, Viola, Cello] contains [Piano, Violin]? false
[Violin, Viola, Cello] contains [Violin, Violin, Viola, Cello]? true
```

The only surprising result may be the last one. How can a smaller collection contain a larger one? Like `removeAll()` and `retainAll()`, `containsAll()` works by calling its single-element equivalent on each of the elements of the collection passed as a parameter. So the last expression in the example

```
stringTrio.containsAll(stringQuartet)
```

is equivalent to

```
stringTrio.contains("Violin")
&& stringTrio.contains("Violin")
&& stringTrio.contains("Viola")
&& stringTrio.contains("Cello")
```

The fact that `stringQuartet` contains duplicate "Violin" elements doesn't really matter—each call to `stringTrio.contains("Violin")` is true, regardless of how many times it has been asked.

iterator()

To retrieve the elements of a collection, you can't just ask for the one in the fifth or ninth position—you don't know if the collection is ordered or not. Instead, you use an object called an *iterator*. This object has a method called `next()` that you call repeatedly to get each element, as well as a boolean method called `hasNext()` that tells you whether there are any more elements. Every `Collection` object supports a method named `iterator()` that constructs an iterator object for you. This provides a simple means of walking through a collection, as shown here:

```
System.out.println("L'Histoire du Soldat is scored"
```

```
   + " for the following instruments:");

Iterator it = hsTrio.iterator();
while (it.hasNext()) {
   String instrument = (String) it.next();
   System.out.println("    " + instrument);
}
```

The output of this code is as follows:

```
L'Histoire du Soldat is scored for the following instruments:
   Violin
   Clarinet
   Piano
```

Later in this chapter, we'll look at Iterator and its related interfaces in more detail.

toArray()

Finally, the Collection interface provides a bridge between collections and arrays with the toArray() method:

```
String[] instruments =
   (String[]) pianoQuartet.toArray
      (new String[pianoQuartet.size()]);

for (int i = 0; i < instruments.length; i++)
   System.out.println
      ("instruments[" + i + "] = " + instruments[i]);
}
```

There are two forms of this method: one that takes no parameters, and one that takes an Object array parameter, as shown in the preceding example. The no-parameter form is equivalent to calling the second form with a value of new Object[0].

The toArray() method allocates an array of the type specified in its parameter that is large enough to hold all the elements in the collection, then copies each element into the array. If the array in the parameter has a nonzero size and is large enough, toArray() will use it as the resulting array rather than allocating a new one. Since the method is declared to return Object[], you must cast the result to the specific array type you want. Naturally, the objects in the underlying collection must be compatible with being cast to the specified type, or a `ClassCastException` will occur.

The `List` Interface

Recall that a `Collection` object is not known to be in any particular order. Usually, however, order is important. For collections of this type, there is the `List` interface.

`List` is a subinterface of `Collection`, so it has all the same methods described in the preceding section. In addition, it has methods that support storing and retrieving elements by their location. A `List` is conceptually very similar to an array, in that both of them are addressed by an integer index: the first element is at index 0, the second at index 1, and so on. The big difference is that a `List` can grow as you add elements to it without your having to do anything special.

Travel Advisory
Remember, when we speak of a `List` object, or the contents of a variable of type `List`, we mean an instance of a class that implements the `List` interface. It may be a `java.util.Stack`, a `java.util.LinkedList`, or any other implementing class, but if you assign it to a `List` variable, you can only call the `List` methods (including those that `List` inherits from `Collection`.)

Referring back to Figure 12-1, you can see that the `java.util` package provides four concrete classes that implement the `List` interface:

- **ArrayList** An array-like list that is optimized for fast random access. In addition to implementing the `List` methods, it has methods that let you grow and shrink its preallocated capacity. (The table does not include the `hashcode()` and `equals()` methods, even though the interface specifies them, because they are defined in `java.lang.Object`, and therefore automatically have at least default implementations in every class.)
- **LinkedList** A `List` whose elements are threaded with a doubly-linked list of pointers (not visible to you). This makes `LinkedList` very fast for element insertions.
- **Vector** An older version of `ArrayList` that has been internally restructured to implement the `List` interface. The main difference between `Vector` and `ArrayList` is that any operation that adds, deletes, or retrieves elements from a `Vector` is synchronized. While this

may be desirable in some cases, there is no need to pay the performance penalty if you don't need synchronization.

- **Stack**   A subclass of Vector that provides the push and pop methods of a pushdown stack. (It could be argued that Stack shouldn't inherit from Vector and shouldn't implement List, since that breaks encapsulation by exposing the inner structure of the stack.)

Table 12.2 describes the methods in the List interface that are different from the ones it inherits from Collection.

TABLE 12.2 Unique Methods in the List Interface	
Method Name	**Description**
void add(int *i*, Object *o*)	Inserts the specified object in the list so that it becomes the new *i*th element. The previous *i*th element and any that follow it are moved down one.
boolean addAll (int *i*, Collection *c*)	Inserts the members of the specified collection in the list, with the first element becoming the new *i*th element and the rest inserted following it.
Object get(int *i*)	Returns the *i*th element of the list as an Object.
int indexOf(Object *o*)	Searches for the specified element in the list, returning its index or −1 if it is not found.
int lastIndexOf(Object *o*)	Works like indexOf() but searches from the end of the list backward.
ListIterator listIterator()	Returns an iterator over the list that can enumerate elements forward or backward.
ListIterator listIterator(int *i*)	Returns a bidirectional list iterator that starts at the specified element.
Object remove(int *i*)	Removes the element at the specified index from the list.

(Continued)

TABLE 12.2	CONTINUED
Method Name	**Description**
Object set(int *i*, Object *o*)	Stores the specified object in the list at the specified position, replacing any previous element at that position.
List subList (int *i1*, int *i2*)	Return the sublist of the list having the specified starting and ending index. The *i1* element is included; the *i2* element is not. The sublist looks through to the parent list, so that changes in either one are reflected in the other.

The functions of most of these methods are obvious from their names, although the last one (subList) has some subtleties:

- The element at the first index is included in the sublist; the element at the second index is not. In this respect, it is analogous to the substring() method in java.lang.String.
- The sublist "looks through" to the main list, meaning that it points to the same objects and in the same order. If you change the order of elements in the sublist, the order changes in the main list as well. If you update an element through the sublist, the element also changes in the main list. If you clear the sublist, its elements are removed from the main list as well.
- If you modify the size or structure of the main list (other than through operations on the sublist), the effects on the sublist are undefined.

The Set Interface

Remember the two characteristic structural features of the Collection interface?

1. Elements are not assumed to be in any particular order.
2. Duplicates and null elements are permitted.

We have just seen that List eliminates the first constraint by declaring the order of the elements to be important. Set is a Collection subinterface that modifies the second assumption: there are no duplicate elements permitted, and at most one null element. You use a Set object when the important property of a collection is being able to determine whether a particular object is a member of the collection or not.

You might use a Set object, for example, if you are writing a program to download web pages, scan them for links, and then follow the links recursively to download other pages. To prevent infinite loops due to cyclic page references, you need to keep track of which pages you've already downloaded. You can do this by creating a Set of visited URLs that you add to each time you download a page. If a URL link in a page you are parsing is already in the set, you can bypass it. For this purpose, you don't care in what order you have downloaded pages, only whether or not you have downloaded a given page.

Although Set is a subinterface of Collection, it does not define any methods that are not already in Collection. Referring back to Figure 12-1, you can see that Set has one concrete implementing class (HashSet), and one subinterface (SortedSet).

SortedSet

The elements of a set are not retrievable by their relative position, but they may have a "key" that implies an order, such as alphabetical. This order is automatically supplied if the elements belong to a class that implements the Comparable interface, which has a compareTo() method.

You can customize the ordering of a SortedSet by supplying a Comparator object that defines a compare(Object *o1*, Object *o2*) method.

Local Lingo
The order implied by the Comparable interface is referred to in the JDK documentation as the *natural ordering*.

Table 12.3 describes the additional methods in the SortedSet interface that are not already in Collection.

TABLE 12.3 Methods in the SortedSet Interface

Method Name	Description
Comparator comparator()	Returns the comparator used by this sorted set, or null if it uses natural ordering.
Object first() Object last()	Returns the set element with the lowest (highest) key value.

(Continued)

TABLE 12.3	*Continued*
Method Name	**Description**
`SortedSet headSet(Object o)` `SortedSet tailSet(Object o)`	Returns the subset of all elements whose key is less than (greater than or equal to) the key of the specified object.
`SortedSet subSet` `(Object from, Object to)`	Returns the subset of all elements whose keys are greater than or equal to the *from* object key and strictly less than the *to* object key

`SortedSet` has one concrete implementation, `TreeSet`.

Mapping Interfaces and Classes

The other major branch of the collections framework is the Map interface and its descendants, illustrated in Figure 12-2. Mapping refers to associating a key object uniquely with a value object. Maps have no duplicate keys and can have at most one `null` key.

Maps are very common data structures. You might use a map to associate a country code and its full name, to store a financial object so that it can be accessed by its stock ticker symbol, or to link an IP address to a host name—anywhere you need to connect a value with a key.

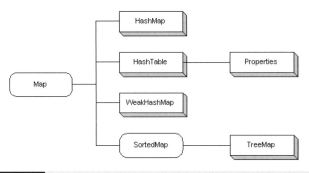

| FIGURE 1-2 | The Map interface and its descendant classes and interfaces |

The Map Interface

The Map interface and its implementing classes provide methods to add, delete, and change mappings; to retrieve values given keys; and to get information about the number of mappings and their key and value sets.

Exam Tip

In general, any type of object can be used for either the key or the value in a Map, not just strings. Watch out for sample code in exam questions that don't cast values retrieved from a Map or that assume that the keys are strings.

Table 12.4 lists the methods common to all Map classes in the java.util package.

TABLE 12.4   Distinct Methods in the SortedMap Interface

Method Name	Description
void clear()	Removes all keys and mapped elements from the map.
boolean containsKey (Object *key*) boolean containsValue (Object *value*)	Returns true if the map contains the specified object as a key (as a value).
Set entrySet()	Returns the keys/value pairs in the map as a Set of Map.Entry objects.
Object get(Object *key*)	Returns the value object associated with the specified key object, or null if no such mapping exists.
boolean isEmpty()	Returns true if the map has no elements.

(Continued)

TABLE 12.4	*Continued*

Method Name	Description
`Set keySet()`	Returns the keys objects in the map as a Set.
`Object put (Object key, Object value)`	Maps the specified key to the specified value. Returns the value previously associated with this key, if any.
`void putAll(Map m)`	Adds all the mappings from the map parameter to this map.
`Object remove(Object key)`	Removes any mapping for the specified key. Returns the value that had been mapped to the key, if any.
`int size()`	Returns the number of mappings currently in the map.
`Collection values()`	Returns all the value objects in the map as a `Collection`.

The `java.util` package contains four concrete classes that implement `Map`:

- **HashMap**   An implementation of all the methods in the `Map` interface (and nothing else). Allows any type of object to be used as either a key or a value, including `null`.
- **Hashtable**   An older functional equivalent of `HashMap`. Does not allow null keys. All retrieval and storage operations are synchronized, unlike `HashMap`.
- **Properties**   A subclass of `Hashtable` that accepts only strings as keys or values. Includes `getProperty()` and `setProperty()` methods with string parameters, as well as methods to save and restore the properties from a stream.
- **WeakHashMap**   A map whose keys are weak references, meaning that they do not prevent garbage collection when they are the only remaining reference. This means essentially that mappings are removed when their keys are not elsewhere referenced. This class is highly specialized and is seldom used.

The **SortedMap** Interface

In addition to these classes, Map also has an important subinterface named SortedMap. Iterators over the key set of a SortedMap will return the keys in sorted order, according to their natural ordering or one supplied by a Comparator. SortedMap has one concrete implementation class, TreeMap. Table 12.5 lists the methods defined by the SortedMap interface beyond what it inherits from Map.

TABLE 12.5	Distinct Methods in the **SortedMap** Interface
Method Name	**Description**
Comparator comparator()	Returns the Comparator object used to determine the sort ordering, if one was specified in the constructor.
Object firstKey() Object lastKey()	Returns the lowest key (highest key) in the map.
SortedMap headMap (Object *toKey*) SortedMap tailMap (Object *fromKey*)	Returns the submap consisting of all mappings whose key is less than (greater than or equal to) the specified key.
SortedMap subMap (Object *fromKey*, Object *toKey*)	Returns all mappings whose key is greater than or equal to *fromKey* and strictly less than *toKey*.

Using the **Map** Methods

The following example illustrates the principal methods of the Map interface in action. It reads a list of operas, organizes them by composer, and then prints each composer's list along with information about the composer.

```
import java.util.*;


public class MapDemo
```

```
{
    private static final String[] input = {
        "Aida,Verdi",
        "Billy Budd,Britten",
        "Das Rheingold,Wagner",
        "Die Walküre,Wagner",
        "Die Zauberflöte,Mozart",
        "Ernani,Verdi",
        "Gloriana,Britten",
        "La Bohème,Puccini",
        "La Fanciulla del West,Puccini",
        "La Forza del Destino,Verdi",
        "La Traviata,Verdi",
        "Le Nozze di Figaro,Mozart",
        "Lohengrin,Wagner",
        "Macbeth,Verdi",
        "Madama Butterfly,Puccini",
        "Manon Lescaut,Puccini",
        "Peter Grimes,Britten",
        "Rigoletto,Verdi",
        "Tosca,Puccini",
        "Turandot,Puccini",
    };

    public void run()
    {
        // Create a map that links a composer name
        // to an information string that lists the
        // full name, nationality, year of birth,
        // and year of death.

        Map infoMap = new HashMap();

        infoMap.put("Verdi",
                "Guiseppe Verdi (Italian, 1813-1901)");
        infoMap.put("Puccini",
                "Giacomo Puccini (Italian, 1858-1924)");
        infoMap.put("Mozart",
```

```
                 "Wolfgang Amadeus Mozart (Austrian, 1756-1791)");
         infoMap.put("Wagner",
                 "Richard Wagner (German, 1813-1883)");
         infoMap.put("Britten",
                 "Benjamin Britten (British, 1913-1976)");


         // Create a map that will associate a composer name
         // with a set of operas by that composer

         Map operasByComposer = new TreeMap();
         for (int i = 0; i < input.length; i++) {

             // Get each line of input and split it
             // into the title of the opera and the
             // name of the composer

             String line = input[i];
             int p = line.indexOf(",");
             String opera = line.substring(0, p);
             String composer = line.substring(p+1);

             // If this is the first time we have encountered
             // this composer, map the composer name to an
             // empty set

             if (!operasByComposer.containsKey(composer)) {
                 operasByComposer.put(composer, new TreeSet());
             }

             // Retreive the set of operas by this composer
             // and add the new one

             Set operas = (Set) operasByComposer.get(composer);
             operas.add(opera);
         }

         // Retrieve the set of composers
         // and report the number found
```

```
      Set composers = operasByComposer.keySet();
      int n = composers.size();
      System.out.println
         ("There are " + n + " composers in the list:");


      // Iterate through the composer set

      for (Iterator it = composers.iterator(); it.hasNext(); ) {
         System.out.println();

         // Get the composer short name and look up
         // the full name and information string

         String composer = (String) it.next();
         String info = (String) infoMap.get(composer);
         System.out.println(info);

         // Retrieve the set of operas by this composer

         Set operas = (Set) operasByComposer.get(composer);

         // Iterate through the set and print each element

         for (Iterator it2 = operas.iterator(); it2.hasNext(); ) {
            String opera = (String) it2.next();
            System.out.println("   " + opera);
         }
      }
   }

   public static void main(String[] args)
   {
      new MapDemo().run();
   }
}
```

The program initially loads a map of composer names to information strings, listing the composer's full name, nationality, year of birth, and year of death. It then creates a `TreeMap` object that will be used to associate a composer name with a `SortedSet` of opera names. The input is a list of opera and their composers contained in an array of strings in comma-separated values format. The program reads each list entry and separates it into a composer name and opera name. Using the composer name as a key, it retrieves the set of operas from the map. If no such set exists (that is, when the composer's name first appears in the input), it creates a new `TreeSet` and stores that in the map. Either way, it adds the new opera name to the set for this composer.

When the list is fully processed, the program extracts the set of composers found in the input, using the map's `keySet()` method. From the set's `size()` method, it can determine the number found. Next, it gets an iterator over the set so that it can retrieve the keys one at a time. Since this is a `SortedMap`, the names supplied by the iterator will be in alphabetical order. As it reads each name, it looks up the information string for that composer in the other map, and prints a header. It then gets the set of operas to which the composer name is mapped and prints them.

Iterators

It doesn't do you much good to put items in a collection if you can't get them back out. With a `List`, you can retrieve elements by their index number, and with a `Map`, you can retrieve them by key. But what do you do with a `Collection` or a `Set`? There isn't any particular notion of which element is the first, second, and so on. That's where *iterators* come in.

An iterator is a helper object that lets you retrieve the elements of a collection one at a time. You do this by repeated calls to an iterator method that gets the next element, figuring out when you're done by calling another method. With one minor exception, an iterator allows only one pass through the collection. (The `ListIterator` interface supports forward and backward iteration.)

Iterators are useful for several reasons:

- They provide a simple, standard interface to a variety of collections without requiring you to know the inner structure of the collection.
- They offer better protection for the underlying collection. Rather than providing a method that returns a `List`, from which elements can be added, deleted, changed, and reordered, a developer can write a method that returns an iterator that simply allows the list to be traversed.
- Multiple iterators over the same collection can be used simultaneously. This is better than having a `getFirst()`/`getNext()` approach built into the collection class itself, which limits the collection to one reader at a time.

However, they also have a few minor disadvantages:

- If all you have is an iterator over a collection, you can't tell how many elements it has except by counting them as you iterate.
- If you add or delete elements from a collection while you are iterating over it, the iterator will throw an exception.
- Using an iterator requires creating a new object. This is usually trivial, but inside a tight loop, there could conceivably be some slight performance implications.

The `java.util` package provides three iterator interfaces: `Iterator`, `ListIterator`, and `Enumeration`. There are no concrete classes because an iterator doesn't make sense outside of the collection to which it is attached. You don't create an iterator with new; you get one by calling a method on the collection.

The `Iterator` Interface

The primary interface in the `java.util` package is `Iterator`, which defines three methods, as shown in Table 12.6.

TABLE 12.6   Methods in the `Iterator` Interface

Method Name	Description
`boolean hasNext()`	Returns true if the next call to `next()` will return an object.
`Object next()`	Returns the next object in the collection.
`void remove()`	Removes from the underlying collection the object last returned by `next()`. This method is optional; if an implementation does not support removal, it must throw an `UnsupportedOperation Exception`.

You can get an iterator over any `Collection` object (and therefore over any `List` or `Set`) by calling its `iterator()` method. Traversing the collection then simply involves calling `next()` repeatedly until `hasNext()` returns false.

The `ListIterator` Interface

`Iterator` has one subinterface: `ListIterator`. As its name suggests, it is designed to work with `List` objects, not `Collection` objects in general. In addition to the three `Iterator` methods, this interface adds two capabilities:

1. It can operate in either direction.
2. It allows you to add, delete, or change elements in the underlying list.

Table 12.7 describes the methods that `ListIterator` defines.

TABLE 12.7 Additional Methods in the `ListIterator` Interface	
Method Name	**Description**
`void add(Object o)`	Adds the specified object to the list just before the next element in the iteration. (Optional—may throw `Unsupported OperationException.`)
`boolean hasPrevious()`	Returns true if the next call to `previous()` will return an object.
`int nextIndex()`	Returns the relative index of the element that will be returned by the next call to `next()`, or the list size if there are no more elements.
`Object previous()`	Returns the previous element in the list.
`int previousIndex()`	Returns the relative index of the element that will be returned by the next call to `previous()`, or −1 if there are no more elements.
`void set(Object o)`	Replaces the last element read from the list with the specified object. (Optional— may throw `UnsupportedOperation Exception.`)

The `Enumeration` Interface

The third iterator in `java.util` is the older `Enumeration` interface. Although this interface is not deprecated, its use is discouraged, since `Iterator` offers the same functionality in addition to providing the `remove()` method. Note that Enumeration is not a subinterface of Iterator but instead defines the two methods shown in Table 12.8.

TABLE 12.8	Methods in the `Enumeration` Interface
Method Name	**Description**
`boolean hasMoreElements()`	Returns true if the next call to `nextElement()` will return an object. Functionally equivalent to `Iterator.hasNext()`.
`Object nextElement()`	Returns the next object in the enumeration. Throws `NoSuchElementException` if there are no more elements.

`Enumeration` is unlikely to disappear any time soon because a number of methods in other packages return it. The `java.util.Collections` utility class provides a static method that returns an `Enumeration` from a `Collection` for compatibility with older APIs.

Utility Classes

The last category of classes in the collections framework you need to be familiar with consists of the two utility classes, `java.util.Arrays` and `java.util.Collections`. These classes contain static methods that apply frequently used algorithms to the various collections objects we have considered.

The `Arrays` class provides methods that operate on arrays of objects or primitive data types. These operations include:

- Converting an array to a `List`. This allows you to work with arrays using iterators, comparators, sublists, and other features of the collections framework.
- Performing a binary search of an array for a specific value.
- Comparing two arrays for element-wise equality.

- Filling an array or a portion of it with copies of an object.
- Sorting an array or a portion of it.

The `Arrays.asList()` conversion method is especially convenient for initializing a list, a capability that `List` otherwise lacks:

```
List favoriteNumbers = Arrays.asList(new String[]
  {"06", "28", "02", "05", "03", "07", "68412"}
);
```

Note that the returned list looks through to the array and consequently its size is fixed.

The `Collections` class provides similar functionality on collections. Its features include:

- Constants representing empty `List` and `Set` objects
- Binary search of a list
- Copying from one list to another (comparable to `System.arraycopy()`)
- Filling a list with copies of an object
- Finding the minimum and maximum element of a sortable collection
- Creating a list with a specified number of copies of an object
- Reversing the order of a list
- Randomizing the order of a list
- Sorting a list
- Getting synchronized or immutable versions of a collection, list, or map

Exam Tip

Do not confuse the `Collections` class with the `Collection` interface.

CHECKPOINT

✔ **Objective 12.01** Make appropriate selection of collection classes/interfaces to suit specified behavior requirements. The main behaviors to keep in mind and the classes that implement them are these:

- Simple, fixed-size grouping of elements: array
- Simple grouping that can grow or shrink: `Collection`

- Collection in which order is important: `List`, `ArrayList`, `LinkedList`
- Only membership is important: `Set`, `HashSet`
- Collections with no duplicates allowed: `Set`, `HashSet`
- Elements in sorted order: `SortedSet`, `TreeSet`
- List with synchronized access: `Vector`
- Key/value pairs: `Map`, `Hashtable`, `HashMap`
- Keys in sorted order: `SortedMap`, `TreeMap`
- Iterating through a collection: `Iterator`, `Enumeration`
- Iterating bidirectionally: `ListIterator`

REVIEW QUESTIONS

1. Which of the following statements correctly describe the results of executing the code below?

```
Collection menu = new TreeSet();
System.out.println(menu.add("spam"));
System.out.println(menu.add("eggs"));
System.out.println(menu.add("spam"));
```

- **A.** The code will print "spam", "eggs", and "spam", in that order.
- **B.** The code will print "eggs", "spam", and "spam", in that order.
- **C.** The code will print "eggs" and "spam" only, in that order
- **D.** The code will print "true", "true", "false", in that order
- **E.** The last line will throw a `DuplicateElementException` when run

2. Which of the following statements will cause a runtime exception if the forms object is initialized as shown here?

```
Set forms = new TreeSet();
forms.add("Oratorio");
forms.add("Sonata");
forms.add("Theme and Variations");
```

- **A.** `String[] a = (String[]) forms.toArray(new String[0]);`
- **B.** `Object[] a = forms.toArray();`
- **C.** `String[] a = forms.toArray();`
- **D.** `String[] a = (String[])`

E. `forms.toArray(new String[] {});`

F. `String[] a = (String[]) forms.toArray();`

3. What will be the output of the following code?

```
Map regions = new TreeMap();
   regions.put("MA", new Integer(16));
   regions.put("CT", new Integer(32));
   regions.put("FP", new Integer(6));
   regions.put("MA", new Integer(6));
   regions.put("MA", new Integer(8));
   regions.put("CT", new Integer(22));
   System.out.println(regions.values());
```

A. $[22, 6, 8]$

B. $[6, 8, 22]$

C. $[6, 6, 8, 16, 22, 32]$

D. $[6, 8, 16, 22, 32]$

F. $[16, 32, 6, 6, 8, 22]$

4. Which of the following classes have at least the same functionality over the `Collection` classes as `java.util.Iterator`?

A. `Enumeration`

B. `ListIterator`

C. `Vector`

D. `CharacterIterator`

E. `BreakIterator`

5. What will happen if the `Iterator.remove()` method is called before the `next()` method is called for the first time?

A. The first element of the collection will be removed.

B. The last element of the collection will be removed.

C. An unspecified element of the collection will be removed.

D. An `IllegalStateException` will be thrown.

E. No exceptions will be thrown, and no elements will be removed.

6. After the following code is executed, what class of object will K contain?

```
Map map = new TreeMap();
```

```
map.put("Today", new Date());
Set K = map.entrySet();
```

    A. `java.util.Date`
    B. `java.lang.Object`
    C. `java.String.String`
    D. `java.util.TreeMap`
    E. `java.util.TreeMap$Entry`

7. Which of the following methods can be used to determine the number of elements in a `java.util.SortedSet`?

    A. `count()`
    B. `length()`
    C. `size()`
    D. `getLength()`
    E. `getSize()`

8. Which of the following are characteristics of the object returned by `java.util.Collections.singleton("83")`? (Select three answers.)

    A. The object will be an instance of some class that implements the `java.util.Set` interface.
    B. The object will be serializable.
    C. The object will be an instance of subclass of `java.lang.String`.
    D. The object will be immutable.
    E. The object's `toString()` method will return `null`.

9. Which of the following are interfaces that `java.util.TreeMap` implements? (Select two.)

    A. `AbstractMap`
    B. `SortedMap`
    C. `Cloneable`
    D. `Externalizable`
    E. `Iterator`

10. Under what circumstances can a method call throw `ConcurrentModificationException`?

    A. When a `List` is modified in one thread while another thread is iterating over it.
    B. When two threads call `LinkedList.listIterator()`.

   C. When `wait()` is called in a non-synchronized method.

   D. When two `Statement` objects are opened over the same `java.sql.`
   `Connection`.

   E. When `clone()` is called on a Vector in a non-synchronized method.

REVIEW ANSWERS

1. **D** A, B, and C incorrectly assume that `add()` returns the element added. E is wrong because attempts to add a duplicate element to a Set are ignored.

2. **E** A, B, and D are perfectly legal. C causes a compile error, not a runtime exception. E throws a `ClassCastException` because the zero-argument form of `toArray()` will create an array of `java.lang.Object objects`, which cannot be assigned to `String[]`.

3. **A** The `values()` method in TreeMap returns the values in the natural order of their corresponding keys, not the values themselves (which makes B wrong). The other answers fail to catch the fact that the same keys have been mapped multiple times.

4. **B** `Enumeration` comes close, but doesn't offer the `remove()` method. Vector has no direct iterator capability over collections in general. D and E work with text, not collections.

5. **D** No elements will be removed, but an exception will be thrown. This will also be the case if `remove()` is called twice without an intervening `next()`.

6. **E** `String` and `Date` are the key and value, respectively. `entrySet()` returns a Set containing some class that implements `Map.Entry`.

7. **C** `size()` is the only method among the five choices that actually exists in the `SortedSet` interface.

8. **A** **B** **D** The object will be a `Set`, not a `String`.

9. **A** **C** `AbstractMap` is a class, not an interface. D is almost right, except that `TreeMap` implements `Serializable`, not `Externalizable`.

10. **A** B is wrong because multiple threads are allowed to read simultaneously. `wait()` and `createStatement()` have nothing to do with `Concurrent-ModificationException`. Cloning does not modify the underlying collection.

About the CD-ROM

Mike Meyers' Certification Passport
CD-ROM Instructions

To install the *Passport* Practice Exam software, perform these steps:

1. Insert the CD-ROM into your CD-ROM drive. An auto-run program will initiate, and a dialog box will appear indicating that you are installing the Passport setup program. If the auto-run program does not launch on your system, select Run from the Start menu and type **d:\setup.exe** (where **d** is the "name" of your CD-ROM drive).
2. Follow the installation wizard's instructions to complete the installation of the software.
3. You can start the program by going to your desktop and double-clicking the Passport Exam Review icon or by going to Start | Program Files | Passport | Java 2 Passport Exam.

System Requirements

- Operating systems supported: Windows 98, Windows NT 4.0, Windows 2000, and Windows ME
- CPU: 400 MHz or faster recommended
- Memory: 64MB of RAM
- CD-ROM: 4X or greater
- Internet connection: Required for optional exam upgrade

Technical Support

For basic *Passport* CD-ROM technical support, contact Hudson Technical Support:

- Phone: 800-217-0059
- E-mail: mcgraw-hill@hudsonsoft.com

For content/subject matter questions concerning the book or the CD-ROM, contact MH Customer Service:

- Phone: 800-722-4726
- E-mail: customer.service@mcgraw-hill.com

For inquiries about the available upgrade, CD-ROM, or online technology, or for in-depth technical support, contact ExamWeb Technical Support:

- Phone: 949-566-9375
- E-mail: support@examweb.com

About the Online Code Samples

Samples of the code used in this book are available free at **http://www.osborne.com**. Just click on the "free code" link.

Career Flight Path

Being certified as a programmer for the Java 2 platform is a little bit like finishing your first year of college. As a college freshman, you take pretty much the same courses as everybody else, whether they are music majors or anthropology majors. Everybody needs to be grounded in the basics before undertaking more specialized studies. Similarly, once you've proved your skill in the basics of the Java language and class libraries, you are ready to tackle more advanced topics in your chosen specialty.

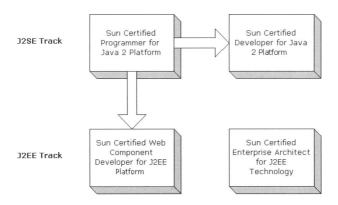

There are three other professional certifications offered by Sun for Java Technology:

- Sun Certified Developer for Java 2 Platform
- Sun Certified Web Component Developer for J2EE Platform
- Sun Certified Enterprise Architect for J2EE Technology

Sun Certified Developer for Java 2 Platform (310-027)

This certification is a logical next step for someone who wants to demonstrate skill in application development. There are two requirements for the certification:

1. Develop an application according to detailed specifications. The application goes beyond the "Hello World" type of program, testing your skill with data handling, caching, remote method invocation, and other production application techniques.
2. Pass an essay examination that demonstrates that you understand what you did in the application and why.

Sun Certified Web Component Developer for J2EE Platform (310-080)

This certification is for programmers who want to demonstrate skill in servlet and JSP development. It covers the servlet model, the structure of web applications, servlet containers, exception handling, session management, security, threading, beans, and tag libraries. These are skills that are especially useful to someone working with the presentation layers of J2EE.

Sun Certified Enterprise Architect for J2EE Technology (310-051 and 310-061)

The "Ph.D." of the Sun Java Certifications is the Enterprise Architect test. This consists of three parts:

1. A multiple choice test that covers all the J2EE technologies. There are 48 questions, and a 75-minute time limit. The passing score is 68 percent.
2. A project that requires skill in the J2EE technologies. There is no time limit, and the passing score is 70 percent.
3. A 90-minute essay exam on the results of your project.

Index

ExamWeb is a leader in assessment technology. We use this technology to deliver customized online testing programs, corporate training, pre-packaged exam preparation courses, and licensed technology. ExamWeb has partnered with Osborne - McGraw-Hill to develop the CD contained in this book and its corresponding online exam simulators. Please read about our services below and contact us to see how we can help you with your own assessment needs.

www.examweb.com

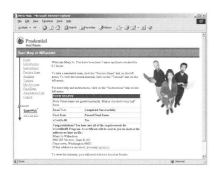

Corporate Assessment

ExamWeb can customize its course and testing engines to meet your training and assessment needs as a trainer. We can provide you with stand-alone assessments and courses or can easily integrate our assessment engines with your existing courses or learning management system. Features may include:

Technology Licenses and Partnerships

Publishers, exam preparation companies and schools use ExamWeb technology to offer online testing or exam preparation branded in their own style and delivered via their websites. Improve your assessment offerings by using our technology!

Check www.examweb.com for an updated list of course offerings.

✓ Corporate-level access and reporting

✓ Multiple question types

✓ Detailed strength and weakness reports by key subject area and topic

✓ Performance comparisons amongst groups

click. study. pass.™

Coming soon:

CCNA™ Passport / A+™ Passport / Server+™ Passport / Network+™ Passport / Java™ 2 Passport
MCSE Windows 2000™ Professional Passport / MCSE Windows 2000™ Server Passport
MCSE Windows 2000™ Directory Services Passport
MCSE Windows 2000™ Network Infrastructure Passport

For more infomation, please contact corpsales@examweb.com or call 949.566.9375